FIRST EDITION

WHO WE ARE
AND
HOW WE LEARN

EDUCATIONAL ENGAGEMENT AND JUSTICE FOR DIVERSE LEARNERS

written and edited by

Jose Lalas, Angela Macias, Kitty M. Fortner, Nirmla Griarte Flores, Ayanna Blackmon-Balogun, and Margarita Vance

cognella®
academic publishing

Bassim Hamadeh, CEO and Publisher
Michael Simpson, Vice President of Acquisitions and Sales
Jamie Giganti, Senior Managing Editor
Miguel Macias, Graphic Designer
Seidy Cruz, Senior Field Acquisitions Editor
Gem Rabanera, Project Editor
Elizabeth Rowe, Licensing Coordinator
Rachel Singer, Interior Designer

cognella
academic publishing

www.cognella.com   800-200-3908

CONTENTS

FOREWORD

E ducation continues to be a central point of political conversation in the United States and abroad. Over the years, multicultural education and social justice concepts in education have begun to make headway in the educational discourse. In 2014 and 2015, the themes at two major conferences reflected this continued thrust for educational justice. At the University Council Education Administration in 2014, the conference theme was "*Righting Civil Wrongs: Education for Racial Justice and Human Rights*," and at the American Educational Research Association conference in 2015, the theme was "*Toward Justice: Culture, Learning, Language, and Heritage in Education Research and Praxis.*" In continuing the push for social justice in education, the American Educational Research Association 2016 annual conference theme is "*Public Scholarship to Educate Diverse Democracies.*" At this critical juncture in world history, a paradigm shift appears to be occurring in the field of education. The old paradigm which has left out historically underserved groups is being challenged by educational scholars.

The intent of this this series, *Multicultural Education and Social Justice,* is to galvanize critical scholarship that can contribute to making schools and communities more responsive to the needs of historically underserved groups. The series is not intended to be a discussion of cultural artifacts but to disrupt the status quo that has limited people's abilities to reach their full human potential. As such, concepts in critical educational theory are at the center piece of the series.

What makes the series unique is that it produces critical scholarship through the publication of textbooks. Typically textbooks attempt to use a kinder, gentler language to attract the largest number of readers. Contrary to textbooks that are driven by a *for-profit* mentality that locks out critical discourse and that skirts around the real issues, the textbooks in this series stir emotions, causing it readers to reflect and act, forming *praxis* to rethink education and schools. Additionally the series seeks to produce scholarship that stretches across the education spectrum to eradicate the "isms" that limit human beings from knowing themselves.

In this inaugural volume, *Who We Are and How We Learn-Educational Engagement and Justice for Diverse Learners*, the contributors have compiled a much-needed textbook that will contribute to the transformation of teaching, learning, and leading in schools. This textbook is timely in that it aligns with the contemporary educational movement that is galvanized around concepts of diversity and social justice.

The editors have brilliantly structured the book around critical social theory to intentionally produce a book that is "analytical, critical—even emancipatory sometimes … " The contributors to this volume superbly engage the reader by reminding us that those shaping educational policy should take into consideration the voices of those they seek to educate: thus its title, *Who We Are and How We Learn*, suggests that we can't effectively teach students that we don't know. Lalas succinctly notes, "Knowledge about the student and how they learn is key in educating them properly, effectively, equitably, and justly." Drawing from the revolutionary work of Paulo Freire and others, the contributors demonstrate why there is a need for critical scholarship that not only critiques but offers ways to effectively address the educational challenges in the twenty-first century.

At the forefront of these educational challenges are issues of diversity, equity, and social justice in education. The older Western-centric lens that has dominated the educational discourse will no longer be able to effectively educate the masses for the new world that is on the horizon. James Banks (2014), a leading educational scholar, highlights that the traditional canon will continue to be challenged in the twenty-first century. He then questions the role of educators in making a decision to work for the transformation of schools so that they are just and equitable for all students.

The contributors in this volume use qualitative research to offer its readers a more nuanced understanding of how to implement diversity and social justice concepts in education. At the end of each chapter are reflective questions and small case studies to combine theory and practice. The book offers much insight for educators—teachers, counselors, educational leaders, and others concerned about the plight of education for historically underserved groups.

Reference

Banks, J. (2014). *An introduction to multicultural education* (6th ed.). Boston, MA: Allyn and Bacon.

ABOUT THE EDITORS

Dr. Jose Lalas is a professor of literacy and teacher education at the University of Redlands. He has been involved in teacher education for twenty-six years as a faculty member in both public and private universities (fourteen years at CSU Dominguez Hills; currently, twelve years at University of Redlands). He earned his Ph.D. from the University of Washington in Seattle, Washington. Prior to his teacher education experience, Jose was a junior high school classroom teacher. He has served as an associate dean, director of teacher education, and coordinator of credential programs. In addition, he also directs the University of Redlands' Center for Educational Justice, a forum that sponsors research efforts, policy symposia, and critical awareness training on issues related to K-16 education and leadership for social justice.

In addition, Jose is very active in the California Council on Teacher Education (CCTE). He has served CCTE as a member of the board of directors and is currently the chair of the Special Interest Group on credential coordinators and a member of the awards committee. He participates in the California Commission on Teacher Credentialing institutional review teams for university accreditation purposes. He co-authored two published books: *A Teaching and Learning Framework for Social Justice* (2006) and *Instructional Adaptation as an Equity Solution for English Learners and Special Needs Students: Practicing Educational Justice in the Classroom* (2007). His research agenda includes critical literacy, authentic student voices, teacher education, adaptation pedagogy, and second-language acquisition. His most current research work focuses on student engagement and the achievement gap and the influence of social and cultural capital, social class, funds of knowledge, language, and poverty. He works with doctoral students conducting dissertation research studies on K-12 issues and leadership in K-12 schools.

Jose Lalas is currently an elected school board member of the Corona-Norco Unified School District, a seat that he held from 1990 to 2003 and from 2008 to the present. He has served as a member of the Corona-Norco Unified School District for twenty years.

Dr. Margarita Vance is a professor at Collin College in Plano, Texas, and a member of the Texas Community College Teachers Association . She is currently serving as a faculty advisor for Students in Entrepreneurship and Economic Development , a Collegiate Entrepreneurs'

Organization, and a mentor and academic coach to developmental students at Collin College. She has taught as an associate faculty member at the University of Redlands in Redlands, California, and at Drury University in Springfield, Missouri. She served as department chair for the business administration and retail management programs at Central New Mexico (CNM) Community College in Albuquerque, New Mexico. During her tenure at CNM, she was the recipient of the Teacher Excellence Award from the Accreditation Council for Business Schools and Programs . Dr. Vance has fifteen years of professional work experience in higher education. She earned her master of business administration from the University of Redlands in Redlands, California, and was inducted as a member of the Whitehead Leadership Society. She also received her doctorate from the University of Redlands in Redlands, California. Dr. Vance has presented at conferences on issues of cultural capital and student engagement. Her research interests include cultural and social capital, funds of knowledge, bilingual education, and multicultural education.

Dr. Ayanna Blackmon-Balogun is a professor of literacy at the University of Redlands and a public school administrator. She has been in public education for the last twenty-one years and began her tenure as a first-grade teacher, teaching five- and six-year old students the joy of reading. She has educated every grade within the K-12 setting and currently serves as an assistant principal at Frisbie Middle School in the city of Rialto, California. She earned her doctorate from the University of Redlands in Leadership for Educational Justice after a unique learning and teaching experience with males in a single-gendered class. She has reviewed proposals for *American Educational Research Association* for several years and presented at several conferences on cultural responsiveness and its effects on writing and on the significance of gender and culture in the classroom. In addition, Ayanna is very active in her community and at one point served as a school board member in the city of Fontana. She is a member of Teachers College Record and a member of the International Literacy Association. During the summer months, she enjoys writing poems, daily devotionals, and children's books. Her first children's book was published in 2009, entitled *Because I Love You So Much: The Influence of Motherly Love.* For the past four years, she has also enjoyed being a contributing author to *Zoe Life Inspired: A Daily Devotional.* Ayanna is a wife and mother of two children, Ashanti Devon (twenty-one) and Genesis Moriyat (ten), and a host of Frisbie Falcons. She is passionate about the work she does and believes it is a calling to serve students and her community.

Dr. Nirmla Griarte Flores is a cohort advisor for the School of Education, University of Redlands (UofR), at the Temecula satellite campus. She also mentors the teacher candidates with the Teacher Performance Assessment tasks. In addition, she is an adjunct faculty member of the UofR, teaching courses such as Language and Literacy, Teaching and Learning in Secondary Schools, as well as Multiple Subject Methods and Curriculum. She earned her doctorate degree with a major in Educational Leadership for Social Justice from the UofR. In addition, she serves as a university supervisor for teacher candidates who are in the process of completing their student teaching assignments.

She has also presented at various staff development and teacher training events/workshops/conferences held at the California Association for Bilingual Educators (CABE Regional and National), American Educational Research Association, California Association of Professors of Educational Administration, and the Corona-Norco Parent Advisory Council. In addition, she has co-facilitated a variety of educational forums organized at the School of Education (UofR) and the Institute for Educational and Social Justice.

Her presentations involved issues on parental involvement, social justice, diversity, equity, closing the achievement gap, and teachers helping teachers.

Dr. Kitty M. Fortner is an adjunct professor at the University of Redlands' School of Education. In addition to teaching in the Pre-Service Teacher Program, she supervises student teachers and interns. She has been involved in K-12 education for twenty years in public and public charter schools. She received her doctorate in Leadership for Educational Justice from the University of Redlands. Kitty works with the University of Redlands Center for Educational Justice sharing information with school leaders, teachers, and policy makers on how best to serve diverse students. She began her educational career as a classroom teacher in an elementary school, working with low-income, second-language students and their families. She has served as a lead teacher, BTSA support provider, RTI Coordinator, and SPED Administrative Designee as well as a master/mentor teacher assisting new and veteran teachers in better serving students and their families. Before her work in higher education, she founded two charter schools in Southern California. Her passion is to provide students with the best learning experience for their needs. She believes that leadership plays an imperative role in the fostering of academic success for all learners.

Dr. Angela Macias is an Assistant Professor at California State University, Dominguez Hills. She has been a Southern California educator for ten years, teaching middle school, high school, and college. She graduated with an Ed.D. in Leadership for Educational Justice from the University of Redlands. Her research focused on funds of knowledge concerning working-class Latino students and student engagement. She presented this research at the American Educational Research Association conference and the California Bilingual Education conference in 2012. In addition to teaching secondary English, she also teaches education courses, college English courses, and leads professional development on culturally relevant instructional strategies. Macias is actively involved in contributing to local educational issues as the chairperson of Civics and Technology for Youth and by running a series of free conferences called Teachers Helping Teachers through the Center for Educational Justice at the University of Redlands.

INTRODUCTION

There is a tremendous promise and opportunity to improve the student achievement of American K-12 students, including the early college- and career-bound young adults across the variety of available educational experiences and established disciplines. As the "smartest kids in the world" are reported to be found in faraway places such as Finland, Poland, South Korea, Japan, China, Singapore, and other parts of the world (Ripley, 2013; Tucker, 2014, 2011), and "achievement gap" in the United States between whites and Asians on one side and Latinos and African American school-age students on the other is a perennial challenge (Howard, 2010), educators are actively seeking explanations and remedies in order to make education more effective, equitable, and academically rigorous for all students. Bryk, Gomez, Grunow, and LeMahieu (2015), who wrote a book on "improvement paradigm," challenged our public schools to advance three aims: improved academic effectiveness, greater cost efficiency, and enhanced human engagement. For academic efficiency, numerous programs, approaches, and strategies abound and are being implemented, including such current innovations as Common Core, social emotional learning, digital multimodal literacy, content area academic language, STEM, and expanded use of technology as in E-books and tablets. States and local school districts have instituted local control funding formulas and other initiatives to meet mounting financial burdens and for greater fiscal efficiency. While education researchers, academicians, and practitioners continue to do their serious work of attempting to better understand the challenges faced by educational institutions and communities in providing opportunities for all students to learn, they rarely collaborate on concrete matters that explicitly integrate education theory and practice in a comprehensive manner in K-12 settings to solve specific classroom problems and enhance human engagement.

Who We Are and How We Learn: Educational Engagement and Justice for Diverse Learners intends to present an effective integration of theory, research, and best practice for improved student engagement. My co-authors and chapter contributors are all active K-12 practitioners and researchers—two administrators, four classroom teachers, one counselor, two former special education teachers, one educational administration professor, and a teacher education professor. We all agree that all well-intentioned school and classroom innovations are only going to work if we know who our students are and how they learn. Knowledge about the students and how they learn is key in educating them properly, effectively, equitably, and justly.

Thus, in this collaborative book for teachers, counselors, administrators, and education professors, we have attempted to integrate theory, research, and practice to foster a perspective that recognizes and respects the inherent social and cultural contexts and characteristics of any interaction and decision-making events that occur in the place we call school. All the chapters of the book have a set of conceptual frameworks, similar to what Jean Anyon called "theoretical arsenal of powerful concepts" (Anyon, 2009, p. 2). Six chapters of the book are drawn from completed doctoral dissertations of my co-authors, whom I chaired as part of the thematic dissertation research that I personally designed and they participated in as doctoral students entitled *Social and Cultural Capital, Social Class, Funds of Knowledge, Language, and Student Engagement in Selected Settings: A Narrative Inquiry.* We employed critical social theories in creating the conceptual framework that guided each study that was later developed into a chapter of this book. This intentional effort produced dissertations that are analytical, critical—even emancipatory sometimes—and sensitive to the practical needs of students, teachers, administrators, counselors, parents, and staff in schools and class-rooms. Aside from providing research-based information to improve student learning and engagement, the research and field-based findings are explicit in their thorough analysis, conclusion, and implication toward equity, access, and educational justice. The underlying thread that dominates the exploration, discussion, analysis, findings, conclusions, and recommendations in each chapter is educational engagement and justice for student success.

Engagement and Motivation

It is important to understand that student success depends on how engaged students are in the classroom. According to Newmann (1992, p. 12), engagement is "the student's psychological investment in, and effort directed toward, learning, understanding, or mastering the knowledge, skills, and crafts that academic work is intended to promote." It implies that for any engagement with curriculum to succeed, teaching and learning must go beyond the acquisition of basic skills and concepts through rote memorization and must engage students in critical thinking, analysis, synthesis and evaluation of data, and personal and societal decision-making. Of course, students could be engaged if they are attending school regularly, avoiding chronic absenteeism, participating in school activities actively, feeling a sense of school belongingness, and not dropping out of school. It is imperative to think about student engagement as requisite to any school reforms and innovations. What does student engagement really mean? Is it synonymous to motivation? What factors influence student engagement?

It is very tempting and natural to think and use the terms motivation and engagement interchangeably. However, current scholars view these two terms as different: student engagement may occur because of motivation; engagement is action, and motivation is the intention to do something; engagement is defined by observable, action-oriented behaviors, while motivation is considered an internal process that carries an intention. According to Reschly and Christenson (2012), student engagement is action-oriented and has been found to be helpful in preventing student dropout and fostering high school completion. Skinner and Pitzer (2012) asserted their view of "engagement as the outward manifestation of motivation" (p.22). The common unifying factor about motivation and engagement is the notion that both are influenced by context and individual differences and link to student outcomes. For example, according to Skinner and Pitzer (2012), student engagement in the classroom context with learning activities driven by certain curriculum may be motivated by the teacher and positive interaction with peers, friends, and classmates. The school and/or classroom contexts and student engagement promote the development of academic assets such as learning, coping, and resilience. School administrators and teachers have to be very intentional in providing students with learning activities and engagement in social institutions such as community and family, school content areas and extracurricular activities such as sports, clubs, and other academic projects, and challenging curriculum in the classroom that emphasizes critical thinking and other metacognitive strategies such as learning from the text, self-monitoring of understanding, questioning the author, and critical analysis.

Recent empirical studies on enhancing engagement in the classroom point to the role of motivation through instruction in mediating the interaction between the teacher and the students. Tasks, use of certain strategies, what students are allowed and expected to demonstrate, and the routine social culture of the classroom provide opportunities for student engagement. The study by Turner, Christensen, Kackar-Cam, Trucano, and Fulmer (2014) on enhancing students' engagement reported that motivation constructs such as belongingness, competence, autonomy, and meaningfulness are helpful in explaining why students engage or disengage in school tasks. After a three-year intervention with middle school teachers, their findings suggest that teachers who employed motivation by providing opportunities for students to experience belongingness in the classroom, competence in performing and organizing a particular task, autonomy in pursuing their individual interests and beliefs, and meaningful learning had students who were more engaged. In short, the more the teacher motivates his or her students, the greater the degree of student engagement.

A current related empirical study by Cooper (2014) underscores the role of identity development in eliciting student engagement in the high school classroom. The study identified three groups of teaching practices to engage students that have emerged from the research literature: connective instruction, academic rigor, and lively teaching. It has been demonstrated in several bodies of research that connective instruction operates at certain levels of contact—where students connect with the subject matter content that they find relevant and appropriate, where teachers connect with their students by recognizing and affirming them, and where the delivery of instruction allows connection among teachers, students, and classroom contexts through opportunities that involve students to develop competence (Martin & Dowson, 2009). In Cooper's study (2014), academic rigor is identified as a category or set of teaching for engagement practices that provide challenging work, emphasize hard work and academic success, and convey passion for content (Wolf, Crosson, & Resnick, 2005). Lively teaching is the category of engaging practices that emphasize active delivery of lessons, such as using games and fun activities, assigning projects, and doing collaborative group work (Cooper, 2014). Interestingly, Cooper's study found that while lively teaching and academic rigor are engaging practices, connective instruction shows stronger influence on student engagement. Cooper explained that "compared with academic rigor and lively teaching, which center on teachers' decisions about how to set an academic tone or present content, … connective instruction acknowledges who students are as people … The engaging element of connective instruction under this conceptualization is that such instruction honors who the students are—acknowledging that they are particular people with particular interests, points of views, personalities, and experiences" (p. 367).

Types of Student Engagement

There are different theoretical models of describing student engagement. It is demonstrated through a variety of activities and may be described as behavioral, which shows efforts; cognitive, which shows deliberate use of strategy; emotional, which shows expression of interest and affection; and agentic, which shows attempts to contribute to learning activities (Fredericks, Blumenfeld & Paris, 2004). One of the most current formulations of engagement was offered by Finn and Zimmer (2012). According to them, there are four types of student engagement: academic engagement, social engagement, cognitive engagement, and affective engagement.

Academic engagement refers to observable behaviors in the classroom and at a student's home that are directly connected to the learning process, such as attentiveness and completing assignments in class and at home or supplementing learning through other academic extracurricular activities. This engagement reflects ongoing participation, focus, hard work, involvement, concentration, and/or effort in doing academic-related work at school, home, and in the community.

Social engagement refers to observable appropriate behaviors that a student demonstrates in school and in his or her interaction with the teacher and his or her classmates in the classroom, such as attending school regularly, coming to school and class on time, exhibiting kindness and a caring attitude toward other students, and not withdrawing from classroom participation in class activities or disrespecting other students. This engagement reflects appropriate interaction with classmates and the teacher, attention to relevant class activities, following directions, and speaking politely.

Cognitive engagement is the thorough, thoughtful, and purposeful effort to comprehend complex ideas in order to achieve mastery of the subject matter. Student behaviors linked to cognitive engagement include: asking critical questions; concentration in understanding challenging academic concepts; willingness to participate in dealing with difficult tasks; reading more references than the assigned material; revisiting content area materials and following through on topics that are learned previously; using self-regulation, self-monitoring, and other cognitive strategies to guide learning; and examining ideas, concepts, and events carefully by using research and other authentic sources.

Affective engagement involves an emotional response characterized by feelings of belongingness and being involved in school as a positive and caring place where activities are relevant and worth pursuing. Affective engagement provides students the enthusiasm, enjoyment, satisfaction, and pride to participate in school activities and to be resilient in dealing with peers and the challenges in doing school tasks. Affective engagement refers to the student's emotional feeling of belongingness in the school community of learners, teachers, administrators, and parents and understanding that school prepares him or her with knowledge, skills, abilities, and disposition for current and future out-of-school tasks and challenges.

The current study by Turner, Christensen, Kackar-Cam, Trucano, and Fulmer (2014) informs us that for students to be engaged in classroom learning activities, there has to be an attainment of a certain degree of comfort and confidence through classroom opportunities for students' sense of belongingness, competence, autonomy, and meaningful learning. In addition, the work of Cooper (2014) on eliciting engagement in the classroom emphasizes the centrality of the emotional and meaningful connections of the teacher, the content, and the instruction to the learner's personal background, identity, and experiences, which relate to Pierre Bourdieu's social and cultural capital (Grenfell, 2008; Swartz, 1997; Bourdieu, 1983) as applied to describing and identifying the learner, including his or her race and social class.

Framing Engagement from a Socially and Culturally Situated View

In this book, we have put forth the idea that social and cultural capital influence student engagement. Throughout the process of conducting a series of qualitative research, we have discovered that student engagement is, indeed, influenced by students' social capital and cultural capital, in which we have included the cultural notions of race, social class, funds of knowledge, and literacy.

Social capital refers to the network of relationships and social connections that provide additional opportunities or resources available for individuals who are members of the group. According to Coleman (1990), it is vested in the structure of relations between persons and among persons. Once social relations begin, the person or persons involved in the relationship may become obligated to reciprocate favors between them or among them, share sources of information, and maintain norms and sanctions to make social capital effective, functional, and dynamic. It provides students with access to resources by way of whom they already know in a particular class or by their familiarity with the teacher and the school. It is, therefore, a set of networks of social relations and resources that provide the cognitive, social, affective, and academic support that the students and their families can use to navigate through the school system. As one can gather from the studies described or implied in the chapters, social capital influences student engagement by providing students with the necessary feeling of belongingness in school as a comfortable place with friendly and supportive teachers, administrators, and classmates. It also fosters positive interaction with teachers and peers and, therefore, promotes positive social and affective growth as well as increased student achievement. Applied to schooling of young children and young adults, teachers must make sure that all students develop their social capital, including their positive and caring relationships with the school personnel and their peers, in order for them to gain a sense of belongingness to the school community and a feeling of being cared for to increase their school participation and pride.

Cultural capital refers to culturally based common practices and/or resources possessed by individuals that may put them at an advantage over others. As described in the research conducted and reported in the current book, examples of culturally based resources, materials, or practices include understanding the school tradition and philosophy of teaching, cultural awareness of the regional origins of the students in the class, knowledge about educational and school discipline practices, going to the museums and art exhibits, educational credentials of teachers and administrators, academic qualifications or degrees, access to computers, and aesthetic preferences such as taste of music, art, food, and other creative forms. Cultural capital can be acquired through social origin by way of one's family or through education or schooling (Winkle-Wagner, 2010) and could be identified easily as one's set of doing things or disposition accumulated from childhood or as a possessed set of skills, works of art, and scientific instruments that require specialized cultural knowledge and abilities to use. Applied to educating children and young adults, teachers, administrators, and parents must make sure that all students, regardless of socioeconomic status, acquire or are exposed to cultural capital or practices that match the content and rigor of the school and classroom curriculum and instruction.

To elicit engagement, it is imperative to connect instruction to the learner's social and cultural capital that comprise his or her personal identity. As operationalized by Cooper (2004), to connect teaching to a learner's personal identity, the teacher must promote relevance, demonstrate care, show understanding of students, provide praise and appreciation, relate to students through humor, and allow students to express themselves. Sense of belongingness, special, caring relationships among peers, parents, and teachers, opportunities for meaningful learning, and the appropriate match between home and school cultural practices of rigorous curricular and instructional delivery are influential themes for fostering student engagement. Thus, this book reminds educators that there is a need for a theoretical and practical view that is "socially and culturally situated" for understanding the connections among concepts, perspectives, approaches, policies, and classroom practices related to the teaching and learning of all students, especially the diverse learners. Influenced by Bourdieu's notions of social and cultural capital, "socially and culturally situated" means viewing objects, things, and events with an eye of taking into strong consideration the impact of one's social background and connections and one's established cultural ways of doing and handling things. My co-authors and chapter contributors believe that everything that relates to teaching and learning is social and cultural because the set of knowledge, practices, dispositions, and even policies that is dealt with on a regular basis is deeply linked to who we are, how we view and work with others, and what common beliefs and practices we hang on to. All learning and teaching activities we engage in "play out in human lives, and are not solely discussed as explanatory of, but also as contributing to and even shaping human and societal initiatives and development" (Hawkins, 2013, p. 8).

In a book edited by Hawkins (2013), she tried to present through current theories, research, and best practice why and how "children who differ from the mainstream in language use, ethnicity, cultural background, socioeconomic status and dis/ability status experience school failure" (Hawkins, 2013, p. 3). She featured an exciting collection of scholars who are mutually complementary in projecting the importance of social, cultural, and historical contexts in learning, language development, and literacy education. She highlighted the use of languages and literacies between people in situated social and communicative practices. In one of its chapters, Luke (2013) stressed the balance of the role of authentic voices of participants in cultural situations for transforming social relations and material conditions and understanding critical discourse analysis. He pointed out that "all texts are potentially ideological, and hence should be the subject of critical analysis and scrutiny" (p. 145).

Does Race Still Matter?

Similarly, *Who We Are and How We Learn* emphasizes the importance of social and cultural contexts in understanding and enhancing student engagement. It also includes the recognition of race as an issue in influencing the interaction among teachers, students, administrators, and parents and in understanding what students can and cannot do, especially those students who come from different racial, cultural, and linguistic backgrounds. Theoretically and pedagogically, there is now an established line of inquiry called critical race theory (CRT) and culturally relevant/responsive instruction that all evolved from the effort to understand the low school performance of African American students (Ladson-Billings, 2004; Ladson-Billings & Tate, 1995). According to CRT, racism still plays a role in the U.S. society, particularly in the educational system, where unfair disciplinary measures in suspending and expelling minority students, hostile learning environments, and unfriendly attitude of failing to see the value of one's personal history, racial background, and cultural experiences are still prevalent. This theory is an important foundational background in contextualizing the minority participants in all the research studies that are featured in the chapters of this book.

Starting from the effort of legal scholars such as Derrick Bell, Alan Freeman, Kimberly Crenshaw, Cheryl Harris, Mari Matsuda, Richard Delgado, and many others, critical race theory (CRT) became a helpful theoretical tool for examining educational issues involving race, racism, and culture (Delgado & Stefancic, 2001; Ladson-Billings and Tate, 2005). Specifically, CRT is used as a research tool in understanding the role of race in the broader context of society and its connection to student achievement. Ladson-Billings and Tate (1995) identified several principles of CRT in education, such as the inherence of race and racism in American society, critical examination of the problems caused by neutrality, objectivity, and colorblindness, the need to focus on the importance of maintaining a commitment to social justice, the importance of experiential knowledge, and whiteness as a property that includes the right to disposition, enjoyment, reputation, and the right to exclude (Harris, 1993).

CRT also recognizes the positive impact of "counter-storytelling," or listening to the authentic stories of minority students. Counter-storytelling serves as a tool for providing a different viewpoint on historical information found in textbooks and everyday events published in various social media. In examining the experiences of Hispanic students, Latino(a) critical race theory, or LatCrit, came about to specifically address how institutionalized racism has affected the lives of Latino and Latina students based on immigration status, language proficiency, accent, and even surname (Solórzano & Yosso, 2002; Solórzano, Ceja, & Yosso, 2001).

Both CRT and LatCrit provide opportunities for the authentic voices, experiences, and perspectives of the marginalized African American, Hispanic American, and other students of color to be heard through counter-storytelling. They afford the avenue for minority students' sense of belongingness, positive identity development, autonomy, meaningful learning, and self-confidence by challenging the dominant viewpoints and sharing their stories with others. The courageous discussion about race and social class in education and the socially and culturally situated perspectives, insights, and practices highlighted in the qualitative studies featured in this book are provocative vehicles for educational engagement and justice for all learners, including the linguistically and culturally diverse students.

Educational/Social Justice for Diverse Learners

Commonly, many educators and researchers view fostering educational and social justice in schools as simply a way of achieving equality, equity, and fairness for all children as well as recognizing, respecting, and valuing the roles played by teachers, administrators, counselors, parents, students, and other school personnel (Marshall & Oliva, 2010; Sandel, 2009). It has been asserted by current researchers and classroom practitioners that social justice can be cultivated on students by recognizing diversity, honoring identity, encouraging individual voice, and understanding issues related to privilege, deficit thinking, poverty, heteronormativity, and immigration and humanitarian concerns (Gorski, Zenkov, Osei-Kofi, & Sapp, 2013; Macias & Lalas, 2014). In addition, social scientists have highlighted the lessons learned from how leadership for social justice has been formulated in and influenced by several disciplines that include philosophy, anthropology, Black studies, sociology, political science, public policy, and psychology (Normore & Brooks, 2014). Even school counselors now view social justice as part of their advocacy work in paying attention to the social and cultural capital of students and their families (Bemak & Chung, 2005). Other researchers frame promoting social justice as a lifelong process of engagement that involves understanding one's identity, examining how inequality affects opportunities of different people, exploring experiences and how those inform a person's unique worldviews, perspectives, and opportunities, and evaluating how schools and classrooms can operate to value diverse human experiences and enable learning for all students (Darling-Hammond, French, & Garcia-Lopez, 2002).

Brown (2004) explained that administrators and leaders for social justice need grounding in learning theories, transformative pedagogy, and reflective practice to "guide others in translating their perspectives, perceptions, and goals into agendas for social change" (p. 99). Similarly, Cochran-Smith (2004) argued for "the necessity of a social justice agenda in a democratic and increasingly diverse society" (p.168) and even proposed "inquiry as stance," or "a way of knowing and being in the world of educational practice that carries across educational contexts and various points in one's professional career and that links individuals to larger groups and social movements intended to challenge the inequities perpetuated by the educational status quo" (Cochran-Smith & Lytle, 2009, p. viii).

Further review of research and professional literature reveals some common principles that are relevant, appropriate, and translatable to classroom teaching that involves the learner, teacher, and classroom context (Lalas, 2007). These principles imply how the learner and the teacher use their life experiences, personal beliefs, world knowledge, abilities to construct and represent knowledge, and dispositions in facilitating learning to occur in the classroom. The classroom context where the interaction, generation, and negotiation of meaningful experiences happen includes the physical classroom arrangement, classroom discipline, instructional materials, assessment instruments, assignments, and many other supplementary materials. It is through the dynamic interchange of the learner, teacher, and classroom context that teaching for social justice can be demonstrated. The common principles gathered from the research literature imply a socially and culturally situated classroom context where a classroom teacher and learner interact, share, negotiate, and generate knowledge. These principles include understanding oneself in relation to another individual or group of individuals, appreciating diversity and promoting equity, recognizing inequities and how to diminish them, equitable participation and allocation of resources, creating a caring and culturally responsive learning environment, working together as a learning community, engagement in classroom inquiry, and critical thinking and reflection (Lalas, 2007).

The Book: Socially and Culturally Situated Chapters Toward Engagement and Justice

As a teacher educator, mentor of doctoral students, school board member, and former classroom teacher with consistent connection with school-age students, I am always in the middle of making decisions and responding to inquiries about what is the best way to teach young children and youth. Every time I give my opinion, I worry about being labeled as impractical because I am theoretical; that is, I always recommend people to determine their own theoretical perspectives or the set of conceptual lenses they are comfortable wearing when confronted with challenges related to school concerns, curriculum, instruction, policy, and other services. I believe that an understanding of one's own view of the world, other people's viewpoints, and other specific concepts, approaches, and perspectives related to teaching, leading a school, and counseling entails an understanding of the context in which they were created. I think I know now, with the help of experience, my interaction with graduate students and faculty and many teachers, and my political and civic involvement in the community as a local district policy-maker, that everything one does is socially and culturally influenced by the context in which it is connected. One must be theoretical in understanding and talking about "socially and culturally situated" context to be practical!

Thus, this collection of research-based chapters includes a variety of theoretical frameworks that have been used in studying the issues and responding to research questions. My co-authors and I believe that the practical application and discussion activities we have at the end of each chapter are best understood when the socially and culturally situated research contexts, findings, and implications are read, discussed, and reflected on critically.

It will be obvious to the readers that all the chapters are recommending for practitioners to know who their students are and how they learn. Identity development of the students appears to be the common thread that connects all the lessons learned in each chapter. This introduction is lengthy because it aims to introduce the key theories, concepts, and insights that the readers will encounter in the chapters. The main concepts covered in this introduction are operationally defined and used in creating the theoretical frameworks for each chapter.

In Chapter 1, cultural capital is defined and discussed as a powerful factor in influencing student engagement. Home and school cultural capitals are studied with the help from the authentic voices of students, teachers, parents, and administrators. Chapter 2 follows the discussion of cultural capital as it pertains to funds of knowledge or family and community resources that are available at the homes and communities of working class Latino(a) high school students. Parents, students, and teachers were interviewed, and photovoice as a technique was used by students to take pictures of objects, events, and ideas around their homes and communities. In Chapter 3, the issue of social class is defined as it relates to the experiences of African American high school students and their parents. The social class as a concept is broadly presented and interviews with parents, students, teachers, and administrators were conducted to determine how social class has impacted the academic performance of the students. In Chapter 4, an interesting framework of social and cultural domains of parental involvement is introduced. It provides parents and teachers with helpful recommendations on what parents must do to foster student engagement. Chapter 5 presents a way of doing literacy using culturally relevant and responsive instruction. Inspired by the tenets of critical race theory and culturally relevant instruction as a pedagogical approach, the curricular and instructional issue of writing as a communication skill is explored in this chapter. Chapter 6 presents the exciting impact of social and cultural capital in the school involvement of African American parents. It documents the increase in GPA of African American students from 1.7 to 3.4 in the span of three to five years that was attributed to the strong parental involvement of the African American fathers. In Chapter 7, the influence of social and cultural capital on student engagement is explored from a school counselor's perspective. Like the other chapters, a narrative inquiry method was employed to gather the authentic voices of parents, teachers, and administrators. In Chapter 8, a model of transformative leadership is presented by a former school administrator and now a professor of educational administration. The author suggests a culture of excellent leadership that takes into account social and cultural capital, social class, funds of knowledge, and other socially and culturally situated contexts. Finally, a reprint of the article about making instructional adaptations for English language learners is included as Chapter 9. This article presents the rationale for making adaptations, discusses the different types of adaptation strategies, and demonstrates a practical technique of making adaptation. The adaptation strategies presented are also applicable to learners with special needs.

It is fundamental to view teaching, leading a school, and counseling from a socially and culturally situated perspective! Meaningful learning and caring and academically rigorous teaching can only occur if we know our students well and we are willing to develop their identities by providing them with opportunities to experience belongingness, cognitive challenges, academic competence, self-worth, and autonomy in a socially and educationally just environment.

— Jose W. Lalas, Ph.D.
University of Redlands

References

Anyon, J. (2009). *Theory and educational research: Toward critical social explanation.* New York, NY: Routledge.

Bourdieu, P. (1983). The forms of capital. In J.G. Richardson (Ed), *Handbook of theory and research for the sociology of education.* Westport, CT: Greenwood Press, 241–58.

Brown, K. (2004). Leadership for social justice and equity: Weaving a transformative framework and pedagogy. *Educational Administration Quarterly, 40*(1), 77–108.

Bryk, A. S., Gomez, L. M., Grunow, A., & LeMahieu, P.G. (2015). *Learning to improve: How America's schools can get better at getting better.* Cambridge, MA: Harvard Education Press.

Cochran-Smith, M. (2004). *Walking the road: Race, diversity, and social justice.* New York, NY: Teachers College Press.

Cochran-Smith, M. & Lytle, S.L. (2009). *Inquiry as stance: Practitioner research for the next generation.* New York, NY: Teachers College Press.

Coleman, J. S. (1990). Foundations of social theory. Cambridge, MA: The Belknap Press of Harvard University Press.

Cooper, K.S. (2014). Eliciting engagement in the high school classroom: A mixed method-methods examination of teaching practices. *American Educational Research Journal, 51*(2), 363–402.

Darling-Hammond, L., French, J., & Garcia-Lopez, S. (2002). *Learning to teach for social justice.* New York, NY: Teachers College Press.

Delgado, D. & Stefancic, J. (2001). *Critical Race Theory: an introduction.* New York, NY: United Press. Bemak, F. & Thompson, E. (2005). Social justice in the classroom. *Educational Leadership,* September 2005, 48–52.

Finn, J. D., & Zimmer, K. S. (2012). Student engagement: What is it? Why does it matter? In S. L. Christenson, A. L. Reschly, & C. Wylie (Eds.), *Handbook of research on student engagement* (pp. 97–131). New York: Springer.

Fredericks, J. A., Blumenfeld, P. C., & Paris, A. H. (2004). School engagement: Potential of the concept, state of the evidence. *Review of Educational Research, 74,* 59–109.

Gorski, P.C., Zenkov, K., Osei-Kofi, N. & Sapp, J. (2013). *Cultivating social justice teachers.* Sterling,VA: Stylus Publishing.

Grenfell, M. (2008). *Pierre Bourdieu key concepts.* Durham, UK: Acumen Publishing Limited.

Harris, C. (1993). Whiteness as property. *Harvard Law Review, 106,* 1707–1791.

Hawkins, M.R. (2013). *Framing languages and literacies: Socially situated views and perspectives.* New York: NY: Routledge.

Howard, T.C. (2010). *Why race and culture matter in schools: Closing the achievement gap in America's classrooms.* New York: NY: Teachers College Press.

Ladson-Billings, G. (2004). New directions in multicultural education: Complexities, boundaries, and critical race theory. In J.A. Banks & C.A. McGee Banks (Eds.), *Handbook of research on multicultural education.* San Francisco, CA: Jossey Bass.

Ladson-Billings, G., and Tate IV, W. F. (1995). Toward a critical race theory of education. *Teachers College Record, 97*(1), 47–68.

Lalas, J.W. (2007). Teaching for social justice in multicultural urban schools: Conceptualization and classroom implication. *Multicultural Education, 14*(3) 17–21.

Luke, A. (2013). Regrounding critical literacy: Representation, facts and reality. In M.R. Hawkins (Ed.). *Framing languages and literacies: Socially situated views and perspectives.* New York: NY: Routledge.

Macias, A., & Lalas, J.W. (2014). Funds of knowledge and student engagement: A qualitative study of Latino high school students. *Learning Landscapes, 7*(2), 195–217.

Marshall, C. & Oliva, M. (2010). *Leadership for social justice: Making revolutions in education.* New York, NY: Allyn & Bacon.

Normore, A. H. & Brooks, J.S. (2014). *Educational leadership for ethics and social justice: Views from the social sciences.* Charlotte, NC: Information Age Publishing, Inc.

Reschly, A. L., & Christenson, S. L. (2012). Jingle, jangle, and conceptual haziness: Evolution and future directions of the engagement construct. In S. L. Christenson, A. L. Reschly, & C. Wylie (Eds.), *Handbook of Research on Student Engagement* (pp. 3-19). New York: Springer.

Ripley, A. (2013). *The smartest kids in the world and how they got that way.* New York, NY: Simon & Schuster.

Sandel, M.J. (2009). *Justice: What's the right thing to do?* New York, NY: Farrar, Straus and Giroux.

Skinner, E. A., & Pitzer, J. R. (2012). Developmental dynamics of student engagement, coping, and everyday resilience. In S. L. Christenson, A. L. Reschly, & C. Wylie (Eds.), *Handbook of Research on Student Engagement* (pp. 21–44). New York: Springer.

Solórzano , D., Ceja, & Yosso, T. (2001). Critical race and LatCrit theory and method: counterstorytelling Chicana and Chicano gradúate school experience. *Qualitative Studies in Education*, *14*(4), 471–495.

Solórzano , D. & Yosso, T. (2002). Critical race methodology: Counterstorytelling as an analytical framework. *Qualitative Inquiry*, *8*(1), 23–44.

Swartz, D. (1997). *Culture and power: The sociology of Pierre Bourdieu.* Chicago, IL: The University of Chicago Press.

Tucker, M.S. (2014). *Surpassing Shanghai: An agenda for American education built on the world's leading systems.* Cambridge, MA: Harvard Education Press.

Turner, J. C., Christensen, A., Kackar-Cam, H.C., Trucano, M. & Fulmer, S.M. (2014). Enhancing students' engagement: Report of a 3-year intervention with middle school teachers. *American Educational Research Journal*, *51*(6), 1195–1226.

Winkle-Wagner, R. (2010). Cultural capital: The promises and pitfalls in educational research. *ASHE Higher Education Report*, *36*(1), 1–144.

CHAPTER 1

Cultural Capital and Its Influence on Student Engagement

Hispanic working-class immigrant students have historically struggled with the notion of how to keep and maintain their own native culture, way of life, and native language, as well as cultural traditions, mores, norms, and values, while simultaneously fighting to find a way to acculturate and assimilate into the dominant society. This predicament is exacerbated when Latino students are required to attend an American school system that is *subtractive* (Valenzuela, 1999) because it devalues the students' native language while replacing it with English without giving any consideration to the *cultural capital* (Bourdieu, 1986) and the *funds of knowledge* (Moll, Amanti, Neff, & Gonzales, 1992) minority students bring from home to school, thus perpetuating a cultural deficit thinking ideology that interferes with student engagement. "According to this hypothesis, introduced by Bourdieu and Passeron (1977) and called cultural reproduction theory, preferences, attitudes, and behaviors that are dominant in the higher social classes are rewarded by the school system and thus reproduce social inequalities" (De Graaf, De Graaf, & Kraaykamp, 2000, p. 97).

Consequently, academic achievement for minority Hispanic students continues to be a subject of discussion among educational leaders, policy-makers, researchers, and teachers. Extensive literature exists on schools' culture and the culture students bring from home, which has a direct influence on student engagement. This chapter uses Bourdieu's (1986) theoretical framework of cultural capital to understand how the role of cultural capital from home and school settings influence student engagement of Hispanic working-class students.

What do we know about Cultural Capital

For the purposes of this chapter, cultural capital is defined as "knowledge, meanings, and symbolic markers that are considered legitimate in a given society and contribute to the reproduction of dominance and privilege in the society" (Ramos-Zayas, 2004, p. 37). Sullivan (2002) explained "Bourdieu states that cultural capital consists of familiarity with the dominant culture in a society, and especially the ability to understand and use educated language" (p. 145). In education, capital is perceived as possessing non-financial social assets necessary to successfully access the school's culture to attain academic achievement. According to Webb and Norton (2009), there are four levels of school culture. They are as follows: (1) language, symbols, and artifacts; (2) norms; (3) values and beliefs; and (4) assumptions. Webb and Norton further explained that "language is the most visible manifestations of culture" (p. 51) because it focuses on the different dialects students inherit from home. Hispanic students' family culture includes language, religion, good manners (*modales*), family traditions, and rituals that include "birthdays, baptisms, confirmations, 'coming out' rituals (*quinceañeras*), wedding showers, weddings, Christmas dinners, outings, and visitations" (Velez-Ibanez & Greenberg, 2005, p. 59). Figure 1.1 depicts the interconnectedness between cultural capital from home and school settings that influence student engagement.

In this chapter, funds of knowledge are construed as a set of practices, values, norms, and traditions that are part of cultural capital. Bourdieu (1986, as cited in Stuart, Lido, & Morgan, 2011) made reference to this set of skills as *habitus* and viewed them as "possessing the necessary habits and dispositions required to effectively navigate the educational system" (p. 490). Children acquire and develop *habitus* early in their lives from their families, who are influential in the development of cultural capital. Bourdieu (1986) saw cultural capital as having three distinctive forms: "*embodied* state, i.e., in the form of long-lasting dispositions of the mind and the body; *objectified* state, in the form of cultural goods (pictures, books, dictionaries, instruments, machines, etc.); and in the *institutionalized* state, a form of educational qualifications" (p. 243). Unfortunately, minority Hispanic students continue to be perceived by educators in the American school system as lacking the cultural capital necessary to attain educational success in the dominant group's culture.

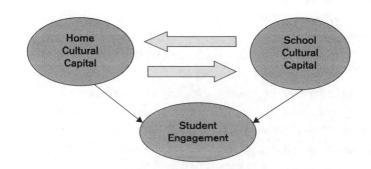

Figure 1–1. Cultural Capital Interconnectedness to Student Engagement

Crosnoe (2005) explained that "Hispanic students have long been considered at-risk in the American educational system" (p. 561), and they continue to struggle with academic achievement.

Some factors that support this perception include poverty among minority Hispanic students, language barriers, and persistent low academic attainment. McLaren (2009) observed, "Schools systematically devalue the cultural capital of students who occupy subordinate class positions" (p. 81), either because the minority parent, the student, or both do not use the same linguistic styles of the school or do not know how to navigate the school's hierarchical authority. Moreover, minority parents may not have a clear understanding of the American school curriculum, and as a result, they are perceived as lacking language skills, knowledge skills, and social skills to help their children be engaged in the learning process. These skills are also necessary to propel Hispanic students to experience academic achievement. The truth is teachers' perceptions of minority students' culture and language continues to be distorted and inaccurate because it is not valued the same as the dominants' society. Macedo (2000) conceded,

> There is a radical difference between a dominant speaker learning a second language and a minority speaker acquiring the dominant language. While the former involves the addition of a second language to the dominant speaker's linguistic repertoire, the latter usually provides minority speakers with the experience of subordination in speaking both their own language, which is devalued by the dominant values, and the dominant language they have learned often under coercive conditions. (p. 20)

Bourdieu (1986) observed, "Thus the more the official transmission of capital is prevented or hindered, the more the effects of the clandestine circulation in the form of cultural capital become determinant in the reproduction of the social structure" (p. 254). Musoba and Baez (2009) explained that "capital involves oppression that functions in a covert and natural way which privileges those in the dominant group" (p. 152). Macedo (2000) argued, "By cultural reproduction I refer to collective experiences that function in the interest of dominant groups rather than in the interest of the oppressed groups that are objects of its policies" (p. 21).

In their article "Teachers, Schools and Academic Achievement," Rivkin, Hanushek, and Kain (2005) wrote, "Academic achievement at any point is a cumulative function of current and prior family, community and school experiences" (p. 422). On one hand, upper- and middle-class students who display strong family cultural capital that is congruent with the school's cultural capital are better able to enjoy academic achievement. On the other hand, minority Hispanic students are automatically perceived as either lacking family cultural capital or possessing less valuable capital and are unable to access the school's cultural capital necessary to attain academic success. Lareau and McNamara Horvat (1999) observed that "one of Bourdieu's major insights on educational inequality is that students with more valuable social and cultural capital fare better in school than do their otherwise comparable peers with less valuable social and cultural capital" (p. 37). Extensive research exists denoting that Hispanic students do not possess the dominant groups' cultural capital; thus, their culture and language are dismissed as having no value. The fact remains that the cultural differences between Hispanics and White students are perpetuated by an educational system that produces and "reproduces power relations by systematically disguising them" (Moore, 2004, p. 447).

Therefore, minority Hispanic children need to have the same educational accessibility that their White counterpart students have irrespective of cultural backgrounds, language skills, and socioeconomic status to help ensure academic attainment through improved curriculum, modified teaching methodologies, and changed standardized testing guidelines to meet the needs of a rapidly changing student population. Anyon (2005) said, "We have long known that social class, or socioeconomic status (SES), is highly correlated with educational achievement" (p. 65).

However, a symptomatic problem exists in our American school system that first blames minority Hispanic students because they are perceived as lacking the ability to learn due to English language barriers. Next, the family is blamed because Hispanic or Latino parents are perceived as not being interested in their child's education because they do not participate in school activities and/or events. Additionally, the community is blamed for not being more supportive of the educators' difficult job to teach a changing student demographic in a highly politically driven educational system.

According to Nieto (2009), "One consequence of accepting these deficit views is that because only students of backgrounds visibly different from the mainstream are thought to have a culture, culture itself is defined as a problem" (p. 477). Valenzuela (1999) observed that "schools . . . are organized formally and informally in ways that fracture students' cultural and ethnic identities, creating social, linguistic, and cultural divisions among the students and between the students and the staff" (p. 5). The educational system is not only divided on how to address these critical educational issues, but also necessitates a shift in instructional pedagogies to meet the cultural background needs of all students irrespective of race, ethnicity, gender, social class, socioeconomic status, religion, and sexual orientation.

This chapter presents some instructional recommendations for educators, which they may want to consider, while tapping into the students' rich cultural family backgrounds, language skills, and knowledge that influence student engagement.

Why Examine Cultural Capital?

It is important to note that Bourdieu's (1986) cultural capital theory is being used as a point of reference to illuminate and to bring awareness to educators of the perpetuation of the deficit lens in the academic setting, which exacerbates the academic gap of marginalized Hispanic children. Bourdieu (1986) believed that "the construct of capital makes it possible to explain the unequal scholastic achievement of children originating from different social classes by relating academic success" (p. 243). Bourdieu provided the following explanation of social classes' distinctions as they relate to academic achievement:

> The notion of cultural capital initially presented itself to me, in the course of research, as a theoretical hypothesis which made it possible to explain the unequal scholastic achievement of children originating from the different social classes by relating academic success, i.e., the specific profits which children from the different classes and class fractions can obtain in the academic market, to the distribution of cultural capital between the classes and class fractions. (p. 243)

Bourdieu (1986) further explained that the three forms of capital—economic, social, and cultural—are "derived from economic capital" (p. 252). These forms of capital are essential for survival in a diverse society. "Bourdieu asserts that cultural capital (i.e., education, language), social capital (i.e., social networks, connections) and economic capital (i.e., money and other material possessions) can be acquired two ways, from one's family and/or through formal schooling"(Yosso, 2005, p. 76). Hispanic parents pass on to their children the value of fostering family ties, earning money, and getting an education.

Nash (1990) explained that "societies and social groups within societies, must reproduce as well as produce, in fact, it might be said that they produce in order to reproduce" (p. 432). Minority Hispanic parents understand the need to break the chains of poverty, and they work to inform their children about the importance of becoming the first generation of students who are afforded better educational and professional opportunities in the future. However, "Bourdieu argues that schools and teachers aid and abet this family-based reproduction process by rewarding possession of elite cultural capital in students and by setting up elitist standards rigged to favor upper and middle class children and exclude others" (Tzanakis, 2011, p. 76). Researchers such as Kingston (2001) agreed that cultural capital is used for "social and cultural exclusion" (p. 89). He explained that "cultural capital is not, then, just a general resource available and valuable to everyone; it is largely the property of the existing elite. The elite benefit because their particular cultural signals, not others, are rewarded" (Kingston, 2001, p. 89). Bourdieu (1974) wrote,

> Although success at school directly linked to the cultural capital transmitted by the family milieu, plays a part in the choice of options taken up, it seems that the major determinant of study is the family attitude to the school which is itself, as we have seen a function of the objective hopes of success at school. (p. 35)

There is a commonly held belief that high-class students are rewarded and therefore included in the educational process by teachers who share the same inclusive cultural capital, and working-class students are excluded from necessary academic resources because they do not share the teacher's "cultural signals" of power and privilege. That is, "pedagogic actions reproduce power relations and the system of cultural arbitraries. So the whole education system reproduces culture and social or power relations" (Bourdieu & Passeron, 1977, p. 12). "This pedagogic action subjects working class or minority pupils to a form of *symbolic violence* forcing them into a competitive mechanism that rewards only dominant cultural capital" (Tzanakis, 2011, p. 77). Bourdieu and Passeron (1977) argued that cultural capital "is first and foremost a power to shape other peoples' lives through exclusion and symbolic imposition" (p. 18). Lamont and Lareau (1988) wrote, "In particular, it [cultural capital] is a power of legitimating the claim that specific cultural norms and practices are superior; and of institutionalizing these claims to regulate behavior and access to resources" (p. 159). Therefore, it is through the exclusionary act that schools continue to perpetuate the achievement gap of minority students who are perceived as lacking cultural capital.

Current Research, Findings, Implications

The purpose of this narrative inquiry was to specifically examine the role of cultural capital from home and school settings and its influence on student engagement through the use of the authentic "voices" of the participants. Sperling and Appleman (2011) explained that "voice is a language performance—always social, mediated by experience, and culturally embedded" (p. 71). By listening to the "oral history" (Creswell, 2007, p. 55) of the participants, the researcher gained a deeper understanding of how student engagement is impacted by the role of culture capital emanating from home and school settings.

Participants

The participants came from a small town situated in a rural bedroom community located in the largest county in Southern California. Although in recent years the town has seen an increase in population, it still only has one high school. The selection of the participants was purposefully done to allow for a richly diverse group of participants that included nine female Hispanic students, ranged between fifteen and eighteen years of age, and nine female parent participants, seven of which were of Hispanic descent with the exception of two female parents, one Canadian and one Caucasian. The three counselors were female, white, middle and upper class. The seven teachers' ethnicities were as follows: one female Asian-American, one female from Latin America, one male from Mexico, and four Caucasian females. The two administrators were upper class, one female Hispanic and one male African American. Each of the teacher participants varied in teaching experience from seven years to twenty-five years.

The Setting

The town is located in Southern California. The current student population ethnicity is as follows: 60.9% White, 33% Hispanic, 1.6% Black or African American, 1.7% Asian and 2.8% other. Approximately 32% of the students who participated in the study were eligible for the free-lunch program and classified as low socioeconomic status (Ed-Data, 2012).

According to Denzin (1978), "Triangulation can take many forms, but its basic feature will be the combination of two or more different research strategies in the study of the same empirical units" (p. 308). By comparing information gathered from all the participants, the researcher was able to see whether there was corroboration among participants, such as the teachers, administrators, counselors, parents, and students. A careful review of the transcribed, audio-taped interviews was conducted, and responses were compared from the participants to identify commonalities in emerging themes; "basically, triangulation is a comparison of information to determine whether or not there is corroboration" (Wiersma & Jurs, 2005, p. 256). The result of the triangulation findings provided answers to the research questions of the current study. Additionally, in an effort to maintain both privacy and anonymity, Table 1.6 reflects the pseudonyms assigned to each of the participants with a corresponding code letter and number.

Summary of Data Findings

Table 1.1 reflects summaries of the participants' perceptions of the interconnectedness between cultural capital from home and school and significant quotes regarding recommended solutions to achieve student engagement.

Table 1–1. Summaries of Participants' Perceptions and Recommended Solutions

Participants	Influence on student engagement		Significant Quotes
	Home Cultural Capital	School Cultural Capital	Recommended Solutions for student engagement
A. 1 Administrator Mr. Manning	• Different family backgrounds encounter dissimilar family experiences • Students learn work ethics at home • No computers at home • Work experience provides students with strong work ethics	• Academic rigor • Good teachers • School pride • Tutoring • Computer lab • Positive social links with administrators • Parents visit the school daily in person • Academic success is the result of good studying habits and hard work	"Parents know that they are always encouraged to visit the school" "We provide our students with a whole variety of academic, social, and career opportunities, so when they leave here they are well-rounded citizens" "Learning takes place when you see students working and collaborating together in developing and completing a product or a project" "It takes a team effort from educators, the students, and their parents to ensure students' success"
A. 2 Administrator Mrs. Garcia	• Two types of parents Haves and have nots • Parents tell kids about the value of education • "Sheltered" community and limited diversity • Some students struggle with academics	• Good school and strong curriculum • Hispanic parents do not visit school due to language barriers, work, and family demands • Some teachers need to be reminded that students lack technology at home	"I feel very strongly that it is this school's responsibility to make sure that everyone's needs are being met, including both the high achievers and the low achievers." "It is important to build good relationships between students and teachers" "Give students hands-on opportunities and training to help them make a connection to the community"
A. 3 Counselor Mrs. Bloom	• Different home backgrounds • Racial tensions originate at home • Some parents are college educated • Bad behavior affects student engagement	• She is an alumni and loves the kids • Positive school climate • Resilient students achieve success • High retention and graduation rates	"Our main goal is to present different assemblies on topics of diversity to educate them about appreciating differences" "The students know that we are approachable" "I think we work very well together to make every student successful"*(Continued)*

A. 4 **Counselor** **Mrs. Sierra**	• Old family values regarding race • Family backgrounds varied, some positive and some negative • Poverty makes kids feel inadequate • Students do not have same skill set	• Not very diverse campus • Teachers want to help students • Counselors and teachers work as a team • School provides information both in English and Spanish	"I think our students really try to stand up for each other, and for the most part the kids tolerate each other" "We are kind of the liaison. We keep the communication going between parents and teachers and teachers and students." "I think parents are more willing to visit the school when they see that good things are going on."
A. 5 **Counselor** **Mrs. Range**	• Community very conservative • Some parents train children from infancy to be successful in life • Some parents enable children to make bad choices	• Gay and Lesbian Alliance was a big challenge for the community to accept • Diversity a reality on campus • Teachers have high expectations • Caring teachers	"Students [in ROP] are interested in the hands-on experiences they gain, and they are very engaged in the learning process" "But we have to continue to keep on working on educating our students about diversity." "We must ask—what are some of the causes affecting student motivation, and what can we do to help them?"
A. 6 **Teacher** **Mrs. David**	• Students involved with their own church • Some parents teach great things and others have low expectations • Students help to take care of siblings	• Alternative school for students who struggle academically is a good thing • Some groups of students feel alienated • The squeaky wheel gets the grease	"Students need to learn how to ask for help, and they also need to ask questions" "I always like to tell my AVID students that you are not just learning what I am teaching you, but you are also learning how to learn." "Some parents think that their children are entitled to things that other people do not have, which they are able to get because of who they know in the district office"
A. 7 **Teacher** **Mrs. James**	• Family sets the tone about education • Parents support school's athletic program	• Opportunities for college-bound students • Overcrowded classrooms impact learning	"I believe that students who are disciplined at home can accomplish academic things that they may not necessarily want to do, but that they recognize that they should to gain an education"

A. 8 Teacher Mr. Brown	• Parents teach the value of education • Large percentage of parents have a college education • Parents are very supportive and involved in their child's education • Hispanic students cannot afford to be involved in sports	• AVID classes • Academic programs meet needs of all students • Not all cultural activities represent other ethnicities on campus • Students who lack technology at home struggle with academics	"The school offers after-school tutoring services and both the library and computer lab are available for all students, including ELL students" "When a student is organized it is going to reflect on their grade." "The environment at home makes a big difference in helping students with learning" "Using different teaching methodologies helps engage students in the learning process"
A. 9 Teacher Mrs. Gomez	• Parents teach children good values • Siblings play an important role • Students are candid and honest	• Many activities and athletics • Tolerance Week teaches students to respect differences • Students graduate and have jobs • Safe school	"Some students are very blessed to have parents that take them everywhere and expose them to everything. It is important to teach them how to socially interact with other people." "It is important to make education relevant to students"
A. 10 Teacher Mrs. Carr	• Students suffer academically because of family problems • Some students come from broken homes and others from affluent homes	• Positive school environment • Students are helpful and kind • Large size of classes impacts learning	"Students can find a niche here or they can find a place where they belong, even if they are not your stereotypical student" "A lot of students do not know how to study, and I encourage students to look at other peers who are successful"
A. 11 Teacher, Mrs. Willard	• Hispanic students cling to their cultural traditions • Community very supportive • Parents support Friday night football	• High percentage of white students and a growing Hispanic student population • School is on the top 20 out of 50 schools in the county	"The Diversity Council was created to make sure that minority students have a voice on campus" "I teach my students to understand that the choices of today can either have positive or negative consequences tomorrow"

(Continued)

A. 12 **Teacher** **Mrs.** **Lawrence**	• Students have a good connection with their families • Hispanic family traditions are important • Hispanic parents do not reach out for help with college information	• The only high school in the small community • Students are a bit "segregated" • Hispanic family values in conflict with school • Parents do not visit the school due to language barrier	"If their friends are involved, then they might feel more inclined to joining a club and the connection helps with student engagement" "You can tell when someone is polite and respectful, and these values come from home" "I try teaching my students that 'Si, Se Puede'—'Yes, We Can'" (Chavez, 2009) "Making the material relevant to the students' lives makes learning fun and interesting"
A. 13 **Parent** **Mrs. Alaniz**	• Taking care of siblings teaches responsibilities • College is expected • Actively involved in child's education	• School celebrates students' successes academically and athletically • School does a good job keeping parents informed	"It is interesting to hear students complain about the school, but they have no idea how good they have it here, unlike other schools where there are so many gangs" "Everyone at this school wants my daughter to succeed"
A. 14 **Parent** **Mrs. Linderos**	• Father has college degree • Mother is very involved in child's education. • Mother has experience navigating the school system • Mother has high hopes for her children	• School has good curriculum and high graduation rates • Daughter did not make the basketball cut • CASHEE testing very stressful for students • Positive things happening at the school	"I see my daughter as having the same success standards as her dad because he has a college education" "I thought this school would be a good fit for my children because I wanted them to feel equal to people of other ethnicities and not less because they are a minority" "I tell them to ask the teacher, or to ask me, or to ask somebody else. I try to teach them that the more you ask, the more you learn."
A. 15 **Parent** **Mrs. Olivares**	• Computers are available at home to do homework • Respect and family religious values • Value of education	• Only school in town • School has good teachers • Racism a problem • Drugs affect student engagement	"I have taught my daughter about the importance of not getting pregnant like I did when I was seventeen years old" "I have taught my daughter not to be a quitter"

A. 16 Parent Mrs. Cordova	• Choosing good friends is important • Family is important • Mother is a resource to her children	• The school has a good football team • School has high graduation rate • School keeps parents informed • Teenage pregnancy a distraction	"The school also offers remedial classes for students who are struggling" "I think it is important that parents find ways to keep their children involved in school in some sort of activity to keep them interested in learning and out of trouble"
A. 17 Parent Mrs. Orozco	• Children previously attended Magnet schools in Los Angeles • Respectful to teachers and others • Important to keep Mexican cultural traditions • Taught children needed information to succeed in life	• After-school tutoring • Library and computers at school • Athletics fees not affordable for Hispanic students • Drugs on campus • Gays and lesbians • Dress code not enforced	"I tell my children—yes, it is true, we are not professionals but we are able to provide you with all of the necessary information to support you morally, economically, and spiritually" "I tell my daughter that as the new generation they have to break the chains of poverty and build a chain of opportunity through education." "We are fighters, we are fighting to get ahead"
A. 18 Parent Mrs. Hernandez	• Parent checks child's grades • Value of a college education • Family is important • Important to complete household chores— teaches initiative and responsibility	• Peer pressure a barrier to learning • Meet with counselors and teachers • School sends out information via e-mail and telephone • Teachers want parents to be involved, but teachers need to make time to meet with parents	"We do not have a computer at home, but I take my children to the city library to use the computer" "All we can do for our kids is to try to be there for them in any way that we can" "Teachers need to teach real-life lessons, and they need to do more hands-on activities to make the subject more interesting to get the student's attention and to connect the material by making it relevant"

(Continued)

A. 19 Parent Mrs. Soto	• Daughter formerly enrolled in GATE • Importance of getting an education stressed at home • Choosing bad friends can be a distraction to learning • Mother has an associate degree and very involved in child's education	• After-school tutoring • Students form "cliques" and are not friendly to others • Front office staff not very welcoming • Counselor has ignored parent request to change student's ELL status	"I tell her, use your social skills for a good use because your friends are a reflection of who you are" "I keep my daughter busy with after-school extracurricular activities such as karate to keep her active and out of trouble" "The more parents know about what the children are studying at school, the better able they will be at helping their children at home"
A. 20 Parent Mrs. Cervantes	• Respectful to elders and others • Daughter has self-respect, self-esteem, and confidence • Religion very important • Hispanic parents do not visit the school because of work	• Not a lot of options—only one high school in town • Good academic classes • Strong football team • Latino Club	"The school also offers after-school tutoring and computer labs to help students graduate from high school" "I know how to find solutions to problems. I am not afraid to go to the school district to find someone who can help me" "I feel that teachers are a great resource of information. Teachers are always available to help and to counsel students"
A. 21 Parent Mrs. Escobar	• Daughter provides parents with class schedule • Good manners and respect • Education is important • Religion part of family tradition and culture • Social connection with counselors	• Closed campus • Community library has computers available for the youth • High cost of school activities prevents daughter from participating in school events • Drugs on campus a barrier to learning	"My daughter has been taught to ask for help if she does not understand something, and she knows to ask another student for help when she has problems with a subject she is learning, and she is always able to complete her homework." "I don't want her doing manual labor like me or her dad. I want her to have a career where she can use her intelligence."

A. 22 Student Cecilia Alaniz	• Parents have taught her to be polite, to be respectful, to be responsible, and to ask questions • Taking care of siblings teaches her to be responsible • Parents keep in contact with teachers via e-mail	• Instruction and curriculum are great • Parents visit school to visit with teachers and counselors • Some students do not want to learn; others get involved with the wrong people	"I do not particularly like going to school, but the school environment is positive because all of the teachers work really hard and put in so much effort and time." "My parents, my grandparents, aunts, and uncles have repeatedly told me—if you can dream it, you can achieve it" "I plan on attending the local community college first, and then I want to transfer to a four-year university."
A. 23 Student Katarina Linderos	• Student loves drawing and reading mystery books • Telling the truth is a family value • Education is important • Parents keep in touch with teachers via e-mail	• Proud of good sports team • School climate both negative and positive • After-school tutoring • Teachers available to help students	"Keep students involved through hands-on projects that are of interest to the students, and use social media like Facebook, which is an exciting thing to use at this time" "Having students just sitting, reading, and taking notes does not work anymore, some classes have a creative process and some classes don't"
A. 24 Student Cristina Olivares	• Good manners • Making good choices • Take responsibility for own actions • Parent involved with PTA • Religion important when making decisions	• School offers good classes, electives, and sports • Hispanic students are unable to "make the cut" in sports • Students not asking questions can hinder learning	"I want to either be an immigration officer or a special education teacher because I do not want to get stuck doing something I do not like for the rest of my life." "Do things that are interesting to the students that will grab the students' attention, and make the subject relevant to what students are currently experiencing."
A. 25 Student Maria Cordova	• Good manners • Being respectful to others important • Being late is never okay • Parent keeps in touch with teachers • Not everyone has computers at home	• Great teachers • Positive school climate • Students too afraid to ask questions • Some students lack motivation • Proud of curriculum	"My future goals and aspirations are to become an attorney-at-law" "I think all the teachers should incorporate more class interactions because it is a great way for the students to really learn about the subject" "There are a lot of smart students at school"

(Continued)

A. 26 Student Alejandra Orozco	• Religion is important • Value of education • Family cultural traditions • Parents do not visit the school due to work demands • Mother keeps in touch with teacher via e-mail • Father has college education	• School offers informational meetings for parents and students • A few good teachers • A lot of school spirit • Racism and bullying a problem • Lectures too boring	"I am highly motivated and driven to achieve many things in life because I want to make my parents proud of me. I am driven to expand my education because I have been raised in a family where money has always been a problem because of a low education. Seeing the struggles of not having an education motivates me to choose another path." "We need teachers who actually like their job, and we also need more interaction with our own counselors"
A. 27 Student Juana Hernandez	• Not every parent can afford to buy a computer at home • Home life very peaceful, respectful, and polite, unlike school • Alumni parents know the school culture • Religion a family value	• School clean and safe • Good curriculum • Computer labs and library • After-school tutors • School celebrates student success • A lot of "cliques" on campus • Counselors never give up on students	"Both my parents graduated from this school and they both attended college, and they have high expectations for me to finish high school and get a college education just like them." "My mom has taught me to never give up, and my parents have always encouraged me to work hard" "Teachers should do more hands-on activities or use some type of props to keep the students interested in learning."
A. 28 Student Alma Soto	• Importance of having good grades and planning for the future • Parents very involved with extracurricular activities outside the school	• School climate both positive and negative • Peers are a distraction to learning • Parents do not feel comfortable visiting the school	"The standard of instruction is good because my teachers are involved with my education" "All of my skills that I use have been taught to me by my mother. I want to either be an astronomer or hold a high government job so that I can have power"

A. 29 Student Gloria Cervantes	• Strong family values • Parents trust her ability to handle school issues • Mom has work flexibility to meet with counselors and/or teachers • Mom has taught her about mortgage interest rates and the economy	• Both good and bad school climate • Library and a computer lab • Good curriculum • Career Center • Student clubs and athletics • Clean school and safe • Counselors too busy to meet with students	"The school has a great learning environment and offers many resources to help students succeed academically" "My mom has taught me about the importance of getting an education to be able to live comfortably. She has always reminded me that I need to be able to support a family with or without having a man." "Every teacher has different teaching styles and some teachers are more effective than others"
A. 30 Student Esther Escobar	• Education is important • Self-efficacy • Parents do not speak English and do not visit the school • Parents trust daughter to handle own school issues	• School climate very calm • Racial and gender tension • Some students are afraid to ask questions in class • Some teachers are caring and flexible	"I know that education is necessary to help me break the chains of poverty because I see how much my parents struggle financially because they did not get a college education and they don't speak English." "My mother has taught me that education will benefit me in the long run because I can pass this on to my future kids and show them that anything is possible."

As you can see in Table 1.1, Hispanic students' home cultural capital had both a positive and a negative impact on student engagement: positive because of parents' strong support, high expectations, and strong family values, good manners—*modales*—and religious beliefs; negative because some students experienced economic challenges and others had difficult family backgrounds but demonstrated self-reliance in order to achieve academic success amidst the many barriers in their daily lives. The school's cultural capital, for the most part, was positive, as described by the administrators, counselors, teachers, parents, and students. However, the participants acknowledged factors of drugs on campus, peer pressure, cell phones in the classroom, "cliques" and racial tensions, students' lack of motivation, and teachers' difficulty adjusting to an increased minority-students population. In addition, Table 1.1 depicts the participants' perspectives regarding cultural capital resources both from home and school to help both "high achievers and low achievers" with student engagement.

In summary, the research findings revealed the following: (1) according to parents, education is an important goal to attain for their children to help stop the cycle of poverty. Parents also expressed a commitment to working with school administrators, teachers, and counselors to help ensure their child has the same access to school resources as their white counterparts; (2) according to administrators and counselors, students who come from difficult home environments tend to demonstrate a high degree of tenacity, resilience, and determination to complete their high school education and move on to higher education; (3) according to teachers, parents who are involved in their child's education have a positive influence on the student's ability to achieve academic success; and (4) according to the students, teachers who demonstrate a genuine concern for the students' success, both academically and personally, can have a lasting positive influence on the students' lives. The students also acknowledged their mother's strong commitment to helping them get an education to improve their quality of life.

Converting Cultural Capital to Student Engagement

Figure 1.2 reflects the cultural capital conversion and interconnectedness between home cultural capital and school cultural capital, which influence student engagement. It is important to note that Hispanic mothers in this study exerted a strong influence on their children by teaching them to "fight to get ahead" and get good grades by maintaining close-knit family ties, talking to counselors to handle school issues, asking teachers questions, and having high expectations for their children to both complete high school and to get a college education to break the chains of poverty. Some Hispanic mothers also understood the value of social and cultural capital and the need to develop networking connections with teachers and counselors to help them not only navigate the American school system, but also to help their children achieve academic success by giving them access to community resources.

The administrators, counselors, teachers, parents, and students in this study presented their own viewpoints and used their own "voices" to share their perspectives. Figure 1.2 also revealed additional home-school cultural capital dimensions identified through the personal interviews with the participants, which clearly "debunks the myth" (Valencia & Black, 2002, p. 99) that Hispanic working-class students do not value education. Specifically, in this current study, interviews of the participants revealed that the home cultures of the Hispanic students value education and expect their children to do well in school, exhibit high family involvement, trust their older children to care for their siblings, provide the opportunities for bilingualism to prosper, and view religion as an important part of family socialization, and expect their children to do well in school.

Table 1.2 depicts further additional findings that compare the deficit view of the Hispanic cultural capital and the more positive perspective that dispels the deficit thinking ideology and highlights the home cultural capital strengths parents and students in this study identified through personal interviews.

Implications

This research demonstrated that Hispanic students possess cultural capital, which has been transmitted from their parents via the family's cultural traditions, religious celebrations, native language skills, and close-knit family ties, which positively influence student engagement. As this chapter implied, we need to move toward a more inclusive educational system that recognizes minority Hispanic students' native language as valuable and also move toward appreciating the cultural capital Hispanic students possess and bring to the classroom. As Dewey (2009) proposed a democratic society, Ladson-Billings (2006) argued that it is imperative that we move away from simply talking about the academic achievement gap between

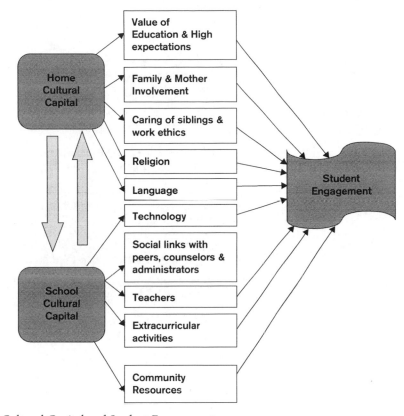

Figure 1–2. Cultural Capital and Student Engagement

Whites and Hispanics, Whites and African Americans, and Whites and Native Americans. She said, "We seem to study them but rarely provide the kind of remedies that helps them to solve their problems" (p. 3).

Therefore, there is a need for courageous educational leaders who are willing to fight for academic opportunities for all children. The creation of learning environments that not only challenge the students to gain new knowledge and skills at school, but also tap into the knowledge and skills that they bring from home should be the focus of educational leaders. Attention needs to be given to changing current school policies and procedures that both "profile" and "track" minority students into a never-ending pathway of deficiencies that leads to academic failure. Valenzuela (1999) suggests that by "making schools and schooling affirmative, truly educational experiences for all students requires implementing changes that reach deep into the structure of the educational system" (p. 99). In her book *Radical Possibilities*, Anyon (2005) wrote, "We have been attempting educational reform in U.S. cities for three decades" (p. 3). She calls for a new social movement to make radical changes to education reform. This social movement should start in the American school classrooms with teachers who are committed to acting as true social change agents to benefit all children, irrespective of the color of their skin, the native language they speak, the clothing they wear, the cultural traditions they practice, the music they listen to, or their socioeconomic background.

Table 1–2. Perceived Deficits and Strengths of Hispanic Parents and Students According to Faculty, Counselors, and Administrators.

Deficits	Strengths
Language barrier	Hispanic parents and students use native language at home to teach values, manners, and respect to others.
Taking care of siblings prevents students from completing homework	Caring for siblings teaches responsibility while parents go to work, and it helps to develop strong work ethics.
Hispanic parents do not attend school activities	Hispanic parents trust and encourage students to handle school issues, which teaches them responsibility and self-efficacy.
Parents do not value education	Hispanic parents have high expectations, hopes, and dreams for their children.
No computer access at home	Some parents provide computers at home, and those without computers at home use the community library.
Parents do not know how to navigate the school system	Hispanic parents are not afraid to contact the counselor or district personnel, and they ask for an interpreter to help them with school issues.
Hispanic parents "hang on to cultural traditions"	Hispanic parents teach the value of keeping strong and close-knit family ties and religious traditions and celebrations.
Difficult family backgrounds	Family economic struggles serve as a motivator for their children to escape poverty.
Increase ethnic diversity and racial tensions	Hispanic parents teach students to make good associations and avoid bad friendships.
Current curriculum does not meet the cultural needs of students	Minority students' culture and language are assets to help them convert home cultural capital into student engagement.
Hispanic students are not involved in school's athletic program	Although the school's athletic fees are too costly for some Hispanic students, they do participate in extracurricular activities outside the school.
Hispanic students are perceived at-risk in the American school system	Hispanic students have a strong sense of perseverance, resiliency, determination, and a desire to improve their quality of life.

Applications/Discussion Questions/Activities

Applications for Administrators

- Organize outreach projects to build collaborative bridges with the community they serve.
- Share information about resources and services in the community that can be beneficial to minority immigrant families and their children.

- Teach minority Hispanic parents about the American school system (i.e., curriculum, access to counselors, administration, and teachers, and advocacy for their children).
- Provide professional development to help teachers connect to the cultural capital students bring from home.
- Research and identify the schools' cultural capital to identify areas of improvement to help all students achieve academic success.

Applications for Teachers

- Move away from directed instruction to a more collaborative approach by creating learning environments that not only include technology, but also hands-on activities.
- Use real-life scenarios to help students make the connection to what they are learning in the classroom to enhance student engagement.
- Conduct home visitations with appropriate school staff support to gain a deeper understanding of the student's cultural capital.
- Engage parents in their child's learning process to remove barriers and misconceptions.

Applications for Counselors

- Participate in culturally sensitive training to better serve minority Hispanic students.
- Work collaboratively with both teachers and parents to help students break the failure rates through access to school resources.
- Conduct research to identify the motivating factors students use to be resilient amidst the many obstacles and challenges they face at school because of language acquisition, ethnicity, and race.
- Improve scheduling issues to allow students quality time to visit with the counselors.

Discussion Questions

- How do you create understanding of minority Hispanic students' cultural capital? What type of questions would you ask to avoid being intrusive? What type of classroom activities would you use to solicit information in a group setting?
- Why do you think it is important to conduct home visits? What are some of the misconceived notions you have personally experienced about this process? How would you go about overcoming said notions?
- What can you do as an educator, a counselor, and/or an administrator to better serve not only the students, but also the community? Why is it important to build positive working relationships with parents and their children?

Activities

1. A new teacher, Mr. Jones, comes to you for advice regarding a Hispanic student who is always sleeping during the first period. What advice would you give Mr. Jones to help him understand

the student's personal situation before he makes wrongful and judgmental assumptions, not knowing that the student is responsible for working at night to help feed his seven siblings?

2. You just attended a workshop on cultural capital and student engagement, and you do not agree with the concept because you don't understand how you could possibly apply it in your classroom. You share your feelings with your colleague, Mrs. Brown. She, in turn, asks you the following question: Have you thought about developing a classroom activity where the students share either family or religious traditions to gain a better understanding of their cultural capital?

3. You just overheard a seasoned teacher, Ms. Lopez, express a desire to organize a community outreach project to teach minority Hispanic parents how to tap into the school's cultural capital. How would you go about helping Ms. Lopez gather information to give to the parents to help them access school resources, to teach them to use their "voice" to advocate for their children, and to guide them through the educational hierarchal system?

References

Age, J. (2009). Developing qualitative research questions: A reflective process. *International Journal of Qualitative Studies in Education, 22*(4), 431–447.

Altshuler, S. J., & Schmautz, T. (2006). No Hispanic student left behind: The consequences of "high stakes" testing. *Children & Schools, 28*(1), 5–14.

Anyon, J. (2005). *Radical possibilities: Public policy, urban education, and a new social movement.* New York, NY: Routledge, a Taylor & Francis Group, LLC.

Aronowitz, S. (2009). Against schooling: Education and social class. In A. Darder, M. P. Baltodano & R. D. Torres (Eds.). *The Critical Pedagogy Reader* (2nd ed.). New York, NY: Routledge, a Taylor & Francis Group, pp. 109–110.

Bogdan, R. C. & Biklen, S. K. (2003). *Qualitative research for education: An introduction to theories and methods* (4th ed.). New York, NY: Pearson Education Group, p. 111.

Bourdieu, P. (1973). Cultural reproduction and social reproduction. In R. Brown (Ed.), *Knowledge, education, and cultural change: Papers in the sociology of education.* London: Tavistock, p. 96.

Bourdieu, P. (1974). The school as a conservative force: Scholastic and cultural inequalities. In J. Eggleston (Ed.), *Contemporary research in the sociology of education.* London: Methuen, p. 35.

Bourdieu, P. (1977). *Cultural reproduction and social reproduction.* In J. Karabel & A. H. Halsey (Eds.), *Power and ideology in education.* New York, NY: Oxford University Press, p. 494

Bourdieu, P. (1986). The forms of capital. In J. G. Richardson (Ed.), *Handbook of theory and research for the sociology of education.* New York, NY: Greenwood Press, pp. 241–258.

Bourdieu, P. & Passeron, J. (1977). *Reproduction in education, society and culture. Translated from the French by Richard Nice.* Beverly Hills, CA: Sage Publications, p. 73.

Castellanos, J., & Jones, L. (2003). *The majority in the minority: Expanding the representation of Latina/o faculty, administrators and students in higher education.* Sterling: VA, Stylus Publishing, LLC, p. ix.

Chase, S. (2005). Narrative Inquiry: Multiple lenses, approaches, voices. In N. Denzin & Y. Lincoln (Eds.), *The Sage handbook of qualitative research,* (3rd ed.). Thousand Oaks, CA: Sage Publications, p. 657.

Chavez, C. (2009). Cesar E. Chavez Campaign, Si Se Puede! Yes We Can! Retrieved from http://www. cesarechavezfoundation.org/uploads/Si_Se_Puede_Curriculum_2009_-_Middle_School.pdf.

Connelly, F. M., & Clandinin, D. J. (2006). Narrative inquiry. In J. L. Green, G. Camilli & P. B. Elmore (Eds.). *Handbook of complementary methods in education research.* Washington: DC: Lawrence Erlbaum Associates Publishers, pp. 477–488.

Creswell, J. W. (2007). *Qualitative inquiry & research design; Choosing among five approaches* (2nd ed.). Thousand Oaks, CA: Sage Publications, p. 37.

Crosnoe, R. (2005). The diverse experiences of Hispanic students in the American educational system. *Sociological Forum, 20*(4), pp. 561–588.

De Graaf, N. D., De Graaf, P. M., & Kraaykamp, G. (2000). Parental cultural capital and educational attainment in the Netherlands: A refinement of the cultural capital perspective. *Sociology of Education, 73*(2), 92–111.

Denzin, N. K. (1978). *The research act: A theoretical introduction to sociological methods.* (2nd ed.). In W. Wiersma & S. G. Jurs. (Eds.), *Research methods in education: An introduction* (8th ed.). Boston, MA: Pearson Education, Inc., p. 257.

Dewey, J. (2009). *Democracy and education: An introduction to the philosophy of education.* Charleston, SC: ReadaClassic.com, p. 5.

DiMaggio, P. (1982). Cultural capital and school success: The impact of status culture participation on the grades of U.S. high school students. *American Sociological Review, 47*(2), 189–201.

Ed-Data. (2012). Countywide profile: Fiscal year 2011–2012. Retrieved on October 12, 2012 from http://www.ed-data.k12.ca.us/App_Resx/EdDataClassic/fsTwoPanel.aspx?#!bottom=/ layouts/ EdDataClassic/profile.asp?level=05.

Fernandez, L. (2002). Telling stories about school: Using critical race and Latino critical theories to document Latina/Latino education and resistance. *Qualitative Inquiry, 8*(1), 48.

Fredricks, J. A., Blumenfeld, P. C., & Paris, A. H. (2004). School engagement: Potential of the concept, state of the evidence. *Review of Educational Research, 74*(1), 59–109.

Freire, P. (1970). *Pedagogy of the oppressed.* New York, NY: The Continuum International Publishing Group.

Gándara, P. & Rumberger, R. W. (2009). Immigration, language, and education: How does language policy structure opportunity? *Teachers College Record, 111*(3), 750–782.

Gibson, M. A., & Obgu, J. U. (1991). *Minority status and schooling: A comparative study of immigrant and involuntary minorities.* In R. D. Stanton-Salazar & S. M. Dornbusch, (Eds.), Social capital and the reproduction of inequality: Information networks among Mexican-origin high school students. *Sociology of Education, 68,* 116–135.

Giroux, H. A. (2009). Teacher education and democratic schooling. In A. Darder, M. P. Baltodano & R. D. Torres (Eds.), *The critical pedagogy reader* (2nd ed.). New York, NY: Routledge Taylor & Francis Group, p. 47.

Guba, E. G., & Lincoln, Y. S. (1981). *Effective evaluation.* In S. B. Merriam. (Ed.), *Case study research in education.* San Francisco, CA: Jossey-Bass, Inc., Publishers, p. 135.

Harker, R. (1990). Bourdieu—Education and reproduction. In C. Mahar, R. Harker & C. Wikes (Eds.), *An introduction to the work of Pierre Bourdieu: The practice of theory,* London: MacMillan, pp. 86–108.

hooks, b. (2009). Confronting class in the classroom. In A. Darder, M. P. Baltodano & R. D. Torres (Eds.). *The critical pedagogy reader* (2nd ed.). New York, NY: Routledge Taylor & Francis Group, p. 138.

Huber, J., & Whelan, K. (1999). A marginal story as a place of possibility: negotiating self on the professional knowledge landscape. In J. W. Creswell (Ed.), *Qualitative inquiry & research design; Choosing among five approaches* (2nd ed.). Thousand Oaks, CA: Sage Publications, Inc., p. 57.

Hursh, D. (2007). Assessing no child left behind and the rise of Neoliberal education policies. *American Educational Research Journal, 44*(3), 493–518.

Khalifa, M. (2010). Validating social and cultural capital of hyperghettoized at-risk students. (Doctoral Dissertation), University of Texas at San Antonio. In *Education and Urban Society, 42*(5), 620-646. doi: 10.1177/0013124510366225.

Kingston, P. W. (2001). The unfulfilled promise of cultural capital theory. *Sociology of Education, 74*, 88–99, Extra Issue: Current of thought: Sociology of Education at the Dawn of the 21st Century. American Sociological Association.

Ladson-Billings, G. (1995). Toward a theory of culturally relevant pedagogy. *American Educational Research Journal, 32*(3), 465–491.

Ladson-Billings, G. (2006). From the achievement gap to the education debt: Understanding achievement in U.S. Schools. *Educational Researcher, 35*(3), 3–12.

Ladson-Billings, G. (2009a). *The dream-keepers: Successful teachers of African American children* (2nd ed.). San Francisco, CA: Jossey-Bass, A Wiley Imprint. p. 19.

Ladson-Billings, G. (2009b). Fighting for our lives. In A. Darder, M. P. Baltodano & R. D. Torres (Eds.), *The critical pedagogy reader* (2nd ed.). New York, NY: Routledge Taylor & Francis Group, pp. 460–468.

Lamont, M. & Lareau, A. (1988). Cultural capital: Allusions, gaps, and glissandos in recent theoretical developments. *Sociological Theory, 6*(2), 153–168.

Lareau, A. (1987). Social class differences in family-school relationships: The importance of cultural capital. *Sociology of Education, 60*(2), 73–85.

Lareau, A., & McNamara Horvat, E. (1999). Moments of social inclusion and exclusion race, class and cultural capital in family-school relationships. *American Sociological Association, 72*(1), 37.

Lareau, A. & Weininger, E. B. (2003). Cultural capital in educational research: A critical Assessment. *Theory and Society, 32*, 567–606. Special issue on the Sociology of Symbolic Power: A special Issue in memory of Pierre Bourdieu.

Lichtman, M. (2006). *Qualitative research in education: A user's guide.* Thousand Oaks, CA: Sage Publications, Inc., p. 12.

Lin, N. (2001). *Social capital: A theory of social structure and action.* New York, NY: Cambridge University Press, pp. 33–40.

Lincoln, Y. S. & Guba, E. G. (1985). *Naturalistic inquiry.* Beverly Hills, CA: Sage.

Lipman, P. (2009). Beyond accountability: Toward schools that create new people for a new way of life. In A. Darder, M. P. Baltodano & R. D. Torres (Eds.) *The critical pedagogy reader* (2nd ed.). New York, NY: Routledge Taylor & Francis Group, p. 371.

Macedo, D. (2000) The colonialism of the English only movement. *Educational Researcher, 20*(3), 15–24.

Martin, N. D. & Spenner, K. I. (2009). Capital conversion and accumulation: A social portrait of legacies at an elite university. *Research in Higher Education, 50*(7), 623–648.

McLaren, P. (2009). Critical pedagogy: A Look at the major concepts. In A. Darder, M. P. Baltodano & R. D. Torres (Eds.), *The critical pedagogy reader* (2nd ed.). New York. NY: Routledge Taylor & Francis Group, pp. 61–83.

Merriam, S. B. (1988). *Case study research in education: A qualitative approach.* San Francisco, CA: Jossey-Bass, Inc., Publishers, p. 84.

Moll, L. C., Amanti, C., Neff, D., & Gonzales, N. (1992), Funds of knowledge for teaching: Using a qualitative approach to connect homes and classrooms. *Theory into Practice, 31*(2), 132–141.

Moore, R. (2004). Cultural capital: Objective probability and the cultural arbitrary. *British Journal of Sociology of Education, 25*(4), 445–456.

Musoba, G. & Baez, B. (2009). The cultural capital of cultural and social capital: An economy of translations. In J. C. Smart (Ed.), *Higher Education: Handbook of Theory of Research, 24*, pp. 151–182.

Nash, R. (1990). Bourdieu on education and social and cultural reproduction. *British Journal of Sociology of Education, 11*(4), 431–447.

Nieto, S. (2009). Bringing bilingual education out of the basement. In A. Darder, M. P. Baltodano & R. D. Torres (Eds.). *The critical pedagogy reader* (2nd ed.). New York, NY: Routledge a Taylor & Francis Group, p. 478.

Norrid-Lacey, B. & Spencer, D. A. (1999). Dreams I wanted to be reality: Experiences of Hispanic immigrant students at an urban high school. *A paper presented at the Annual Meeting of the American Educational Research Association.* Montreal, Quebec: Canada.

Ochoa, G. L. (2000.). Mexican Americans' attitudes toward and interactions with Mexican immigrants: A qualitative analysis of conflict and cooperation. *Social Science Quarterly, 81*(1), 84–87.

Perez, M. (2009). Low-income Latina parents, school choice, and Pierre Bourdieu. In J. Anyon (Ed.), *Theory and educational research: Toward critical social explanation.* New York, NY: Routledge, a Taylor & Francis Group, pp. 135–148.

Ramos-Zayas, A. Y. (2004). Implicit social knowledge, cultural capital and "authenticity" among Puerto Ricans in Chicago. *Latin American Perspectives, 31*(5), 34 56.

Ream, R. K. (2003). Counterfeit social capital and Mexican-American under achievement. *Educational Evaluation and Policy Analysis, 25*(3), 237–262.

Ream, R. K., & Rumberger, R. W. (2008). Student engagement, peer social capital, and school dropout among Mexican American and Non-Latino white students. *Sociology of Education, 81*, 109–139.

Rivkin, S. G., Hanushek, E. A., & Kain, J. F. (2005). Teachers, schools, and academic achievement. *Econometrica, 73*(2), 417–458.

Roscigno, V. J., & Ainsworth-Darnell, J. W. (1999). Race, cultural capital and educational resources: Persistent inequalities and achievement returns. *Sociology of Education, 72*(3), 158–178.

Salkind, N. J. (2010). Narrative research. *Encyclopedia of Research Design.* Thousand Oaks, CA: Sage Publications, Inc., pp. 869–947.

Singh, D. (2009). *Ethnographic studies in education,* Vol. 2. Retrieved from http://schoolofeducators. com/2009/12/volume-2-month-12-day-26-ethnographic-studies-in-education/.

Smrekar, C. (1996). *The impact of school choice and community: In the interest of families and schools.* Albany, NY: State University of New York Press.

Sperling, M., & Appleman, D. (2011). Review of research: Voice in the context of literary studies. *Reading Research Quarterly, 46*(1), 70–84.

Stanton-Salazar, R. D., & Dornbusch, S. M. (1995). Social capital and the reproduction of inequality: Information networks among Mexican-origin high school students. *Sociology of Education, 68,* 116–135.

Stuart, M., Lido, C., & Morgan, J. (2011). Personal stories: How students' social and cultural life histories interact with the field of higher education. *International Journal of Lifelong Education, 30*(4), 489–508.

Sullivan, A. (2002). Bourdieu and education: How useful is Bourdieu's theory for researchers? *The Netherlands' Journal of Social Sciences, 38*(2), 144–166.

Trueba, E. T. (1999). Critical ethnography and Vygotskian pedagogy of hope: The empowerment of Mexican immigrant children. *Qualitative Studies in Education, 12*(6), 591–614.

Tzanakis, M. (2011). Bourdieu's social reproduction thesis and the role of cultural capital in educational attainment: A critical review of key empirical studies. *Educate, 11*(1), 76–90.

UFW: The official web page of the United Farm Workers of America. (2006). *Education of the heart: Quotes by Cesar Chavez.* Retrieved from http://www.ufw.org/_page.php?menu=research&inc.=history/09.html.

United States Department of Commerce, Bureau of the Census (2000). *Census 2000 brief: Overview of race and Hispanic origin.* In R. K. Ream, (Ed.). Counterfeit social capital and Mexican-American under achievement. *Educational Evaluation and Policy Analysis, 25*(3), 237–262.

United States Department of Education. (2001). *No Child Left Behind Act of 2001.* Washington, DC: United States Department of Education.

Valencia, R. R., & Black, M. S. (2002). Mexican Americans don't value education!"— On the basis of the myth, mythmaking and debunking. *Journal of Latinos and Education, 1*(2), 81–103.

Valenzuela, A. (1999). *Subtractive schooling: U.S.-Mexican youth and the politics of caring.* Albany, NY: State University of New York Press.

Velez-Ibanez, C.G., & Greenberg, J. (2005). Formation and transformation. In N. Gonzales, L. Moll & C. Amanti (Eds.), *Funds of knowledge: Theorizing practices in households, communities and classrooms.* Mahwah, NJ: Lawrence Erlbaum Associates, Inc. p. 59.

Webb, L. D. & Norton, M. S. (2009). *Human resources administration: Personnel issues and needs in education* (5th ed.). Upper Saddle River, NJ: Pearson Education, Inc. p. 257.

Wiersma, W., & Jurs, S. G. (2005). *Research methods in education: An introduction* (8th ed.). Upper Saddle River, NJ: Pearson Education, Inc., p. 257.

Winkle-Wagner, R. (2010). *Cultural capital: The promises and pitfalls in educational research.* Hoboken, NJ: John Wiley & Sons.

Yosso, T. J. (2005). Whose culture has capital? A critical race theory discussion on community cultural wealth. *Race Ethnicity and Education, 8*(1), 69–91.

Yosso, T. J. & Garcia, D. G. (2007). "This Is No Slum!" A critical race theory analysis of community cultural wealth in cultural clash's Chavez Ravine. *A Journal of Chicano Studies, 32*(1), 145–179.

CHAPTER 2

Tapping Into Funds of Knowledge for Student Engagement

What are we missing with student engagement? Although changes in academic standards, content area assessments, and teacher qualifications may change throughout the years, one emphasis in education will never change—the need for student engagement. This issue has remained a quandary for teachers throughout generations. As well-rounded educators, we know that there is no magic solution to a problem that evolves constantly, but we can definitely expand our understanding of what student engagement is and how our schools can address it. There are many personal and contextual factors that contribute to student engagement. Students' goal orientations and self-efficacy are major personal factors that are influenced by prior experiences in school and home life. Instructional contexts also affect student engagement greatly; one of these contexts is real-life significance. Therefore, the research described in this chapter analyzes how student home environment, academic content, and school environment inform teaching and learning strategies through the lens of funds of knowledge. This perspective can help teachers, counselors, school leaders, and community members create a learning environment that provides real-life significance that is informed by students' real personal experiences. The results of the research in this chapter were used to create an approach called *Cross-Educational Teaching* (Macias, 2012). This approach to instruction utilizes learning strategies that take place at home through family dynamics and combines them with common instructional strategies used in the classroom to create a new lesson plan format that uses students' funds of knowledge.

What We Know about Funds of Knowledge

Funds of knowledge is defined as "historically accumulated and culturally developed bodies of knowledge and skill essential for household and individual functioning and well-being; skills, experiences, and values students gain from their home experience and family" (Moll, Amanti, Neff & Gonzalez, 1992, p. 133). To adequately examine the funds of knowledge students bring to school, educators must consider students' personal backgrounds as well as the environment in which they live and go to school. This holistic approach is necessary when using a funds of knowledge lens.

The Need for Funds of Knowledge Studies

Currently in the United States, demographic statistics indicate the diverse population of students served in public schools is changing all the time. However, the diversity of the student population does not match the demographics of teachers employed in the public school system. As of 2011, 84% of educators in the U.S. are white (Crouch & Zakariya, 2012). Although the population of young Hispanic educators entering the teaching field is growing, it is not growing nearly as quickly as the number of Hispanic students in public schools. In fact, the largest growing population of young people in the United States are Hispanic, both native and foreign-born (Crouch & Zakariya, 2012). According to Davis and Bauman (2013), in Southwestern states such as California, Arizona, Nevada, New Mexico, and Texas, at least 40% of students in public schools are Hispanic. The same study shows that 13% of the entire U.S. population is foreign-born. In the future, trends also indicate that there will be no majority group in the United States; all groups will be less than 50%, making the U.S. one of the most diverse societies—if not *the* most diverse society—in the world (Crouch & Zakariya, 2012).

What does this mean for the field of education? Ultimately, the changing demographics are linked to concerns of whether schools are adequately serving minority students. Crouch and Zakariya (2012) explain that some growing concerns with the change in population are the needs to address equity in programs, qualified educators, gaps, and high school completion rates. This does not mean that the differing demographics in teacher and student populations is the sole reason for these concerns, but it does serve as a baseline understanding for a need in studying students' funds of knowledge so that teachers can build appropriate educational environments and develop appropriate instructional strategies. Even if the population of educators begins to match the demographics of students at some point in the future, the strategies used in schools for teaching, counseling, and leading originated under a system of the past with a monocultural approach and a very different population. Therefore, it is likely that educational outcomes will still reflect our current problems, and the achievement gap will persist.

Funds of knowledge is an approach that attempts to remedy the incongruence of a monocultural system and a diverse population. Gonzales, Moll, Floyd-Tenery, Rivera, Rendon, Gonzales, and Amanti (1993) conducted an anthropological ethnography studying Latino students' cultural experiences and skills learned at home in order to help combat deficit thinking. Their study resulted in the theory called funds of knowledge. Teachers studied the skills, experiences, and family dynamics of their students and later applied findings to curriculum and instruction.

Recent studies on funds of knowledge reveal that there are many untapped educational resources in all low-income communities. For example, Licona's (2013) study on a low-income border community found that there were many examples of renewable resources adapted into everyday living that could serve as a wonderful starting point for science lessons. Licona also indicated that many science teachers carry with them some feelings of intimidation related to their own content areas that were most likely instilled in them through college. Thus, the teachers' attitudes prior to this funds of knowledge study were that science was an elite subject, only for the academically advanced. However, even in low-income and low-education communities, examples of very complex scientific action was found that could serve as culturally relevant instructional material.

Another study out of Canada found that funds of knowledge studies can even be applied to students as young as preschool and still prove to be helpful. Massing, Kirova, and Hennig (2013) found that when preschool teachers did home visits and were trained on funds of knowledge, they found ways to incorporate home languages and objects from home to increase success of immigrant and refugee students. Even the challenge of a language barrier was met with neighbors and friends that proved to be a valuable bridge for communication. This study helped the preschool teachers interpret some of the behaviors that they were seeing in students of different backgrounds than themselves.

Larrotta and Serrano's study (2012) involved adult students in a parent class designed to teach Spanish-speaking parents English. Rather than home visits, these researchers conducted a language course designed to utilize funds of knowledge by allowing the adult students to use culturally relevant reading material, group discussions, and creative writing. Selecting topics that parents care about—such as household finances—for reading material, assigning personal glossaries to learn vocabulary after group discussion, and writing culturally relevant stories allowed students to engage with the material and use their funds of knowledge to learn English. The course showed success due to the connection to real life with topics and due to the selection of activities that allowed students to feel respected during the lesson. These are essential elements to a funds of knowledge approach.

The research in this chapter used a similar approach to Licona's (2013), Massing, Kirova, and Hennig's (2013), and Larrotta and Serrano's (2012) funds of knowledge studies. The research in this chapter focuses on student engagement and utilized culturally relevant learning activities and various qualitative methods to identify funds of knowledge students possess and the perspectives on funds of knowledge held by students, parents, and teachers at a Southern California high school.

Current Research, Findings, and Implications

The purpose of this research was to investigate Latino students' funds of knowledge through three qualitative methods: interviews, observations, and document analysis. Narrative inquiry was chosen for this research because funds of knowledge rely on personal experience, cultural background, and social capital. Due to the personal nature of sources that make up funds of knowledge, narrative inquiry seemed an appropriate choice. Chase (2008) wrote that narrative inquiry is a particular subtype of qualitative inquiry (p. 651). A narrative is a retelling of one part or all of a participant's life that serves as a form of discourse in which meanings are constructed. This emphasizes the researcher's role as a facilitator and interpreter, as well as the participants' role as narrators of their own experiences. This approach allows for easier access to funds of knowledge than other forms of research.

Document analysis was used as one process to tell the stories of teachers and students. Teachers' lesson plans were analyzed with the purpose of identifying areas that encouraged or increased student engagement. This was cross-referenced with interviews to verify that these strategies employed in the lessons did seem to increase engagement in academic content. Teachers were fairly consistent in strategies that they employed to increase engagement, and these strategies were often present in lesson plans, indicating a consistent planning-to-practice pedagogy by these educators.

Document analysis was also used with photovoice journals, a project designed to combine funds of knowledge and content standards for a grade level-appropriate writing. Wang and Burris (1997) began the photovoice method in the health industry, and over the last several years, it has found a strong, useful purpose in other fields, such as education.

Photovoice is defined as:

> A process by which people can identify, represent, and enhance their community through a specific photographic technique. It entrusts cameras to the hands of people to enable them to act as recorders, and potential catalysts for change, in their own communities. It uses the immediacy of the visual image to furnish evidence and to promote an effective, participatory means of sharing expertise and knowledge. (Wang & Burris, 1997, p. 369)

This research technique was selected in order to allow for students to be placed in the role of expert concerning what affects their learning. The hope was to enhance their school community by offering personal perspectives on their own funds of knowledge. Students were informed that this project was to help teachers better understand what they care about and what affects their learning.

Additional methods of research employed were interviews and observations. Parents and teachers were interviewed with open-ended questions on topics related to their perspective on student engagement in school. All parent participants were extremely welcoming by inviting the researcher into their homes along with a translator. The experience was very comfortable as well as extremely revealing. These families supported the interest the researcher had in their lives as a teacher and a researcher. Regardless of the language barrier, families were open and seemed grateful for the opportunity to contribute to research that supports their community. Observations were interwoven into this process of the home visits in which the interviews took place for each family. Additional observations were done in class with students as they discussed their photovoice journals in groups. This process was a positive confirmation in value of personal experiences for many students, as they had opportunities to share their topics and journal entries with peers.

Teachers were interviewed in their classrooms and other various locations. This was a wonderful opportunity to get a candid look at teachers' perspectives on topics that rarely get covered in typical faculty meetings. The teachers at this school community were also open and willing to support research on student engagement. They exhibited significant dedication to their profession and their students.

Research Findings

The photovoice journals, observations, interviews with parents, home observations, interviews with teachers, and lesson plans were all analyzed for common themes related to student engagement. Macias (2012) began with the students by looking for common themes between all of the photovoice journals and offsetting this data with any additional field notes taken during classroom observations. Students were given unlimited time over a semester to work on their photovoice journals by selecting topics that affected their learning in and out of school, taking photos that represented these topics, and writing journal entries on each topic selected.

Even though students were given freedom on selecting topics, Macias (2012) found that half of the photovoice journal entries were related to school, indicating the importance of school in the lives of these students. Additionally, nearly half of the journal topics were devoted to specific people, indicating a strong influence of personal relationships that influence the value for school. After identifying the topics students selected, the photovoice journals were analyzed for overall emphasis, and meaningful quotes were selected. Figure 2.1 outlines the social and cultural values implied by the topics and overall emphasis of each photovoice journal.

The parent interviews and home observations resulted in similar topics found in student photovoice journals. Topics of discussion by parents primarily focused on values such as selecting friends, using family and community resources, finding role models, setting academic goals and expectations, and appreciating cultural heritage. There was a clear connection between the parent responses and their children's journals. Furthermore, the rest of the student participants also reflected these same concepts in their journals. This indicates that there may be a fairly consistent set of values in many families across this school community, a finding that could prove to be an extremely valuable component in the process of increasing student engagement.

Another finding that has a huge impact on student engagement was the importance of role models. Almost every student in the study listed a sibling or older relative that guided him or her in schoolwork and personal life. This finding represents a huge untapped resource that teachers could utilize on a regular basis.

Figure 2.2 outlines meaningful quotes and social and cultural values articulated by each parent participant during interviews. These social and cultural values greatly shape students' funds of knowledge. Although there were five parent participants, two participated in one interview. Parent interview 1 represents a father and mother's responses.

Throughout the analysis of the data from teacher interviews and analysis of lesson plans, it was apparent that teacher participants did not recognize many of the resources that parents and students relied upon for school success and student engagement. In the fifty minutes that teachers had with their students to teach their core subject, they made multiple efforts to engage students in learning. Many of these were effective according to teachers' responses, but they still were not described by students and parents when the data was compared. This indicates that all parties have an understanding of student engagement that is built upon different sources and measured by different outcomes. In other words, teachers are not wrong about which of their efforts result in student engagement in class, but there are

	Meaningful Quotes	Social and Cultural Values that Influence Learning
1	"I encourage myself to succeed." "I give thanks to God for sending me this beautiful gift."	Personal Strengths, Religion
2	"Seeing the smile on her face when she looked at my report card was fascinating. Hopefully there will be many more smiles." "We actually compete with each other to see who will get better grades."	Confidence, Competitiveness
3	"I want to make my parents proud of something; make them see that I am something in my life." "She always told me to keep my head up and high and chase after my dreams and goals."	Supportive Relationships, Following Dreams
4	"They affect my studies because when I need their help on any class they try to help me." "I like dancing because it's what my ancestors did back then, and I feel like I need to do this, too, because I want to bring back our culture and where I came from."	Academic Support, Cultural Roots
5	"They always help me in the things I need." "...like my dad, I always know that I could count on him because he is the only thing I have."	Family Support, Parent Relationships
6	"I will only get that car that I want if I go to college." "Church helps my family stay bonded."	Focus on the Future, Family Support
7	"I want to be the first in my family to go to college." "My friends in Honors tell me to stay after school with them for help...Most of them want me to be successful."	Academic Focus, Motivation for Success
8	"My aunt and uncle are the first...to graduate...which inspired me because I want to do the same." "With music, I can be who I really am, instead of pretending to be someone I wish I was."	Motivation for Academic Success, Individuality
9	"My family has so much love inside them." "My friends are like family to me, we are close to each other, and they always have my back."	Family and Friend Support
10	"She affects it [my learning] by giving me so much advice when I need it most." "She makes me be a good role model, so when she's older she follows good paths."	Encouraging Relationships, Role Models

Figure 2–1. Funds of Knowledge Through Photovoice Journals

	Meaningful Quotes	Social and Cultural Values Articulated by Parents
1	"I encourage my daughters to be very selective with their friends so they pick friends who are equally or more educated so that they are around people who elevate them."	Parents trust daughters to communicate problems; Parents teach daughters to choose friends very wisely
2	"I learned that language was not a barrier or an excuse for getting the appropriate education for my child."	Maintaining extremely high expectations for going to college; Parents must be highly involved in children's education
3	"I tell my daughter that this is the time in her life and learning is beautiful. If I could go back in time, I would go get that education."	Hard work will help students achieve goals; Open, honest communication with children allows for better lifelong learning
4	"She needs to try her best, not just be another body or another person there, but to be more than that and to stand out. She is not documented, but that just means she has to try harder."	Utilizing family and friends as a network of support; Family bonding through cultural practices

Figure 2–2. Funds of Knowledge Through Parent Interviews

additional funds of knowledge that are more important to students that could produce a much higher level of authentic student engagement in classroom lessons and school participation overall.

Throughout the entire process of triangulating data from all twenty participants, four themes became evident: friendships, siblings and relatives, communication skills, and decision-making skills. A summary of all student, parent, and teacher perspectives of these funds of knowledge and the implications for student engagement follow.

Student Friendships

The first major theme that is common throughout these findings is student friendships. Figure 2.3 shows the emphasis placed on friendships by students and parents as well as the different views that teachers had about these relationships.

Sibling and Relative Relationships

The following theme, relationships with siblings and relatives, was among the most surprising examples of funds of knowledge. Most families described a very strong influence of older siblings and extended

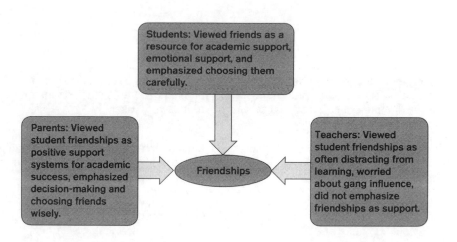

Figure 2–3. Perspectives on Student Friendships as Funds of Knowledge

family as role models. These relationships seem to be a valuable resource that teachers are unaware of for the most part.

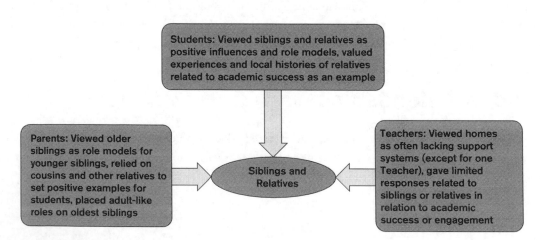

Figure 2–4. Perspectives on Sibling and Relative Relationships as Funds of Knowledge

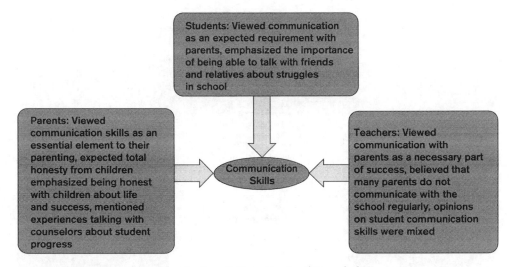

Figure 2–5. Perspectives on Communication Skills as Funds of Knowledge

Communication Skills

This study showed a common theme among teachers that communication with parents is valuable and beneficial for education. Although all of the parents seemed enthusiastic and dedicated to their children's education, only two of them reported contacting teachers or counselors regularly. While the other three parents did mention that they are comfortable doing so, they emphasized the communication with their children in order to become informed on academic progress. Students demonstrated that they know this expectation, and teachers again seemed unaware of the household dynamics of communication.

Decision-Making Skills

Contrary to what teachers seemed to expect, students seemed to perceive decision-making as an extremely important element of growing up with lasting effects on their lives. These values have been taught by parents and were reflected in the parent interviews as well. The major differences between perceptions lay in the size of decisions. Parents tended to focus on large life decisions and lasting wisdom. Students tended to focus on academic goals and how their daily social interactions would affect their long-term goals. Teachers focused on daily, small skill sets and social interactions that have direct academic outcomes.

Implications

Since students see friendships as a resource and both parents and students indicate an importance in choosing friends wisely, it seems that there is a misconception of this value by teachers who view student friendships

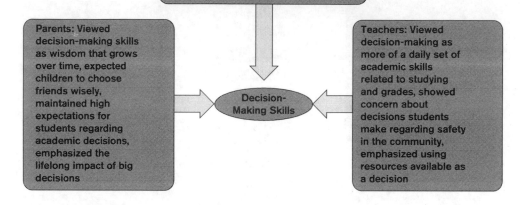

Figure 2–6. Perspectives on Decision-Making Skills as Funds of Knowledge

as distracting. These teachers undoubtedly have witnessed students distracting their classmates to feel that these relationships present problems in learning. One possibility is that the distractions being witnessed are not actually happening between students who have the deep friendships. In the short time that teachers spend with students over one class period, it is difficult to understand the complexities of their relationships. Another possibility is that the distractions are occurring because there is not enough structure in regards to each student's role in the learning activity. Parents and students both indicate very specific ways that students' friendships provide academic support. In addition, students have very specific responsibilities at home. It is possible that some of these distractions teachers discussed may be avoided if students are trained to choose group members wisely, similar to how parents teach them to choose friends wisely, and if roles are clearly defined for the learning activities in the same way they are clearly defined at home.

The strong commitment each family showed for mentoring younger relatives demonstrates a valuable support that teachers could utilize. Teachers could make a point of asking individual students to identify who fulfills this support role in his or her life. Most likely, students will identify an older sibling, a cousin, an aunt, or an uncle. Knowing these people's names and how they influence students' academic success could be valuable for instruction and overall student engagement. Students can interview these people to find out keys to success and be asked to include them in school activities, meetings, or school projects regularly. Students could log responses about these role models' experiences with education. Students could also have these older siblings and relatives sign progress reports or academic goals. Considering these interviews with parents, it seems that some of these relationships with siblings and relatives may actually have a greater impact on academics than parents in many families due to an intentional sharing of family responsibility. These roles in students' lives were not always clear to teacher participants, according to the data. This indicates that the school staff may be unaware that most students have such relationships, or that the school staff may not have a set of strategies for tapping into these resources.

There seems to be a disconnection of expectations about communication skills. Although teachers saw communication with parents as necessary for student success, parent and teacher expectations do not align. These expectations do not imply either party is not fulfilling their role properly. Instead, it seems that teachers could make a conscious effort to build a more personal connection with parents about students' strengths and weaknesses. Parents seemed to be very explicit on students' strengths and weaknesses, and therefore expected students to engage in honest communication at home. Understanding this dynamic could be very influential in increasing student engagement. Students could be required to involve their parents in academic progress and lead conversations about school rather than waiting for parents to call teachers for updates. In this particular school community, such an effort could prove to be more productive and increase communication overall, utilizing the existing funds of knowledge related to communication skills.

The emphasis parent participants had on decision-making shows that students may need to see greater relevance in daily lessons. Since teachers often talked about skills regarding studying and passing classes, implying that this may be somewhat of a weakness with some students, it would benefit students to discuss the lifelong relevance for each lesson. Students' photovoice journals indicated that setting goals comes naturally since many student participants included references to future goals such as college and careers. These funds of knowledge could be applied regularly in class. As objectives and learning activities are introduced, students may become more engaged if they are challenged to explore the lifelong implications of learning goals. Although most teachers would acknowledge the need for real-life applications of content, the results of this study imply that these Latino students need a much more personal connection and time to relate content to their own life goals.

Although funds of knowledge for everyday life and household skills emerged in this study, such as cooking, taking care of children, church activities, and maneuvering around town on the bus, the skills all parents and students focused on were more general life skills for social relationships. The themes of friendships, siblings and relatives, communication skills, and decision-making skills indicate a maturity in student understanding of the overall purpose of school and a common set of values throughout the school community. These values were reflected by parents and students. However, there was a clear fracture in consistency regarding interpretation of these funds of knowledge. The differences in teachers' understandings of these funds of knowledge compared to students and parents indicate that there is a need to create a bridge between home and school educational strategies. Using the data from home observations and parent interviews, Macias (2012) found elements of teaching strategies used for parenting. Each of these strategies was then applied to elements of teacher lesson plans to create a new funds of knowledge approach to lesson planning specifically designed for this school community. Figure 2.7 describes the elements of lesson plans used by teacher participants, the connection to home learning found in the research with students and parents, and a funds of knowledge connection for each element of the lesson plan.

This research can serve as a model for how to combine original research and educational strategies within any school community. If educators cannot do the extensive kind of research involved in this study, there are shorter, simpler ways to access some funds of knowledge that can inform instruction. Examples

Elements of the Lesson Plans	Connection to Home	Funds of Knowledge Connections
A starter or opening question was often given to students as they entered class to begin the lesson.	When students came home, their first interaction with parents was most likely an update of their day, and personal successes or problems are shared.	Rather than a question with a specific answer to be written down, students could be asked to share something more personal related to the content through discussion.
The beginning of lessons often included an objective or essential question to focus on the academic goal for the day.	To teach lessons to their children, parents often shared personal experiences or experiences of close family and friends.	To hook students' interests, personal stories related to content could be shared by the teacher.
Direct instruction, such as PowerPoints with note-taking followed by teacher modeling, was a common method of delivering content.	Rather than passively listening, parents expected children to take on adult-like roles. All members of the family participated equally in a task.	Instead of teachers leading a presentation while students take notes, teachers could give each student some information to share. This way, note-taking becomes a shared group process instead of a passive activity.
Independent practice often followed direct instruction. This involved answering questions or completing a learning activity in pairs and sharing answers with the class.	At home, parents assigned older siblings to lead or supervise younger siblings. Children took this role very seriously. Although younger siblings still had an equal part in a task, they were guided by older siblings, who acted as mentors.	Although the process of working in pairs does seem to reflect the cooperative environment of home life, students could take turns fulfilling a mentoring role throughout assignments. This may better reflect the mentoring role of siblings at home.
Assessments within lesson plans varied from teacher to teacher. Some used written assignments, some used quizzes, and others used projects.	Parents at home were not generally concerned with the details of each lesson or concept. Instead, they focused on the big picture of progress. They assessed this by open and honest conversation.	Although we cannot ignore details with our content areas, we can mimic this oral communication in order to assess comprehension. Rather than assessments being completely written products, an oral element can also be implemented. Students can be required to share the big picture. Students can be given a partial grade on this progress of being able to articulate the main concepts learned orally.
Many lessons concluded with a reflection question that students finished before they left class. This allowed for one final step in checking comprehension with the lesson.	Reflection happened at home as well. Many students wrote about music and how it helped them focus. Parents also discussed how they expected their children to share feelings about problems they faced at school.	The reflection in class can be modeled after this personal reflection that happens at home. It may build importance to the issue if students are allowed to listen to music and quietly focus on the question. Then, discussion in small groups can follow before they turn this in to the teacher. As evident with parent interviews and photovoice journals, students may feel there is more importance attached to a concept if they have to reflect about and share it.

(Macias, 2012)

Figure 2–7. Cross-Educational Teaching

include home surveys, student-led parent conferences, journal writing, student-led interviews with family members and relatives, and intentional focus on home-life connections through group discussions related to content. These are simple ways that educators can access some of the funds of knowledge that may otherwise remain hidden in the classroom. Although many school communities may reflect similar demographics as this study, the most valuable part of this process is getting to know students on a deeper level by investigating funds of knowledge unique to each community.

Applications for Administrators

- Find creative ways to help teachers connect with the school community.
- Learn about the community surrounding the school (events, tours, activities, faith-based community, etc.).
- Conduct surveys to understand the needs of the community.
- Conduct parental and student surveys to understand the types of funds of knowledge available within the school community.
- Establish systematic ways to celebrate diverse cultures in the school.
- Provide trainings on culturally relevant and responsive pedagogy.

Applications for Teachers

- Utilize journals within the classroom setting to allow students opportunity and space to express funds of knowledge.
- Celebrate students' identity and funds of knowledge.
- Incorporate culturally relevant instruction to allow students to contribute to the content.
- Conduct home visitations with support staff (community liaison, counselor, classified staff) to gain insight and appreciation for the value in the home.
- Invite parents to contribute input, resources, materials, etc. on curriculum and unit plans.
- Provide opportunities for parents to participate in instruction as guest speakers.

Applications for Counselors

- Establish communication tools that inform parents on classroom instruction, course content, etc.
- Participate in cultural competency training and engage in ongoing self-reflection to address biases.
- Provide workshops for parents, teachers, and administrators on funds of knowledge and their implication in school.
- Create opportunities to meet students at the start of the year to build rapport and trust.
- Conduct surveys to allow students to share their personal background.

Discussion Questions

- What kinds of hidden funds of knowledge may exist in your school community that may impact instruction? What are some realistic ways teachers, administrators, and counselors can tap into these funds of knowledge in their everyday jobs?
- What kinds of activities can be designed for a school staff/faculty to learn more about the school community and families? How might you structure a funds of knowledge training at your school site?
- What are important rules, procedures, or preparation to set into place before home visits take place?
- What resources may be available in your school community to serve as a bridge to connecting with families in order to learn more about their funds of knowledge? (churches, community organizations, clubs, etc.)
- How might your understanding of funds of knowledge impact counseling a child experiencing trauma or family problems?
- How might your understanding of funds of knowledge impact disciplining a child experiencing behavior problems?

School Scenarios for Discussion

- Mrs. Smith is interested in teaching a small unit on Dia de los Muertos in her class. She has a lot of Latino students, and the holiday is only a few weeks away, so she feels like this will be a really exciting unit of study. She has come to you for help in planning and co-teaching the unit. What advice would you give Mrs. Smith to help her tap into her students' funds of knowledge and be sure that this unit goes as well as she hopes?
- Your school faculty just read an article on funds of knowledge at a professional development training. During the discussion afterward, Mr. Jones makes a comment that he teaches math and so this is irrelevant to him because his subject is culturally neutral. He believes this kind of study is only relevant in elementary school or social studies. What would you say or do following this development to try and help Mr. Jones, and perhaps any others, better understand the concept without insulting their professional opinion?
- Per your respective grade level and subject area, your department has decided to do a short funds of knowledge study. Each of you is supposed to come up with a common core lesson that utilizes the results. Where would you start? What kinds of learning activities or assessments would you develop? What kind of administrative, counselor, or community support would you need to make this successful?

References

Chase, S. E. (2008). Narrative inquiry: Multiple lenses, approaches, voices. In N. Denzin & Y. Lincoln (Eds.), *Collecting and interpreting qualitative materials* (pp. 651–680). Thousand Oaks, CA: Sage.

Crouch, R., & Zakariya, S. B. (2012, May). The United States of education: The changing demographics of the United States and their schools. Retrieved from http://www.centerforpubliceducation.org/You-

May-Also-Be-Interested-In-landing-page-level/Organizing-a-School-YMABI/The-United-States-of-education-The-changing-demographics-of-the-United-States-and-their-schools.html.

Davis, J., & Bauman, K. (2013). *School Enrollment in the United States: 2011*. Retrieved from the United States Census Bureau website: http://www.census.gov/prod/2013pubs/p20-571.pdf.

Gonzalez, N., Moll, L., Floyd-Tenery, M., Rivera, A., Rendon, P., Gonzales, R., & Amanti, C. (1993). Teacher research on funds of knowledge: Learning from house- holds (Educational Practice Report No. 6). Santa Cruz, CA, and Washington, DC: National Center for Research on Cultural Diversity and Second Language Learning.

Freire, P. (1970). *Pedagogy of the oppressed.* (1996 ed.). London, England: Penguin Books.

Jocson, K. M. (2009). Steering Legacies: Pedagogy, Literacy, and Social Justice in Schools. *The Urban Review*. doi:10.1007/s11256-008-0103-0.

Larrotta, C., & Serrano, A. (2012). Adult learners' funds of knowledge: The case of an English class for parents. *Journal of Adolescent & Adult Literacy, 55*(4), 316–325. doi:10.1002/JAAL.00038.

Licona, M. M. (2013). Mexican and Mexican-American children's funds of knowledge as interventions into deficit thinking: opportunities for praxis in science education. *Cultural Studies of Science Education, 8*, 859–872. doi:10.1007/s11422-013-9515-6.

Macias, A. (2012). *Funds of knowledge of working-class Latino students and influences on student engagement* (3549283) (Doctoral dissertation). Retrieved from ProQuest Dissertations and Theses database. (3549283)

Massing, C., Kirova, A., & Hennig, K. (2013). The role of first language facilitators in redefining parent involvement: Newcomer families' funds of knowledge in an intercultural preschool program. *Canadian Children, 38*(2), 4–11.

McLaughlin, D. S., & Barton, A. C. (2012). Preservice teachers' uptake and understanding of funds of knowledge in elementary science. *The Association for Science Teacher Education, 24*, 13–36. doi:10.1007/s10972-012-9284-1.

Moll, L., Amanti, C., Neff, D., & Gonzales, N. (1992). Funds of knowledge for teaching: using a qualitative approach to connect homes and classrooms. *Theory Into Practice, 31*(2), 132–141.

Wang, C. & Burris, M. (1997). Photovoice: Concept, methodology, and use for participatory needs assessment. *Health Education & Behavior, 24*(3), 369–387.

CHAPTER 3

Social Class and Student Engagement

Is There Really a Connection?

S ocial class is commonly viewed from an economic stance. Traditionally, it is defined by tangible, quantifiable measures such as bank balances, property, education, and investments. Several studies have shown that the higher students' social class is, the more engaged students are in the learning process. Consequently, students from low socioeconomic status families with fewer resources tend to start school less prepared for the academic experience (Jeynes, 2007; Lubienski & Crane, 2010; Raag et al., 2011).

Drawing from research on social class and academic growth, aspects of social class influence student engagement in both positive and negative ways. According to the research on social class, students living in the middle and upper class have fewer gaps, obstacles, and issues that hinder their learning process. The one thing many researchers agree on is that children of middle- and upper-class parents have a predictable advantage over children from the lower socioeconomic level (Berliner, 2007). The traditional view of social class, limited to a single perspective that only uses economic measures, restricts the use of social class as a variable in conducting research. Looking at social class in a multifaceted conceptual framework gives researchers, scholars, and educators a clearer understanding of how it plays out in the lives of people. This chapter includes an introduction to a multifaceted conceptual framework of social class that includes concepts of identity, behavior, and structural measures. It looks at how social class impacts student engagement for academic success. It also includes an overview of transformative leadership (Shields, 2009, 2010, 2013) and its connection to the identified elements of social class, namely behavior, identity, and structural measures. The intent of this chapter is to share perspectives and practices related to the notion of social class, discuss transformative leadership and its role, and identify opportunities where the building blocks of social class have demonstrated its influence on student engagement through the involvement of a parent group at a local high school in Southern California.

What We Know About Social Class and A New Way to Look at It

This current research expands the definition of social class to include identity, behavior, and structural measures. The interaction among a person's identity (social networks), behavior (cultural practices), and structural measures (tangible resources) provides a broader scope in examining and analyzing the influence of social class on student engagement. In the multifaceted conceptual framework illustrated below,

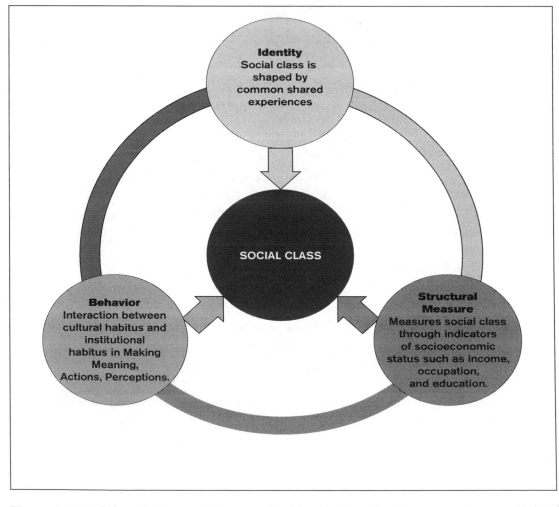

Figure 3–1. Multifaceted Conceptual Framework of Social Class: The Connections Between Identity, Behavior, and Structural Measures

identity, behavior, and structural measures are connected to each other and are the building blocks of social class.

Identity

Identity is an internal block that relies on personal networks. Identity is developed through social connections, political relationships, and learning that occurs through interactions with family, peers, and political associations. For example, through cooperative and collaborative dialogue, identity is formulated (Vygotsky, 1978). Aries and Seider (2007) used the social identity theory in interviewing forty-five students and discussing the importance of social class in the formation of identity. They found that "social class plays an important role both as an independent variable that shapes the formation of identity and as a domain of identity exploration" (p. 151). Students' identities are not constant, according to Pearce, Down, and Moore (2008). Bingham and Okagaki's research described the change that takes place as students interact with their environment, families, and with other social groups (2012). Factors such as race, gender, economic status, ethnicity, language, and sexual orientation shape one's social identity (Nieto, 2008, 2012).

The factors of social-relatedness pertaining to identity, such as relationships with teachers, family, and peers, affect student engagement. Allen (1992) analyzed survey data from 1,800 respondents and found that academic achievement was influenced positively when students had positive social experiences with diverse peers and dialogued with faculty members about their learning. Strayhorn (2010) showed that conversations pertaining to college among black and Latino parents and their sons were extremely important for academic success. Strayhorn's study provided empirical evidence supporting discussions among students and their family, friends, teachers, and parents as having a positive impact on academic achievement, especially for black and Latino boys. Mentoring is another product of relatedness that has been found to contribute directly to engagement and academic gains (Williams & Sanchez, 2011). Marks (2000) studied a sampling of 3,669 students from 143 math and social studies classrooms in 24 elementary, middle, and high schools. Students completed surveys about their attitudes, behaviors, and experiences in school. He reported that when norms of respect, fairness, safety, and positive communication were present in the school environment, student engagement enhanced at all levels. McInerney (2009) found that students were more engaged when the teachers-to-student relationship was built on respect and affirmation, allowing the student to participate in the construction of knowledge.

Behavior

The behavior block of social class encompasses both conscious and unconscious actions. The interaction between the internal and external factors with institutional agencies, such as school, church, or home, affects the way in which a person perceives information and makes decisions. As one interacts with teachers, classmates, and administration, his/her way of thinking is affected, and the way s/he sees the world changes. In the (2013) study, Hambre and his associates observed 4,341 students from preschool to sixth grade and found that effective teaching strategies positively affect student learning. It also showed that staff development specific to teaching strategies had positive effects on teaching. Contemporary research demonstrated how an individual with training and awareness could modify his/her perceptions and the way s/he approaches decision-making and meaning-making challenges (Skinner & Chi, 2012; Skinner & Pitzer, 2012). As noted in the research of Froese-Germain (2009), there was a difference between middle-class and lower-class children when asking for help. As compared to the lower-class children, middle-class children requested the assistance from the teacher more often when they had a problem or needed help (Froese-Germain, 2009). Boyd-Zaharias and Pate-Bain (2008) noted educators played a critical role in bridging the communication gap across groups and encouraging broad participation that could ameliorate the educational situation for all students.

Structural Measures

The final block of social class is structural measures. The structural measures block includes external systems such as level of educational attainment, occupation, and income. These measures are used to indicate levels of economic stability. Currently, the greatest number of people in the United States are identified as middle class (U.S. Census Bureau, 2013).

In summary, the multifaceted conceptual framework of social class broadens the understanding, depth, and complexity of social class. It also opens the conversation to include aspects such as social networking and cultural practices. Some researchers have even included styles of hair, extracurricular activities, choices made in curriculum, styles of clothing, and lipstick and nail polish colors as descriptors of social class when talking about identity (Bettie, 2003). Others have even included the way one dresses or talks as well as when one gets married as descriptors of the behavioral block of social class. The type of car one drives and the school one attends are structural measures of social class.

Student Engagement and Academic Success

In an effort to address students' educational needs, educators, educational researchers, and policy-makers find it hard to agree on the reasons for academic failure of American students. Among the many arguments posed to explain the failure of American students are:

- A lack of qualified teachers (Ahuja, 2012; National Council of Supervisors of Mathematics [NCSM], 2008; National Council of Teachers of Mathematics, 2000);
- Ineffective teaching practices (English, 2010; Griner & Stewart, 2012; Ladson-Billings, 1995; Robinson & Harris, 2013);
- Deficit thinking about students and what they can achieve (Bourdieu & Passeron, 1977; Valencia, 1997; Walker, 2010);
- A lack of understanding of students' diverse backgrounds and needs (de Wet & Gubbins, 2011; Pang, Stein, Gomez, Matas & Shimogori, 2011; Riehl, 2000);
- Issues surrounding parental involvement (Abrams & Gibbs, 2002; Howard & Reynolds, 2008; LaRocque, Kleiman & Darling, 2011; Olivos, 2006);
- Disengaged students (Keiser, 2000; Lysne, Miller & Eitel, 2013; Mokoena & Africa, 2013; Yurco, 2014);

- The need for changes in school policy and how schooling takes place (Berliner, 2005, 2007; Darling-Hammond & Friedlaender, 2008; Darling-Hammond, LaPointe, Meyerson, Orr & Cohen, 2007);
- The need for changes in social policy and how people from various social groups are viewed (Anyon, 2005a, 2005b; Bower, 2011).

Students disengage in school for a variety of reasons. However, students most often disengage because of disconnectedness. In other words, students find it hard to engage in school when they do not have social or cultural connection to the learning process.

On the other hand, engagement is reflected through students' participation in and with school (Finn & Voelkl, 1993; Zhao & Kuh, 2004) through students' persistency and cognitive investment in learning (Hazel, Vazirabadi & Gallagher, 2013) and through students' emotional attachment to, interest in, or ability to influence school (Pomerantz, Moorman & Litwack, 2007). Christenson, Reschly, and Wylie (2012) present student engagement as a process that consists of both definitive and influencing aspects. Definitive aspects, often called indicators, assist in defining what student engagement looks like (Lam, Wong, Yang & Liu, 2012). Indicators are categorized as affective, behavioral, and cognitive. Influencing aspects stimulate student engagement. Influencing aspects are categorized as contextual or personal factors.

Indicators clarify the definition of engagement. Affective indicators directly relate to how a student feels about learning and school. If a child enjoys going to school and likes to participate in the learning process, s/he is more likely to be engaged in school. Behavioral indicators relate to the efforts that students place on the learning process and their involvement in school activities. When students engage behaviorally, they willingly participate in classroom discussions and activities, as well as participate in other school organizations such as sports, clubs, and events. Cognitive indicators relate to the way that students understand the purpose of education. When engaged cognitively, learning becomes a vehicle for personal development or increasing self-efficacy (Griffiths, Lilles, Furlong & Sidhwa, 2012).

Influencers of student engagement are outside of the definition yet essential in motivating students to engage in school. Influencers such as being goal-oriented, having teacher support, or having parent support increase student engagement. Teacher support in and of itself is not student engagement. However, when students receive teacher support, their levels of engagement increase. Influencers are both contextual and personal. Contextual influencers stimulate engagement related to the instructional context (Lam, Wong, Yang & Liu, 2012). When learning has real-life significance, promotes curiosity, or challenges personal ideas, students take more interest and are more engaged in the learning process. Contextual influencing factors address the supports that surround students and how students relate to others in the learning process.

The personal influencing factors address the motivational beliefs of students. When students believe in their own capacity to succeed, they are engaged in all three areas—affectively, behaviorally, and cognitively—in school. A section of data from a survey on student engagement given in a multi-country study involving 822 middle school students from three cities in China reported self-efficacy as positively influencing engagement (Lam et al., 2012). The study showed that the highest correlation to student engagement was effort attribution. Lam and his associates reported that effort attribution helps students believe in their capacity to perform better in school.

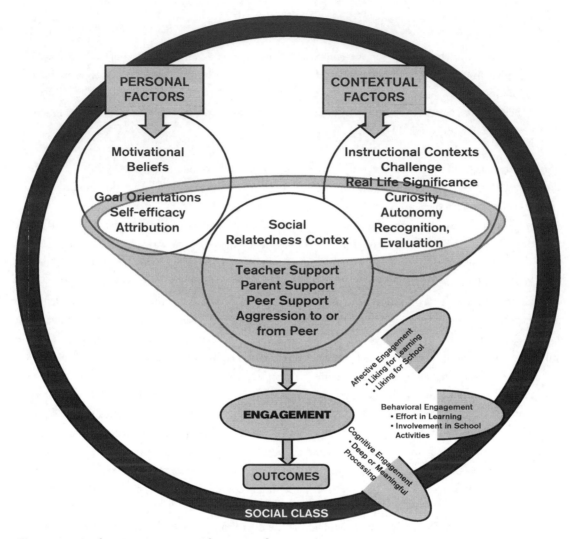

Figure 3.2. Student Engagement: Defining & Influencing Factors

What We Know About Transformative Leadership

According to Foster (1989), leadership is "critically educative" and not only looks "at the conditions in which we live, but it must also decide how to change them" (p.185). Santamaria and Santamaria (2012) report that transformative leadership is an avenue in which leaders become aware of the strengths, weaknesses, and challenges of our school systems, reflect on how the system advantages or disadvantages members, analyze inequities, and take critical action to deconstruct wrongs and reconstruct a more just and equitable system. Transformative leadership starts with the end in mind. The transformative leadership perspective suggests that a leader can be anyone, regardless of formal position, who serves as an effective social change agent (Astin & Astin, 2000; Shields 2013).

Transformative leadership begins by recognizing that the material realities of the wider community impinge on the ability of any organization to achieve success and the ability of individuals within the organization to succeed (Shields, 2009, 2010, 2013). Shields argues that transformative leadership recognizes the uneven playing field that exists in education between low-income students and middle- and upper-class students. She says that a greater effort is needed for change to occur. Weiner (2003) wrote that "transformative leadership is an exercise of power and authority that begins with questions of justice, democracy, and the dialectic between accountability and social responsibility" (p. 89). According to Shields (2013), transformative leadership understands that a safe space must be made for the lived experiences of all children. Shields developed eight tenets of transformative leadership: (1) the mandate to effect deep and equitable change; (2) the need to deconstruct and reconstruct knowledge frameworks that perpetuate inequity and injustice; (3) a focus on emancipation, democracy, equity, and justice; (4) the need to address the inequitable distribution of power; (5) an emphasis on both private and public (individual and collective) good; (6) an emphasis on interdependence, interconnectedness, and global awareness; (7) the necessity of balancing critique and promise; and (8) the call to exhibit moral courage. See the table below outlining the tenets of transformative leadership.

Current Research Findings and Implications
Summary of Research Methodology

This study draws data from a qualitative narrative inquiry study of an upper-middle class high school, St. Paul Preparatory High School (SPP, pseudonym), where a reduced achievement gap has evened the playing field for African American and Latino students. Utilizing a semi-structured, open-ended, conversational interview, purposefully chosen participants shared their lived stories through their authentic voices. The goal of this study was to identity social class blocks and their impact on student engagement. The participants in the study consisted of six students, three administrators, two parents, two teachers, and two community members who were associated with the students in the high school of interest. Information was collected from the participants and using constant comparison with Nvivo 10, nodes were coded and themes emerged and were identified. As a qualitative research tool, this method allowed the researchers to actively utilize the voices of the participants to recreate their stories.

This narrative inquiry was adapted from a pilot study conducted in the Philippines in 2011 and field-tested on more than seventy participants from selected school sites. Participants in the previous studies included teachers, students, parents, and administration. The preliminary findings from the study were presented at the International Conference on Teacher Education in the Philippines in July of 2012. Subsequently, the research design was also used here in the United States in several dissertations that focused on the influence of funds of knowledge, social and cultural capital, and social class on student engagement with 168 participants. Findings from the U.S. studies have been accepted for presentation at the American Education Research Association (AERA) annual conferences.

Although this study was conducted using conversational interviews, general guiding questions were developed that pertained to (a) the school, (b) students' achievement, (c) engagement activities/strategies, and (d) parent participation. Also specific to the leadership group, topics pertaining to their involvement were included. During the conversational interviews, questions were posed based on the information being

Table 3–1. Carolyn Shields' Tenets of Transformative Leadership

The Mandate to Effect Deep and Equitable Change	Transformative leaders address the assumptions, biases, and stereotypes that are held by the dominant culture and have difficult intentional and critical conversations that challenge those assumptions, biases, and stereotypes to create equity.
The Need to Deconstruct and Reconstruct Knowledge Frameworks that Perpetuate Inequity and Injustice	Through critical and difficult conversations, transformative leaders challenge existing knowledge in order to ensure respectful, caring policies and practices. They value the cultural capital and experiences that children bring with them to school without judging or marginalizing the student by focusing on what they do not bring.
A Focus on Emancipation, Democracy, Equity, and Justice	Transformative leaders work to create learning environments that are more democratic, equitable, and socially just. They focus on creating a space where the voices and the lived experiences of children are welcome in the education arena.
The Need to Address the Inequitable Distribution of Power	Transformative leaders recognize that organizations have systemic and institutionalized realities that perpetuate an uneven playing field where power is used inappropriately to oppress and promote inequity. They argue for democracy where power is used for mutual benefit.
An Emphasis on Both Private and Public (Individual and Collective) Good	Transformative leaders are intentional about equity of access, standards, and outcomes, as well as establish relationships that empower students to participate as world citizens who promote community engagement in school activities and vice versa.
An Emphasis on Interdependence, Interconnectedness, and Global Awareness	Transformative leaders consider the world to be the classroom. Fostering global curiosity, understanding, and responsibility helps to create agentic human beings who both understand their ability to take action as well as ways to do so without being hegemonic. By helping students to know themselves as individuals and as a part of a global community, they emphasize connectedness.
The Necessity of Balancing Critique and Promise	Transformative leaders engage in an activist approach where with courageous actions and engagement they confront inequities, addressing aspects pertaining to policies, structures, and pedagogy and looking for ways to ensure hope for a more equitable future for all students.
The Call to Exhibit Moral Courage	Transformative leaders know their "true North" and non-negotiables and in the light of public disdain press forward toward a system of education embracing equity, democracy, and social justice.

(Adapted from Shields, C. M. (2013). *Transformative Leadership in Education: Equitable Change in an Uncertain and Complex World.* New York, NY: Routledge.)

shared and the guiding topics that framed the interview process. The flexibility of using conversational interviews permitted the researcher and the participants to co-create a space for the narrative to develop. Open-ended questions were used as a part of the conversation, and follow-up questions were used as clarifiers and to further understanding.

The participants in the current study were individuals with firsthand knowledge of the St. Paul Prep Parent Advisory Group. Both the participants and the site were selected for the purpose of informing the researcher about social class and student engagement. Participants were chosen because they had the ability to inform the researcher on aspects of background, common practices, and relationships of the parent advisory group, a key participant in the changes at SSP. Participants included both members of and non-members of the parent advisory group. Of the fifteen participants interviewed, eleven were non-members and four were members. Participants who were non-members included district administration, previous school administrators, teachers, students, and community members who had knowledge about the parent advisory group at SSP.

St. Paul Preparatory High School Parent Leadership Group

The St. Paul Prep parent advisory group (SPPAG), a parent leadership group with a mission to assist students, specifically African American students, in being successful in their academics and in life, had significant roles in the transformation of students' educational experience at St. Paul Preparatory High School. SPPAG's mission statement outlined various avenues used to promote students' success and create positive change in the educational experience of children. Their mission statement reads as follows:

To motivate students to excel, not only in the classroom, but in life, by showing them the possibilities and consequences of their decisions, and to work with the community to provide parents with the resources they need to assist their students throughout the educational process. After all, it takes a village.

Their goals or objectives are:

- Mentor … so that our students can achieve academic excellence
- Encourage … the pursuit of respectable career paths
- Motivate … students to contribute to their communities by enriching the lives of others
- Inform … parents and students of the opportunities for success available to them

The work of the SPPAG changed a failing school community. How did this group help to transform their school? How did they assist in narrowing or even erasing the achievement gap? How did they encourage students to graduate and set goals to attend college? How did they help to raise the level of student engagement?

The administration of St. Paul Prep had tackled many of the barriers previously discussed in this chapter. Many had been addressed, reduced, or removed as obstacles for student achievement during the program and curriculum development planning of the school. St. Paul Prep was created with the idea of serving all students regardless of their socioeconomic status. The teachers were hand-picked for their expertise elevating the quality of teachers who would be serving the students. The district went above and beyond to create an effective "flagship" school. The school offered all students a variety of AP classes and a plethora of extracurricular groups and activities to join, and the socioeconomic status of most families negated socioeconomic issues that so often hinder student achievement. However, with all the additions, accommodations, modifications, and focus, the African American population continued to struggle. Consistent with the research on academic achievement, SPP continued to have a significant achievement gap between the black and white students.

Although current research literature reports that students who live in the upper-middle and upper-class levels, socioeconomically speaking, are more successful in school than those in the lower socio-economic levels, academic engagement and academic success were elusive for the African American students in this study. Located in an upper-middle class community, St. Paul Prep High School (SPP, pseudonym) aims to serve students from a variety of socially, racially, and socioeconomically diverse communities and promises them access to rigorous curriculum that could prepare them for a successful future. Focusing on providing all students with the opportunity to achieve, its website boasts of how it accommodates individual learning styles while maintaining high, obtainable expectations for all students. "SPP is quite proud of its rigorous academic, vocational, and athletic programs, as well as its extensive range of extracurricular activities. Staff and parents work together to create a learning environment that promotes academic and social development, teaches responsibility and pride, and models learning as a lifelong venture" (SPP website). With over twenty AP class offerings, fifty extracurricular groups and activities to join, a highly qualified teaching staff (with over 98% of the staff holding a bachelor's plus thirty or more units), and few socioeconomic issues to distract from learning, SPP was truly a place designed for students' success.

> "They put a lot of support in for the students. And with that intentional support, came a lot of successes for the students. So that was wonderful. One thing the SPP found as it grew in size and got older … was that there wasn't that kind of intentional support for African American students." (SPP District Administrator, 2014)

Although the administration and faculty had endeavored to address as many of the potential gaps that hinder students' academic success, there was still a group of students who continued to fail academically. Low graduation rate, low college attrition, and a low GPA of 1.74 were the norm for the African American students until a group of fathers decided to intervene. What happened that caused the academic success of the African American students at this school to change? What caused these African American students to engage in school to the point where their average GPA went from 1.74 to 3.4 and their graduation rate increased to 100%? Students also began to enter some of the best colleges and universities in the country. What aspects of social class played a role in student engagement for these students? The findings in this study give insight into how social class helped to create high-achieving African American students who not only displayed the attitudes and behaviors that are considered critical to academic success, but also worked to impart these attributes to their classmates, creating a community of learners.

Findings

Findings suggest that the social class of the St. Paul Prep Parent Advisory Group provided the opportunity to create space for students to succeed and engage better in school. Students expressed feelings of belonging and pride in their individual accomplishments. Students found themselves in caring relationships where encouragement and motivation created a desire to work harder to be successful in school. In addition, students began to participate in tutoring as needed, field trips, and school life, in general. Students understood the purpose of school and developed abilities to evaluate, self-monitor their own learning, and strategize and set goals for their futures.

Evidence of Student Engagement

When looking at the building blocks of social class, the evidence of student engagement could be seen in the following ways:

1. Cognitive Engagement
    a. Students received positive support from their parents, peers, and teachers in the way of tutoring, grade checks, and caring conversations that lead to improved grades, higher GPA, and higher graduation rate.
    b. Students received positive support from their parents, peers, teachers, and the community in the way of field trips and peer interactions in Baptist Student Union [BSU] a student lead club where through conversations about schooling, education, setting goals and expectations for college-motivated students to engage in the learning process.
2. Affective Engagement
    a. Students became a part of a learning community, had positive feelings about themselves and school, and began setting goals and reaching those goals. Students talked about goals for college, career, and life.
    b. Students are affirmed and recognized for the part that they play in the community. They have a sense of belonging and set goals and reach them.
    c. Students talked about goals for college, career, and life.
3. Behavioral Engagement
    a. Graduation rates increased, and college/university matriculation increased. Students have been accepted to Yale, UCLA, USC, and UCR.
    b. Students participated in the various clubs, events, and activities around campus, providing them opportunities to develop feelings of belonging and connectedness to the school community.

Students responded to the involvement of the parent advisory group with enthusiasm and grew in all areas of student engagement that were connected to the building blocks of social class.

When Looking at Social Class as Behavioral

Understand that the dynamics of social class as behavior are both conscious and unconscious. The interaction between a person and external factors such as school affects the way in which that person perceives changes in his or her environment or in the information being presented. As students learn or interact with teachers, classmates, and administration, their disposition changes and affects the way they see the world. Under this construct of social class, the themes of care, motivation, and relationship were the most prevalent.

Care. The idea of care permeated the conversations of all participants. There was a genuine desire on behalf of the parent advisory group to value each student as well as take responsibility to assist them to grow academically. In addition to taking responsibility, the parent advisory group held students accountable for their personal success. Through conversations that focused on building trust and respect, grade monitoring, and their personal investment of time, students received positive feedback and exhibited improved grades. The parent advisory group committed themselves to the students, and in return, the students committed themselves to academic success. Participants made comments such as: "I'd go there and help with the grade checks and talk with the kids, try to understand why they were not getting good grades, and offer advice, counseling, try to get a verbal contract with them to do better... say, 'I know you can do better'"; "The responsibility of our kids is ours"; and "They (meaning the parent advisory group) committed themselves to being the village elders despite the fact that they no longer have a personal investment in the program, which tells the students, they do care about you."

Motivation

Motivation was another strong factor to consider when looking at student engagement. When students believed in themselves and their capacity to accomplish tasks, they demonstrated persistence and worked hard to reach their goals. While the parent advisory group emphasized work ethics to become successful, they also gave appreciation in the form of award ceremonies, money, and praise for good grades and improved GPAs. The parent advisory group mentored students in small groups as well as one on one. The parent advisory group's constant encouragement motivated students to ask for help and set realistic goals for success. Upon graduation, students began matriculating to prestigious universities and were eligible to receive scholarships due to their grades and active participation in community service. Participants made comments such as: "This year, we are all taking at least one kid and personally mentor one kid and help them to do better in school"; "You gotta give 'em feedback along the way, encouragement, and help. We help them set up tutoring for kids, you know, after school"; and "But because of this mentorship, these kids blossom. They go to good places. They get their degrees."

Relationships

Final in the behavior block of social class, relationships were imperative. The important relationships found in the study were the relationships among teachers and students, teachers and parents, students and parents, and as students to students. The parent advisory group worked diligently to involve parents in the educational process. They held meetings and workshops that informed parents about school events, activities, and assistance available to them. The parent advisory group stepped in to encourage, influence and motivate the students when parents were unavailable. Teachers, counselors, and administrators worked as mentors to students. Teachers conducted after-school tutoring. Students also tutored each other. Through these positive and supportive relationships, students developed an appreciation for school, collaboration, learning, and hard work. Supportive relationships improved student engagement through consistent reinforcement. Participants made comments such as: "Almost every teacher does after-school tutoring at least one day a week" and "But the relationship that parent advisory group has with the teachers and counselors evolved over time."

Connections to Transformative Leadership: A Story of African American Fathers' Involvement

In adherence with the tenets of transformative leadership, the SPP advisory group, a parent leadership group made up of five African American fathers from the community, approached the school administration with concerns for the African American students. One participant recalled how the school administrators welcomed the group when they came seeking equitable solutions. The advisory group spoke about a sense of "having a calling" to press toward equity, democracy, and social justice. Transformative leadership describes this as a call to exhibit moral courage. Specific interventions designed to assist students were planned and implemented. Interventions like grade checks, caring conversations, and tutoring led to improved grades, higher GPAs, and a higher graduation rate for the African American population.

These leaders took responsibility for creating a space where all the stakeholders could take responsibility for student success. All of the men took time out of their busy day to volunteer on the high school campus, talking to students about their grades, mentoring, and tutoring, and letting them know that they believed in them. Although the initial cause that brought the fathers to the school was the inability of their sons to play on the basketball team due to low scores, they did not allow that to be the only reason. Working to empower students and their parents, this group of fathers known as the "village elders" invested themselves in the work of creating a more just system for students. To build trust within that community, the leadership created a small, close-knit family atmosphere that continues to have that "home-town feel" even after growing to 4,000 students. One teacher described himself as living his "calling."

The parent advisory group worked to encourage students to work harder by explaining to them why their education was important. They knew each student individually and stuck to their mantra, "It takes a village to raise a child." The students responded to the encouraging words in a way that went beyond the school principal's expectations. He spoke about times when he would visit classrooms. "You could go there any day and … there would be forty to forty-five kids … at the tables studying. I would walk in and I would go, 'You're kidding me.'"

During their lunch, the students would report to one classroom to study and interact with their fellow classmates. After-school tutoring in math and science, one-on-one mentoring, and parent calls were a regular part of their efforts.

Providing opportunities for students to better engage in school and to improve their grades were the areas of focus. Each student identified as at-risk and in need of intervention received a personalized intervention plan. The ultimate goal was for all students to graduate and have the choice of college. When they began, only 28% of the graduating students were entering college. At this time, 73% of the 98% that graduate are A-G eligible and college is an option.

African American Men of Influence

The men in the parent group were men of influence. There was a firefighter/paramedic, a superior court presiding judge, a regional director for a major corporation, a professor, and a regional manager for local public affairs for a major utility company. They were influential men who used their influence to gain access to the school, engage the community, and influence students to set academic and life goals. They were influential in helping the African American students to raise their GPA from 1.74 to 3.4. Under their influence, more students are going to college or a university immediately after high school. Students are encouraged to have a global vision and be prepared to compete in the world as a global citizen. This year marks the first year that a former student will begin to give financially to support the high school students. Students gained a better understanding of their personal capacity through field trips to museums, colleges, and universities to help them better understand the larger world around them.

The parent group discouraged mediocrity by providing the students with ample opportunities for conversations, role models, and community interactions. All participants began to believe in their capacity to succeed. Adults and students alike attributed success to one's personal desire to be successful. An atmosphere was created where motivation and accountability became the primary indicators of academic success.

When Looking at Social Class as Identity

Identity is an internal construct that relies on one's personal networks. Identity, through a shared experienced with people, can be influenced. The impact that identity has on learning and academic achievement is evidently favoring the mainstream students because most schools located around the vicinity of SPP house and support middle-class and upper-class English-speaking whites. The themes that emerged under social class as identity were black culture, privilege, and role models.

Black Culture.

Since the members of the parent advisory group were African Americans who worked with predominantly African American students, it would make sense that aspects of black culture would be evident in their interviews. They defied the common stereotypes about black men and black people in general. They showed themselves to be educated, focused and sincere, not just angry and looking for someone to blame. They spoke to the students with a voice that they could understand. They took the students on field trips to the African American Museum so that they could better understand their past and the opportunities that were available to them in the future. They worked to build trust and provide positive examples for the students and the community. They wanted to "create a space for students to belong and where they could be proud." Participants made comments such as: "We take the kids to the African American Museum so that they can see and study some of our history"; "The black community has a lack of trust in anybody"; and "We are, all of us, positive, and it is kinda nice to know that we are trying to effect the little kids, and it's kinda nice to see that black men can be positive examples for our kids, and that's one of our mantras."

Privilege

The theme of privilege stemmed from the fact that the school was located in an upper-class neighborhood. All participants spoke of the privilege of living in the area of the school. The school was able to offer a variety of classes, from regular-education classes to AP and honors classes. Statements made by participants showed privilege with district attention to the school in allocating resources and time. A judge, a regional manager, and business owners made up the parent group. They had both privilege in the community and with the school. They used their social and political networks to provide opportunities for students to engage in school and the community in a variety of ways. Field trips were planned, community members were invited to campus to speak, and recognition events were held for improved grades and GPAs. Students began to see school as a means to reach their goals. Participants made comments such as: "I was intrigued with the fact of what was going on, and like I said, there was some shifting and shifting, and it ended up with us five guys. It's a judge, a regional director for a major corporation, a physics professor, a retired firefighter, and I'm a regional manager for local public affairs for a major utility company." They understood that they had already broken stereotypes and stood in places of privilege in their community and were determined to help their children do the same.

Role Model

The parent group believed in having professional role models in front of the students to motivate them and to pique their curiosity for their future. They also felt the need for staff members to feel a "calling" to affect students' lives. The role models played an important role in the engagement of the students. They offered opportunities for internships, mentorships, and specific knowledge in their areas of expertise. The students were able to gain perspective and information from the role models that helped to change their decision-making process for their futures. The students met policemen, secret service agents, engineers, and a judge. These role models encouraged students to dream big and set big goals. Participants made comments such as: "And then these guys would help to kind of mentor them and spend some more time with them" and "We have chefs, engineers, policemen, secret service ... you know ... a wide gambit. And these are all parents who come to talk to the kids. These parents come in and talk to the kids about what they are doing in school."

Connections to Transformative Leadership: African American Fathers Creating Connections

The parent advisory group needed to change the understanding that the school had about African American students and African American men in general. The school principal recalled the moment he met the advisory group for the first time. He had been told that a group of angry black men were waiting to see him. However, contrary to what he had been told, they were black fathers wanting to help make the school a successful place for their children. They wanted their children to identify with black people who were being successful out in the world. They wanted to let the students know that there was more out there for them than just "rap music and basketball." They wanted the students to aspire to success. One of the parent advisory members advised the principal that "our children need people who look like them to talk to them." He felt that the African American students needed a better understanding of the opportunities that were available and that too often the students "don't identity with successful African Americans in the work-place." They took the students on field trips to the African American Museum and constantly reminded them of their heritage and that they could be proud of who they were. They celebrated the school's first black valedictorian, who was the daughter of one of the fathers in the parent group. The parent advisory group worked diligently to create a sense of belonging for all students, but specifically for the African American students. Students who worked with the parent advisory group were required to participate in the Baptist Student Union (BSU), and this became the hub of "the village."

This leadership group entered the school and created connections with students due to the privileged position that they held in the community as well as with the district and school administration. Because of the way in which they carried themselves, the resources that they could provide, and the time that they put into this endeavor, this group was able to forge relationships that moved both students and the school in the direction of academic success. Their work helped to reduce the achievement gap for the African American students at the school. This has opened other doors of privilege for students to receive scholarships for university.

The idea of a student interacting with successful people opens students' minds to think differently about their choices. The parent advisory group members influenced the students to connect with the community, and the African American community stepped up to be role models for mentoring, apprenticeships, recognition, and conversations. Architects, bankers, CIA agents, judges, doctors, and many others participated in the role of helping students understand the options that were available for them as African Americans. The idea of creating a positive identity for the students in order to encourage them to set high and obtainable goals became prevalent.

When Looking at Social Class as Structural Measures

Social class as structural measures looks at the external measures of social class. It takes into account indicators of socioeconomic status such as income, education, and occupation. The relevant themes for this particular construct of social class addressed communication, community, and school culture. The parents in the group were in positions to be able to take time off from work and set aside time for critical conversations with parents, teachers, and students. They were also able to use their connections to influence the community to get involved with the school. They used their social networks to open doors for students to experience life in a different way and influenced the African American students to take advantage of the course offerings, sports, and extracurricular activities that were far more extensive than that of other schools. Table 3.4 is descriptive of the themes and evidence that emerged from the authentic voices of the participants from the view of social class as structural measures.

Communication

The St. Paul Prep Parent Advisory Group used their social status and influence to communicate with community members and parents to create spaces for change. They communicated the importance of being involved in the educational experience of the students at St. Paul Prep. They created opportunities for parents to see their children being successful in school. Inviting parents to workshops, award ceremonies, and school activities allowed parents' voices to become a part of the conversation. They spoke about their efforts to keep parents informed of all available educational options that give parents choices in the education of their child. Through positive communication, students' self-efficacy and perspective changed. They grew to understand that opportunities available to them through improved grades could help them have a bright future. Participants made comments such as: "Continue to try to get those parents in but let's go that route. So when the kids are here they're alright. Let's take care of them. We'll continue reaching out to the parents" and "We have a lot of open houses for parents to be able to come in and check on how their student is doing."

Community

The theme of community was apparent in the way the parent advisory group, school, and community worked together to motivate and encourage students to succeed academically. The members of the parent advisory group are from this upper-middle and upper-class neighborhood and work within the community.

Student Recognition and Success

The school and community became positive pathways for student motivation, recognition, and success. Building strong relationships with the community provided students with opportunities for internships and apprenticeships. Students were able to use school as a means to develop their goals and aspirations. The purpose of school had changed for them. Participants made comments such as "It's the community. It's important to have a strong relationship between the district and the city, chamber of commerce, law enforcement, and civic organizations. We work hard at doing that. We don't take that for granted" and "We thought that it would be a good idea to get more parents involved. So we wanted to put on a workshop to show the community, the parents at large, what we were doing, and to invite them to join us and to help us."

School Culture

All participants commented on the theme of school culture. They spoke about the atmosphere being inclusive and conducive for growth. They talked about the collaboration that went on between staff and students and between parents and staff. The student participants talked about the classes, clubs, activities, and events that were available for them to participate in according to their interests. One parent said that he was attracted to the school because of the sign in front of the school. The sign read "home of the scholars, champions, and athletes." This parent said that he could tell from that sign that this was the place for his kids. He said the fact that the word "scholar" came first was what impressed him. Having options for the students made them feel supported and let them know that they belonged to a supportive community of school administrators, staff, fellow students, parents, and community members. The adults worked to create a campus that supported the various types of students, from the large population of EL students to the small population of African American students. The parent advisory group assisted and encouraged students to prepare for university and to set their goal for graduation from the university rather than just a high school graduation. Participants made comments such as: " … our whole campus is a college-going culture"; "There's a lot of in-class projects, presentations we do … there are a lot of projects"; and "Student leaders were good on following up and hanging out with them during the day and checking up on them in classes and things like that."

Connections to Transformative Leadership: African American Fathers Influencing Others to Get Involved

Understanding the resources that the community was able to offer was integral for the parent group. They understood the need for the partnership to be created where all stakeholders felt that they could make a difference. They created a community environment emphasizing the need to understand and work together for the growth of the students. They worked to redistribute power back into the hands of the students.

Students were empowered as the community members embraced the call to action. Having community and business support became a norm for this leadership group. They created relevant partnerships that acted to serve individual students as mentors and role models, communicating the encouragement that students needed to make gains in the educational system. Community members, accepting this "call to moral courage," would speak to students about opportunities available for the students that were not options when they were younger and challenge students to set goals and work toward achieving them. The parent advisory group believed that community was more than just the neighborhood where students lived. Community for them was about a sense of belonging to all people. Community members who came to speak to the students often spoke about the past and issues that surrounded race and class. One participant noted that the word "community" meant taking responsibility for each student's success. He went on to say, "The responsibility of our kids is ours … more importantly, we're unapologetic about that. We empower the parents and the community to say 'it's our responsibility.'"

Quarterly financial donations from the Rotary Club, restaurant coupons from various fast food and fine dining restaurants, haircuts for boys and manicures for girls, donations of venues for activities, and other incentives were used to communicate to students that having good grades was important. When students had a 3.0 or higher GPA for a grading period, they were able to participate in programs like "Fades for Grades" or "Manicure Time" to encourage them to keep working hard. The African American parents had critical and reflective conversations with students, fellow parents, and other community groups and individuals. They felt that all decisions grew out of needs identified through these conversations or requests for help.

Utilizing the theme of community, the parent group wanted students to understand the value of a community and personalize what community was to them. The students gained a sense of belonging and found the motivation to excel by the inspiration received from the community's investment into their lives. The administration, staff, students, and parents created an engaging community atmosphere in which students can focus and be motivated to reach their goals. Within their corner of the campus, the parent advisory group created a recognition ceremony for students who were progressing toward their goals.

Conclusions and Implications

Considering the building blocks of social class, the findings in this study indicated that when student engagement increased, the students became successful. The results of all their efforts decreased the achievement gap between the African American subgroup and their white counterparts. The achievement gap has decreased from 23% to 4% over the parent advisory group's last ten years of work.

This study supports prior research findings that African American students learn best when schooling is culturally relevant to their identity development and that African American students pursue relationships built on "interest, trust, and shared experiences" (Hale, 1986; Nieto, 1996; Shujaa, 1994). It was shown very strongly in this current study that the ethic of care was foundational for the relationships and successes of the African American students. Creating motivating moments that inspire children to pursue goals of higher education by way of role models, field trips, and mentorships help students to better engage in school and have academic success.

In summary, student engagement was influenced by social class in the following ways:

1. When looking at social class as identity, student engagement is stronger when students have a strong, positive sense of their identity. When they have role models who validate them and dispel stereotypes, students discover within themselves the strength to take risks and to set goals for academic success.
2. When looking at social class as behavior, student engagement increased when they felt that they were cared for. When parents, teachers, peers, and community people give support through caring relationships, students respond positively.
3. When looking at social class as structural measures, student engagement increased as students developed a sense of community. When students communicated more with their parents, peers, and teachers, it opened up other ways of creating and setting life goals.

Overall, students in this study showed increased student engagement, as evidenced by:

1. Improved grades
2. More effort in academic tasks
3. Narrowing of the achievement gap
4. The Number of students continuing on to college increased
5. Students felt more connected to school
6. Students could approach their teachers for discussion
7. Students built more caring relationships
8. Students began volunteering in the community at local elementary schools

Implications for School Leaders

As a school principal, the findings have challenged me to take a closer look at the educational program that I lead to ensure that a student's social class is taken into consideration. I work hard to ensure that students are cared for in the three building blocks of social class. The ethic of care must become foundational to the program of any school. Students participate in activities that promote connection to the school and the community. Parents are invited to participate in the schooling of their child. Emphasis is placed on creating a space where parents, teachers, and students can communicate about their needs and creatively come up with solutions to benefit the students' academic growth. Here are suggested topics for courageous conversation or implementation in school sites:

- Broaden the definition of social class and how it influences engagement in schools.
- Open opportunities to have critical conversations with teachers to help them better understand issues that may hinder student engagement and academic success.
- Create opportunities to embrace and celebrate the identities of students.
- Invite community leaders and businesspersons to act as role models and speak to students, which can inspire and encourage students to engage in school and set goals for life successes.
- Create a space where parents can participate in the schooling process, recognizing that they are their child's first teachers and that they have firsthand knowledge that may be helpful in serving their child.
- Create a supportive learning environment for African American students.

Implications for Teachers

- Understanding the broader definition of social class to allow teachers to create a more complete picture of the student and his/her needs.
- Having ethic of care as the foundation for creating student success can help to build critical relationships with students and lead to better student engagement.
- Communicating with parents and allowing them to advise teachers on the best way to assist students, especially minority students, could open pathways to further the engagement of students in the classroom.
- Creating opportunities to embrace the identities of students and creating a more relevant space for learning to take place.

Implications for Counselors

- Understanding the broader definition of social class to allow counselors to create a holistic picture of the student, the family, and their needs.
- Possessing an ethic of care as the foundation for creating student success can help to build critical relationships with students and lead to better student engagement.
- Utilizing communication as a collaborative approach with a multifaceted lens for early intervention.
- Creating opportunities to embrace the social identities of students and creating a more relevant space for learning to take place.
- Deconstructing the deficit-thinking model that leads to discriminatory practices in course selection, special education referrals, and disproportionate discipline practices.

Discussion Questions/Activities

1. Scenario: A group of parents comes to the school to discuss the achievement of their children. They want to participate in creating a solution. What do you need from the parents? What do you need to know about the parents? What do you say to the parents? Can they be included in the solution? If yes, how will you include them?

2. Complete a neighborhood assessment of the potential business partners who would be able to invest in the creation of a supportive community for the students at your school. Complete the following chart.

Name of organization	Contact person	Do they have students/ family members who attend the school?	Product/service that they can offer to school	Length of time in business	Do they want kids to participate?

3. How does understanding the building blocks of identity, behavior, and structural measures as they pertain to social class assist you in creating an engaging environment for students' academic success?

4. Create a tree map for the influencers of student engagement. Each tree map should be filled with examples of what that specific influence looks like. See example below:

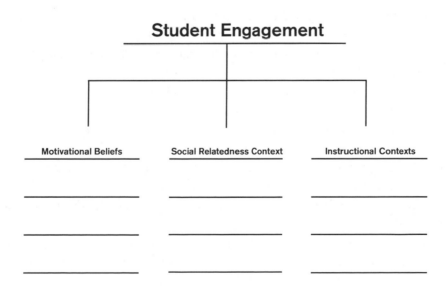

References

Abrams, L. S., & Gibbs, J. T. (2002). Disrupting the logic of home-school relations: Parent involvement strategies and practices of inclusion and exclusion. *Urban Education*, *37*(3), 384–407. doi:10.1177/00485902037003005.

Ahuja, S. (2012). Research results for quality schooling: Bridging the gap between research and practice. *MIER Journal of Educational Studies, Trends and Practices*, *2*(2), 206–214.

Allen, W. R. (1992). The color of success: African-American college student outcomes at predominantly white and historically black public colleges and universities. *Harvard Educational Review*, *62*(1), 26–45.

Anyon, J. (2005a). *Radical Possibilities: Public Policy, Urban Education, and a New Social Movement* (p. 240). New York, NY: Routledge, Taylor & Francis Group.

Anyon, J. (2005b). What "counts" as educational policy? Notes toward a new paradigm. *Harvard Educational Review*, *75*(1), 65–88.

Aries, E., & Seider, M. (2007). The role of social class in the formation of identity: A study of public and elite private college students. *The Journal of Social Psychology*, *147*(2), 137–57. doi:10.3200/SOCP.147.2.137-157.

Berliner, D. C. (2005). Our impoverished view of educational reform. *The Teachers College Record*, *108*(6), 949–995.

Berliner, D. C. (2007). Investing in students lives outside of school to increase achievement inside schools. In G. M. Rodriguez & R. A. Rolle (Eds.), *To What Ends and By What Means?: The Social Justice Implications of Contemporary School Finance Theory and Policy* (p. 227). New York, NY: Routledge, Taylor & Francis Group.

Bettie, J. (2003). *Women without class: Girls, race, and identity.* (p. 246). Berkeley, CA: University of California Press.

Bingham, G. E., & Okagaki, L. (2012). Ethnicity and student engagement. In *Handbook of research on student engagement* (pp. 65–96).

Bourdieu, P., & Passeron, J. C. (1977). *Reproduction in education, society, and culture.* London: SAGE Publications, Inc.

Bower, C. B. (2011). Social policy and the achievement gap: What do we know? Where should we head? *Education and Urban Society*, *45*(1), 3–36. doi:10.1177/0013124511407488.

Boyd-Zaharias, B. J., & Pate-Bain, H. (2008). Class matters —In and out of school: Closing gaps requires attention to issues of race and poverty. *Phi Delta Kappan*, *90*(1), 40–45.

Christenson, S. L., Reschly, A. L., & Wylie, C. (Eds.). (2012). *Handbook of Research on Student Engagement* (p. 840). Boston, MA: Springer U.S. doi:10.1007/978-1-4614-2018-7.

Darling-Hammond, L., & Friedlaender, D. (2008). Creating excellent and equitable schools. *Educational Leadership*, (May), 14–21.

Darling-Hammond, L., LaPointe, M., Meyerson, D., Orr, M. T., & Cohen, C. (2007). *Preparing School Leaders for a Changing World: Lessons from Exemplary Leadership Development Programs*. Stanford, CA: Stanford University, Stanford Educational Leadership Institute.

De Wet, C. F., & Gubbins, E. J. (2011). Teachers' beliefs about culturally, linguistically, and economically diverse gifted students: A quantitative study. *Roeper Review*, *33*(2), 97–108. doi:10.1080/02783193.2011.554157.

English, A. (2010). Transformation and education: The voice of the learner in peters' concept of teaching. *Journal of Philosophy of Education, 43*(S1), 75–97.

Finn, J. D., & Voelkl, kristin E. (1993). School characteristics related to student engagement. *Journal of Negro Education, 62*(3), 249–268.

Foster, W. (1989). The administrator as a transformative intellectual. *Peabody Journal of Education, 66*(3), 5–18.

Froese-Germain, B. (2009). Make child poverty history? Yes we can. Examining the relationship between education and poverty. *Our School Our Selves, Spring,* 189–199.

Griffiths, A. J., Lilles, E., Furlong, M. J., & Sidhwa, J. (2012). The Relations of Adolescent Student Engagement with Troubling and High-Risk Behaviors. In S. L. Christenson, A. L. Reschly, & C. Wylie (Eds.), *Handbook of research on student engagement* (pp. 563–584). Boston, MA: Springer U.S.

Griner, A. C., & Stewart, M. L. (2012). Addressing the achievement gap and disproportionality through the use of culturally responsive teaching practices. *Urban Education, 48*(4), 585–621. doi:10.1177/0042085912456847.

Hamre, B. K., Pianta, R. C., Downer, J. T., Decoster, J., Andrew, J., Jones, S. M., … Hamagami, A. (2013). Teaching through interactions: Testing a developmental framework of teacher effectiveness in over 4,000 classrooms. *The Elementary School Journal, 113*(4), 461–487.

Hazel, C. E., Vazirabadi, G. E., & Gallagher, J. (2013). Measuring aspirations, belonging, and productivity in secondary students: Validation of the student school engagement measure. *Psychology in the Schools, 50*(7), 689–704. doi:10.1002/pits.21703.

Howard, T. C., & Reynolds, R. (2008). Examining parent involvement in reversing the underachievement of African American students in middle-class schools. *Educational Foundations, Spring,* 79–99.

Keiser, N. M. (2000). Principals' and teachers' perceptions of teacher empowerment. *Journal of Leadership & Organizational Studies, 7*(3), 115–121. doi:10.1177/107179190000700308.

Ladson-Billings, G. (1995). Toward a theory of culturally relevant pedagogy. *American Educational Research Journal, 32*(3), 465–4912. Retrieved from http://0-www.jstor.org.library.uor.edu/stable/pdfplus/1163320.pdf?acceptTC=true.

Lam, S., Wong, B. P. H., Yang, H., & Liu, Y. (2012). Understanding student engagement with a contextual model. In S. L. Christenson, A. L. Reschly, & C. Wylie (Eds.), *Handbook of Research on Student Engagement* (pp. 403 –420). New York: Springer.

LaRocque, M., Kleiman, I., & Darling, S. M. (2011). Parental involvement: The missing link in school achievement. *Preventing school failure: Alternative education for children and youth, 55*(3), 115–122. doi:10.1080/10459880903472876.

Lysne, B. S. J., Miller, B. G., & Eitel, K. B. (2013). Exploring student engagement in an introductory biology course. *Journal of College Science Teaching, 43*(2), 14–20.

Marks, H. M. (2000). Student engagement in instructional activity: Patterns in the elementary , middle , and high school years. *American Educational Research Journal, 37*(1), 153–184.

McInerney, P. (2009). Toward a critical pedagogy of engagement for alienated youth: insights from Freire and school-based research. *Critical Studies in Education, 50*(1), 23–35. doi:10.1080/17508480802526637.

Mokoena, S., & Africa, S. (2013). Engagement with and participation in online discussion forums. *The Turkish Online Journal of Educaitonal Technology, 12*(2), 97–106.

National Council of Supervisors of Mathematics (NCSM). (2008). *The prime leadership framework: Principles and indicators for mathematics education leaders*. Indiana: Solution Tree.

National Council of Teachers of Mathematics. (2000). *Principles and Standards for School Mathematics. 2000*. Reston, VA: NCTM.

Newmann, F. M., Wehlage, G. G., & Lamborn, S. D. (1992). The significance and sources of student engagement. In F. M. Newmann (Ed.), *Student engagement and achievement in american secondary schools* (pp. 11–39). New York, NY: Teachers College Press.

Nieto, S. (2008). Culture and education. In *Yearbook of the National Society for the Study of Education* (Vol. 107, pp. 127–142). doi:10.1111/j.1744-7984.2008.00137.x.

Nieto, S. (2012). Teaching, caring, and transformation. *Knowledge Quest*, *40*(5), 28–32.

Olivos, E. M. (2006). Racism and deficit thinking. In *Power of parents: A critical perspective of bicultural parent involvement in public schools* (pp. 41–59).

Pang, V. O., Stein, R., Gomez, M., Matas, A., & Shimogori, Y. (2011). Cultural competencies: Essential elements of caring-centered multicultural education. *Action in Teacher Education*, *33*(5-6), 560–574. doi:10.1080/01626620.2011.627050.

Pearce, J., Down, B., & Moore, E. (2008). Social class, identity and the "good" student: Negotiating university culture. *Australian Journal of Education*, *52*(3), 257–271. doi:10.1177/000494410805200304.

Pomerantz, E. M., Moorman, E. A., & Litwack, S. D. (2007). The how, whom, and why of parents' involvement in children's academic lives: More is not always better. *Review of Educational Research*, *77*(3), 373–410. doi:10.3102/003465430305567.

Riehl, C. J. (2000). The principal's role in creating inclusive schools for diverse students: A review of normative, empirical, and critical literature on the practice of educational administration. *Review of Educational Research*, *70*(1), 55–81. doi:10.3102/00346543070001055.

Robinson, K., & Harris, A. L. (2013). Racial and Social Class Differences in How Parents Respond to Inadequate Achievement: Consequences for Children's Future Achievement. *Social Science Quarterly*, *94*(5), 1346–1371. doi:10.1111/ssqu.12007.

Santamaria, L. J., & Santamaria, A. P. (2012). *Applied critical leadership in education: Choosing change* (p. 193). New York, NY: Routledge.

Shields, C. M. (2009). Transformative leadership: A call for difficult dialogue and courageous action in racialised contexts. *ISEA*, *37*(3), 53–68.

Shields, C. M. (2010). Transformative leadership: Working for equity in diverse contexts. *Educational Administration Quarterly*, *46*(4), 558–589. doi:10.1177/0013161X10375609.

Shields, C. M. (2013). *Transformative leadership in education: Equitable change in an uncertain and complex world* (p. 147). New York, NY: Routledge.

Skinner, E. A., & Chi, U. (2012). Intrinsic motivation and engagement as "active ingredients" in garden-based education: Examining models and measures derived from self-determination theory. *The Journal of Environmental Education*, *43*(1), 16–36. doi:10.1080/00958964.2011.596856.

Skinner, E. A., & Pitzer, J. R. (2012). Developmental dynamics of student engagement, coping, and everyday resilience. In S. L. Christenson, A. L. Reschly, & C. Wylie (Eds.), *Handbook of research on student engagement* (p. 838). Springer.

Strayhorn, T. L. (2010). The role of schools, families, and psychological variables on math achievement of black high school students. *The High School Journal*, *93*(4), 177–194. doi:10.1353/hsj.2010.0003.

U.S. Census Bureau. (2013). American Fact Finder (2008-2012). Retrieved from http://factfinder2.census.gov/faces/tableservices/jsf/.

Valencia, R. R. (1997). *The evolution of deficit thinking: Educational thought and practice* (p. 288). Milton Park.

Vygotsky, L. S. (1978). Readings on the Development of Children. In *Mind and Society* (pp. 79–91). Cambridge, MA: Harvard University Press.

Walker, K. L. (2010). Deficit thinking and the effective teacher. *Education and Urban Society*, *43*(5), 576–597. doi:10.1177/0013124510380721.

Weiner, E. J. (2003). Secretary Paulo Freire and the democratization of power: Toward a theory of transformative leadership. *Educational Philosophy and Theory*, *35*(1), 89–106. doi:10.1111/1469-5812.00007.

Williams, T. T., & Sanchez, B. (2011). Identifying and decreasing barriers to parent involvement for inner-city parents. *Youth & Society*, *45*(1), 54–74. doi:10.1177/0044118X11409066.

Yurco, B. P. (2014). Student-generated cases: Giving students more ownership in the learning process. *Journal of College Science Teaching*, *43*(3), 54–59.

Zhao, C., & Kuh, G. D. (2004). Adding value: Learning communities and student engagement. *Research in Higher Education*, *45*(2), 115–138.

CHAPTER 4

Social and Cultural Dimensions of Parental Involvement

A Predictor of Student Engagement

It is common knowledge now that parental involvement improves student outcomes. While research and common sense support the importance of parent involvement, educators are constantly asking why many parents are not involved in their children's education. As a topic with multiple interrelated, fairly complex components, it is imperative to examine these components to help teachers, administrators, counselors, and parents themselves become more intentional in assisting students and encouraging better parent involvement. The purpose of this chapter is to provide several explanatory conceptual lenses, share a parent involvement study, and present insights and practical suggestions related to effective parental involvement.

Parental involvement can be seen through the lens of Bronfenbrenner's ecological systems model that views the child as embedded in a series of interrelated systems that interact with one another (Xu & Filler, 2008; Tan & Goldberger, 2009; Woo, 2005). These systems are comprised of the microsystem (parents and siblings), mesosystem (peers and siblings), exosystem (community connection), and macrosystem (cultural influence). These four interconnected systems posit that parental involvement is "not a fixed event but a dynamic and ever-changing series of interactions that vary depending on the context in which they occur, the disciplines from which the collaborative team members are drawn, the resources parents bring to the interactions, and the particular needs of the child and the family" (Xu & Filler, 2008, p. 54).

Parental involvement can also be analyzed using Bourdieu's theories of social and cultural capital. Social capital consists of an individual's social connections, obligations, or membership in a group. Cultural capital is related to one's knowledge, skills, and dispositions as well as to one's possession of certain sophistication in certain kinds of art, literature, and other "cultural goods." Certain achievements such as educational certificates or degrees are also part of cultural capital. These theories imply that a set of high-status social connections and cultural knowledge, resources, and skills is valuable and useful in interacting with established bureaucracy and other social agencies (Perez, 2009).

Another way of looking at parental involvement is through Epstein's model, which describes six types of parental involvement: parenting, communicating, volunteering, learning at home, decision-making, and collaborating (Epstein, 2007). Epstein developed this framework of six (6) dimensions, each made up of a group of parental practices. For each dimension, Epstein presented a series of activities or practices that parents adopt when they become involved in their child's education. Her model is known to identify parental practices in the schooling experience of a child and to assist educators in developing school and family partnership programs. It is also useful in classifying the practices of immigrant parents (Beauregard, 2014). This chapter presents several specific explanations and recommendations, as well as a study that explored the links and implications of social and cultural dimensions of parental involvement in influencing student engagement.

What We Know About Parental Involvement

In general, students engage better in school when parents play a positive role in their learning process (Jennings, 2015; Jeynes, 2012; Jeynes, 2011). Students are more likely to make a personal commitment to engage in rigorous learning when they know parents care about how well they do (Hoover-Dempsey et al., 2005; Wang & Sheikh-Khalil, 2014). In a study done by Wang and Sheikh-Khalil (2014), parental involvement predicted academic success and mental health both directly and indirectly through behavioral and emotional engagement. They found that parental involvement in tenth grade improved not only academically, but also emotional functioning among adolescents in eleventh grade. However, among the types of parental involvement (i.e., school involvement, home involvement, and academic socialization), academic socialization had the strongest positive relation with achievement and strongest negative relation with depression. In other words, parents who conveyed the importance and value of education and discussed future plans with their children motivated them to engage in their academic work behaviorally and emotionally.

Obviously, one of the contributory factors to a positive academic journey is the level of parents' positive involvement. In fact, this is true of all groups of students. Research shows when parents are actively taking a part in their children's education, their children do better in school regardless of their own educational level, ethnicity, and zip code (O'Sullivan et al., 2014; Ma et al., 2014). O'Sullivan and associates (2014) explored the relationships between methods of parental assistance (i.e., provision of structure, direct assistance, and autonomy support) and children's achievement in mathematics in low-income families. The results indicated that provision of structure is the most prevalent method of involvement among low-income parents regardless of their child's achievement level. This study (O'Sullivan et al., 2014) also discussed the importance of helping low-income parents realize they can help their children succeed in math even if they cannot provide direct assistance with their homework.

Scholars have indicated that active involvement in schools is crucial to children's academic success, including that of the low-income and limited English-proficient families (Henderson et al., 2006). In another similar study conducted by Perez (2009) on low-income Latino parents in New York City, it was found that equipping parents with Bourdieu's notion of social and cultural capital sharpened their understanding of the school system and improved their advocacy practices for their language-minority children. The Latino parents recognized the power of their cultural knowledge, skills, and dispositions and the strength of their social connections, obligations, and networks of families, friends, and communities. They produced a parent guide and developed "the confidence to question their child's teachers and school principals in ways they had not before" (Perez, 2009, p. 146). Given that so many statistics on the achievement gap tell us that low-income students and limited English-proficient students already face some additional challenges in school, it is imperative that their parents are involved in their children's education in order to increase student engagement.

Additionally, many studies indicate that parent involvement is related to life circumstances of the family, which can also explain why many low-income students are also low-performing. Gordon and Cui's (2014) study asserted that communities high in poverty often struggle with facilitating school-related parental involvement that increases academic achievement. In these cases, parental involvement may be hindered by challenges such as inadequate resources (i.e., Internet-abled computers), lack of knowledge of their adolescents' schoolwork, or unavailability due to inflexible part-time jobs.

Other studies showed that parental aspiration for children's education positively relates to student engagement, whereas school-parent communication regarding student-school problems negatively predicts student motivation across ethnic groups (Goldenberg et al., 2001; Fan & Chen, 2001). In light of all these findings, there are multiple challenges that parents face in their quest to support their children's schooling. More specifically, immigrant parents in the United States are often perceived as disengaged in their children's schooling and not involved in their children's learning (Wamba, 2006).

The Problem of Deficit Thinking

The challenges that parents face in getting more involved and communicating with schools could stem from what is commonly called the theory of deficit thinking and oppression. Paulo Freire (1981) believed that oppression is brought about by a lack of dialogue between those who are in a position of power and those who are not. In his revolutionary book *Pedagogy of the Oppressed*, Freire (1981) pointed out that the ability to make claims and changes in the world around you is what leads to freedom. However, this task must be shared between those in power and those who do not have a position of power if oppression is to end. This explanation is a basis for understanding the deficit thinking we often see in schools. Due to the educators' position of power in schools, educators can often grow to believe that parents are ignorant and are closed-minded to the potential contributions parents may be able to make to their students' education. Therefore, since many parents do not yet feel this power to make changes or influence outcomes, they are, in fact, "oppressed" by the system. Deficit thinking in our educational system continues to be a stereotypical view of the lack of school involvement and participation of immigrant and non-English-speaking families.

Despite the general knowledge that parental involvement has a positive influence on student engagement, not all parents are perceived to have the desire or the time to take part in their child's academic world (Worthy, 2006). It appears that there are parents who seem to avoid getting involved. Sadly enough, they have been branded as the "silent, alienated parents" (Worthy, 2006, p. 6). This group of parents, who are the often the hardest to reach, may have had bad experiences when they were in school, may feel uncomfortable with teachers, and may feel intimidated. Unfortunately, immigrant families coming to the United States are perceived to lack the familiarity with American schools and are less likely to become more involved in the school context (Hidalgo, Siu & Epstein, 2004; Worthy, 2006; Wamba, 2006). These parents often face the fear of criticism and failure. Parents may also fear the differences in the lifestyle or values from that of the teacher. These feelings cause them uneasiness and discomfort in the school setting. Therefore, they avoid participating or becoming involved (Whitaker & Hoover-Dempsey, 2013).

Conversely, there are some immigrant parents who are eager to become more involved, but many do not understand the expectations of the American educational system and do not feel completely welcome (Wamba, 2006). The case study done by Whitmore and Norton-Meier (2008) confirms that although many schools and teachers have goals of increasing parental involvement, they often relegate parents to the position of troublemakers or assume parents just do not care. In this case study (Whitmore & Norton-Meier, 2008), the parents shared assumptions about the schools their children attended. They were unlikely to initiate communication, were uncertain about how to ask questions or voice concerns, and assumed the school was providing the best for their children. It is important to note in the same study that the schools did not initiate contact with their families or make attempts to understand how their home lives contributed to the children's learning. According to Whitmore and Norton-Meier (2008), parental involvement in many settings continues to be narrowly defined by the tasks of selling wrapping paper and cutting and pasting for bulletin boards. This kind of "busy work" and a lack of substantial input toward school policies and instruction represent a huge underestimation placed on parents. Although schools are making great strides to involve immigrant parents, several studies still indicate that effective parent involvement is still a huge issue that must be addressed in many places. If there are parents willing to put up a bulletin board, they are probably willing to do more.

As studies show, many immigrant parents have different educational experiences than their children. This is one reason that extra effort for increasing involvement is so important. Their efforts to help at home may not adequately support the American school system and the efforts made in the classroom. In fact, in Peterson and Heywood's (2007) study, teachers and principals have witnessed that immigrant parents, in particular, are trying to enforce drills upon the children to learn to read because that is how they were taught in school. However, teachers believe that a much more useful technique for learning at home involves meaningful activities that create a "language-rich environment," such as reading the newspaper together (Peterson, Heywood & Daphne 2007, p. 525).

One effective strategy conducted within the study by Peterson, Heywood, and Daphne (2007) was a "workshop for parents to introduce them to teachers' expectations for students and parents and to instruct them on best practices for supporting developing literacy, thereby helping parents to augment their social capital" (p. 526). This kind of unique approach demonstrates an understanding of the challenges parents face, as well as a respect for parents' ability to support their children's education at the same time.

Schools serving diverse populations have long been criticized for having a deficit view of immigrant families. Some critics assert that the deficit perspective leads educators to view culturally and linguistically diverse students and their families as "the problem" rather than to consider and remedy their own deficiencies in working with diverse populations. Immigrant parents are frequently perceived as lacking the resources (e.g., experience, know-how, and education) to provide and support home educational experiences for their children. This deficit perspective suggests that fault and responsibility lay with the population of the English language learners (ELL) rather than the school. It implies that the role of the school is to change the way families interact with schools. Unfortunately, many educators assume that a lack of parental participation is evidence of a lack of parental interest (Arias & Morillo-Campbell, 2008). Howard (2008) explains that from a deficit standpoint, parents are assumed to have little knowledge or capital to advocate on behalf of their children. This cultural deficit approach is indeed a dilemma of parental involvement because it assumes that parents are to be blamed for the academic failure of their children. The excuse that there is no parental involvement because of a lack of interest has plagued underperforming schools for far too long and may be negatively affecting student engagement. It is necessary to look at an alternative paradigm of parental involvement.

Alternative Paradigms for Parent Involvement

In recent years, there have been several proponents of an alternative paradigm for a more positive perspective on parents contributing to school success. Arias and Morillo-Campbell (2008) present this perspective in terms of informal home activities such as nurturing, instilling cultural values, talking with their children, and sending them to school clean and rested. Quezada (2014) sought out to eliminate the negative stereotypes that affect low-income, non-English-speaking, marginalized parents. In fact, Quezada focused on the role that educators play in order to engage in mutual partnerships with culturally and linguistically diverse families to assure children are academically successful. Another view of parent involvement presented by Kabir and Akter (2014) encourages all partners in the education process—parents, children, schools, teachers, and communities—to become involved in the co-construction of shared knowledge.

Such alternative paradigms present a more positive relationship with parents and may prove to have positive educational outcomes for student engagement as well. One example of such an approach to parent involvement can be seen in a study on immigrant parents in Quebec, Canada. Beauregarda et al. (2014) found that parents faced challenges that required them to adjust their roles in order to be perceived as involved parents. The immigrant parents in this study protected their children from challenges related to different issues of injustice, and they maintained the position that teachers and school personnel should be respected in order to ensure that their children learn to respect authority (Beauregarda et al., 2014). This frame of mind suggests to us that parenting roles and practices are shaped by family and school environment.

Environments in which educators recognize the influence of school and home can allow immigrant families to be participants in a sociocultural context in which they bring rich linguistic, cultural, and social resources (Beynon, Larocque, Ilieva & Dagenais, 2005). Family environment may refer to the number of children in the family, the language spoken at home, the availability of the parents, the children's relationships with family members, and other similar factors. The school environment may be defined by factors such as staffing and turnover, identification of children's needs, and the kinds of support provided to children. Additional factors that influence the school environment are parents' experiences with school staff and the attitudes of school staff regarding the community. All of these factors from home and school environment can heavily influence parent involvement and, in turn, student engagement.

Considering the sociocultural context that parents contribute is pertinent to improving involvement. Bolivar and Chrispeels (2011) found that when Hispanic immigrant parents participate in leadership development, they are empowered to affect changes that benefit their children through individual and collective actions. This study described how parent graduates of a leadership program founded organizations that continue to affect the educational system. The authors argued that the concepts of social and intellectual capital can inform parent involvement research and practice because they explain a community's capability to engage in new forms of action. Bronfenbenner's concept of empowerment is relevant to Bolivar and Chrispeel's (2011) study because it describes preparing parents and their communities to establish direct and indirect links to the power structure of the education system. As mentioned previously in a similar study, Perez (2009) describes how low-income Latino parents joined in creating a handbook for all parents that would describe all the high school options. They made joint decisions about the content and design of the guide within the context of their social and cultural capital (Perez, 2009). These examples illustrate the kinds of positive outcomes that can result from school communities that are committed to understanding and improving parent involvement.

Explanations for Parent Involvement

Many research studies agree that parental involvement is multidimensional. Three (3) major explanations are examined as far as the multiple dimensions of parental involvement. The first explanation involves Bronfenbrenner's ecological systems model, as referenced earlier (Xu & Filler, 2008). Bronfenbrenner asserts that a child should have "regular sustained interaction with their parents as opposed to a sporadic quality time—one of the most critical challenges facing society today" (Woo, 2005). According to Bronfenbrenner's ecological systems, which include the microsystem, mesosystem, exosystem, and microsystem, the child both affects and is affected by these interrelated systems while his or her learning occurs "within the context of normally occurring routines in familiar settings" (Xu & Filler, 2008, p. 56).

The second explanation describes Epstein's (2001) model, consisting of six (6) types of involvement: *parenting* (family obligations and support of their child), *communicating* (home-school communication), *volunteering* (family involvement in school life), *learning at home* (parental involvement in the child's schoolwork at home), *decision-making* (parental participation in the decision-making process and in the management and defense of the child's interests), and *collaborating* (partnership with the school, businesses, and other local organizations). Epstein's explanation has been very useful in identifying and classifying the parental practices of immigrant parents in the child's schooling experience (Beauregard et al., 2014).

The third explanation involves Bourdieu's concept of social and cultural capital. According to Bourdieu, social capital involves social relationships or networks that provide access to resources, while cultural capital for parents represents the power to promote their children's academic enhancement (Lee & Bowen, 2006). From these three explanations for parental involvement, this chapter attempts to enrich the conversation about the topic by formulating a viable framework of parental involvement from a socially and culturally driven perspective.

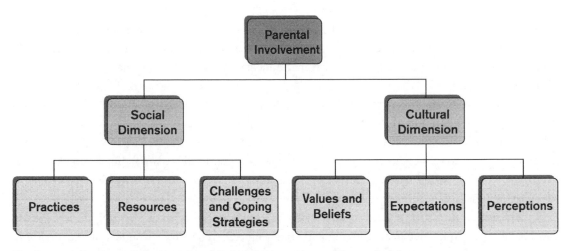

Figure 4–1. Framework for Social and Cultural Dimensions of Parent Involvement

When addressing the development of a framework for the social and cultural dimensions of parental involvement, it is important to gain understanding of human relationships. Additionally, it is important to understand that different cultural groups have unique systems for perceiving and organizing the world around them (Gorinski & Fraser, 2006). From the review of related research literature, both the social and cultural dimensions of parent involvement can be broken into smaller elements. For the current study to be discussed in this chapter, a theoretical framework of the social and cultural dimensions of parental involvement was developed based on substantial works in this field (Carreon, Drake & Barton, 2005; Kao, 2004; Guo, 2006; G. Li, 2006; J. Li, 2004; Hidalgo, Siu & Epstein, 2004).

The <u>social dimension</u> of parent involvement is evident through the ***practices*** parents use to engage in their children's learning (Carreon, Drake & Barton 2005), the ***resources*** a family utilizes (Kao, 2004), ***challenges*** encountered by parents, and the ***coping strategies*** utilized to face challenges (Guo, 2006). The <u>cultural dimension</u> of parent involvement is reflected in parents' ***values and beliefs*** about what children should learn (G. Li, 2006), ***expectations*** about academic success (J. Li, 2004), and ***perceptions*** of the parents' familiarity with school instruction and their communication with mainstream schools (Hidalgo, Siu & Epstein, 2004). This framework of social dimensions and cultural dimensions of parent involvement will be applied to the current study, findings, and implications.

Current Study Findings and Implications

Looking Closely at Filipino American Experience

In the Philippines, poor student engagement and inclination to take prohibited drugs and other delinquent behaviors are attributed to parents who do not have enough time for their children's academic difficulties (Magno et al., 2008). In addition, a significant number of cases of students' lack of engagement in school, such as missing classes, tardiness, absenteeism, and mediocre compliance of performance tasks and subject requirements, continue to proliferate (Niehaus & Adelson, 2014). Moreover, this poor engagement in school contributes to superficial knowledge from class lessons and deviant behaviors such as gangsterism (Oglivie, 2008). In light of the negative effects of poor student engagement due to a lack of parental involvement, as emphasized in the above-mentioned research studies, the current study attempts to investigate some parental involvement dimensions that will serve as a viable predictor of student engagement.

The current study examined the cultural and social practices employed by Filipino American parents in working with their children in K-5 grade levels. One of the main goals of this study was to develop a model of parent involvement that could be generalized across cultural groups. To accomplish this, two research questions were examined. The first research question examined the social dimension of parental involvement of Filipino immigrant families. The second research question explored the elements related to the cultural dimension of parental involvement.

To address these research questions, a qualitative case study that featured face-to-face, in-depth interviews of Filipino immigrant parents and children at their homes was conducted. Conducting and observing moments of dialogue with the Filipino immigrant parents and their children served to highlight the following social dimensions of parental involvement: practices on how parents engage in their children's learning, resources that parents bring to their children's education, challenges faced by immigrants, and coping strategies utilized. In the same way, the extensive interviews paved the way to understand the following cultural dimensions of parental involvement: values and beliefs on how children should learn, expectations on the children's academic success, and perceptions of parents' familiarity with school instruction and their communication with mainstream schools.

As part of the research process, the following interview questions were utilized to seek answers from parents in terms of the three aspects of the social dimension of parent involvement based on the framework previously summarized:

1. *Practices*—As a parent, describe the variety of *practices* you have done and/or are currently doing in order to be engaged in your child or children's learning. How do you help your children with their schoolwork?
2. *Resources*—What are the *resources* you have acquired or would like to acquire in order to support your involvement in your child or children's education? What are the things you need to be helpful to your children? What is your highest educational attainment? What is your present occupation and/or occupational background?
3. *Challenges and Coping Strategies*—Describe the *challenges* or difficulties you have faced as an immigrant parent from the Philippines and the *coping strategies* you have used to overcome these challenges. How do you share your experiences with your kids? Is it important for you to share these experiences?

Another set of interview questions were given to parents to investigate the three aspects of the cultural dimension of parent involvement based on the framework previously summarized:

1. *Values and Beliefs*—Based on your knowledge and experiences, what are your *values and beliefs* on what your child or children should learn?

2. *Expectations about Academic Success*—Describe your *expectations* on how your children would do well in school—academically, socially? How would this relate to your experiences as a child? What made you think of those expectations? What is the basis of your expectations?

3. *Perceptions of the Parents' Familiarity with School Instruction and Their Communication with Mainstream Schools*—What are your *perceptions* of the American education system in terms of the school instruction? Describe your level or degree of involvement in communicating or interacting with your child or children's school (e.g., volunteer regularly, attend parent-teacher conferences and/or family nights, send notes to teachers).

In addition to interviewing parents, the current study also involved interviews with children regarding the social and cultural dimensions of parent involvement outlined in the framework. Children were asked the following questions regarding the three aspects of the social dimension of parent involvement:

1. *Practices*—How does your mother or father help you with homework?
2. *Resources*—What are some of the tools/techniques that your mother or father uses to help you with school?
3. *Challenges and Coping Strategies*—What are some of the stories that your mother or father has told you about coming here to America?

Another set of interview questions was given to children regarding the three aspects of the cultural dimension of parent involvement:

1. *Values and Beliefs*—What are some of the things that your mother or father has told you about what you should learn?
2. *Expectations about Academic Success*—How does your mother or father expect you to become better at school?
3. *Perceptions on Parents' Familiarity with School Instruction and Their Communication with the School*—Describe how your mother or father volunteers at your school, attends parent-teacher conferences and/or family nights, sends notes to teachers, etc.

The framework on parental involvement previously outlined provided the lens to look at the social and cultural aspects involved in the interactions of Filipino immigrant parents and their children. In this particular study, it was found that there were several commonalities among the responses of the participants. These commonalities were grouped into categories based on the occurrences of the responses. These categories were then further analyzed into specific key themes that emerged from these recurring responses. The six key themes identified in this research were (1) *systems approach*, (2) *social/cultural/economic capital*, (3) *cultural mismatch/acculturation*, (4) *good moral character*, (5) *aspiration*, and (6) *resiliency*.

These key themes provided the answers to the research questions on the social and cultural dimensions of parental involvement. For example, in terms of the *systems approach*, it was determined that the Filipino parental practices described in this study established some kind of a systematic routine that enabled the parents to help their children in their schooling. In addition, in terms of the *social/cultural/economic capital*,

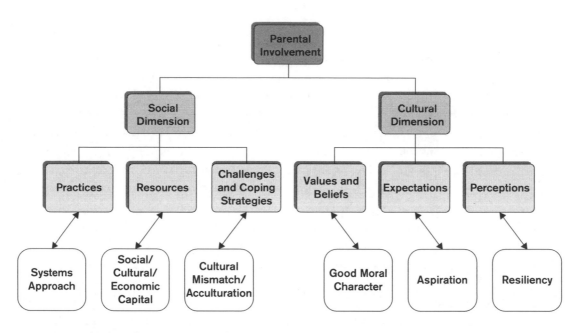

Figure 4–2. The Key Themes Emerging from the Social and Cultural Dimensions of Parental Involvement

it was evident that these Filipino immigrant participants shared a variety of resources with their children to enhance their learning. Moreover, the challenges faced by these Filipino immigrant parents resulted from a *cultural mismatch*, because discrepancies between the mainstream schools and the immigrant families were evident. Nevertheless, through the process of *acculturation*, these parents were able to acquire coping strategies that enabled them to overcome their challenges. Another key theme—*good moral character*—provided the reason why parents wanted to instill in their children some values and beliefs that revolved around the family, education, and spirituality. The key theme of *aspiration* also suggested why parents' high expectations of their children's academic success were apparent. Finally, the key theme of *resiliency* revealed that Filipino immigrant parents could adjust to their new environment and yet maintain their traditional culture while actively being involved in their children's lives. These findings provided insights into the experiences of these immigrant parents and provided guidance to the needs and strengths of these families, which could greatly inform educators on increasing parental involvement among similar populations.

The Social Dimensions of Parental Involvement: Practices

Implications of Systems Approach with Student Engagement

Under the social dimension of the parental involvement framework used in this study, the first aspect is **practices**. Systems approach was identified as a key theme for practices in this study. Systems approach pertains to the parents' ability to create a structure that establishes an organized pattern of supporting their children in their schooling (APA Task Force, 2008). Some examples of the systems approach found in the interviews were practices such as establishing routines, creating patterns, and maintaining an organized schedule. Additionally, participants indicated that they often allow children to do homework on their own. Participants indicated that parents intervene with homework and other tasks when there is a problem or difficulty, at which time parents brainstorm solutions with children. Participants also described enforcing discipline by not allowing their children to watch TV or play before homework is done and discouraging cramming or procrastination with homework. The research also revealed that parents have systems for practicing certain skills like reading aloud, cursive writing, and spelling by conducting household tasks like writing the family's grocery list. Participants indicated regular routines of checking backpacks and notebooks for assignments as well. By way of the systems approach, all parent participants mentioned that they have established some kind of a routine or a system in order to create a consistent pattern and schedule for the children to follow. Overall, parents and children reported high engagement at home and felt that families have accountability due to the systems approach in their household.

The Social Dimensions of Parental Involvement: Resources

Implications of Social/Cultural/Economic Capital with Student Engagement

Another aspect of the social dimension within the parenting framework is **resources**. Social, cultural, and economic capital were identified as key themes. Capital pertains to the parents' contributions that enhance their ability to support their children's success. There are three forms of capital. Social capital refers to the collectively owned skills, experiences, and connections that allow for success, which can be cultural or economic. Cultural capital refers to one's cultural background, knowledge, disposition, and skills that are passed on from one generation to another. Economic capital is reflective of material capital, symbolic of the currency that enters into the exchange system of the school (McLaren, 2003). The interviews described places, people, materials, and after-school activities that represent social, cultural, or economic capital. The analysis revealed that 85% of the parents provided resources for their children by exposing them to places conducive to learning, such as the library, museums, zoos, planetariums, schools, field trips, and educational stores with activities. All these above-mentioned resources point to the fact that when adequate social, cultural, or economic capital is put into place, student engagement is evident.

The Social Dimensions of Parental Involvement: Challenges and Coping Strategies

Implications of Cultural Mismatch/Acculturation with Student Engagement

The third aspect of the social dimension of parental involvement outlined in the framework is **challenges**. Along with challenges are coping strategies used to deal with challenges. In this study, cultural mismatch was identified as a major challenge faced by these immigrant parents. Cultural mismatch pertains to the misalignment of the ways of thinking and doing of parents compared to those of the school. Several details were revealed through the interviews that paint a picture of this cultural mismatch. Some examples of these challenges described by participants are the language barrier, cultural conflict between parents and children, conflict between spouses of different cultures in their child-rearing practices, different math problem-solving strategies from what they learned in the past, low level of reading ability or comprehension skills, and feelings of isolation and depression due to a lack of social networking.

Acculturation was identified as the main coping strategy to deal with these challenges. Acculturation refers to the adjustment of immigrant families into the mainstream culture (Ying & Han, 2008). Some examples of acculturation described by participants were learning the ways of the culture with patience and a positive attitude, maintaining constant communication with children, widening their circle of friends for social networking, engaging in more reading with children, and discussing methods for child-rearing with spouses in private.

The language barrier is one of the most prevalent forms of a cultural mismatch found in this study. Most parents (65%) have the utmost challenge when it comes to communicating with their children. In response to this challenge, the concept of *acculturation* is applied as a *coping strategy*. One parent in this study decided to join a Toastmasters club, where she learned how to speak English effectively and properly. Through this process of learning and widening her range of social networks, she was able to overcome the fear of isolation, depression, and feelings of racism.

Cultural mismatch still existed even among highly educated parents. Despite the fact that most parent participants were highly educated, 25% of them were not accustomed to reading textbooks or any academic books, and most of the homework assignments required a great deal of reading. Overall, these parents found that they could engage their kids intellectually, emotionally, and socially by connecting the past with the present cultures. In this way, children were able to see the comparison and contrast and at the same time appreciate what they have and where they come from.

The Cultural Dimensions of Parental Involvement: Values and Beliefs

Implications of Good Moral Character with Student Engagement

Good moral character was identified as the key theme of the **values and beliefs** cultural element of parental involvement. Good moral character refers to the highest purpose of living where an ideal person shows self-reliance, controls feelings and emotions, maintains harmonious relationships with others, and pursues knowledge to the best of one's ability with a goal of developing an obedient and compliant character (Guo, 2006). Some examples of ways that participants described their parenting for good moral character involve respect to the elders, fear of the Lord, and value of education, integrity, contentment, responsibility, and relationships. Specific areas emphasized by participants in this study were family, education, and spiritual-ity. The highest common value that most Filipino immigrant parents held on to was the family (95%). Every example of *good moral character* can naturally lead students to higher engagement in school. Students who are constantly being reminded of what is right from wrong have a sense of engaging themselves to make the right decisions. These decisions influence overall success and positive experiences in school and therefore lead to higher engagement.

The Cultural Dimensions of Parental Involvement: Expectations

Implications of Aspiration with Student Engagement

Aspiration is the key theme that emerged from the **expectations** expressed by the parent participants. *Aspiration* refers to the educational level the parents hope their child attains (Goldenberg et al., 2001). Some specific examples of expectations drawn from interviews that represent aspirations were having high expectations based on the child's innate ability, having expectations based on the parents' childhood experiences, having expectations that are slightly above standard, and having expectations based on the child's maturity level. Results revealed that 90% of the parents had high expectations based on their child's innate ability. This means that when parents know that their child has the intellectual capacity, he or she is expected to perform well academically. In essence, when children are exposed to a sense of *aspirations*, they tend to be highly engaged in their schooling. Their purpose at school makes more sense when parents remind them of what they want them to achieve.

The Cultural Dimensions of Parental Involvement: Perceptions

Implications of Resiliency with Student Engagement

Resiliency is the key theme identified based on the parents' **perception** of their familiarity with schools. *Resiliency* refers to the ability of parents to adjust to their perceived notion of schools in order to create an atmosphere viable for their level of involvement. In the current study, participants described several examples of perceptions that represent resilience. Parents described learning about the differences between U.S. and Philippine education, and many believed that U.S. teachers have a higher level of education. Parents also indicated that they felt there was more access to information in the U.S. Two negative perceptions that these parents shared were that there is a lack of moral values in U.S. schools and that Filipino teachers impose more discipline. Participants also described how parental involvement is encouraged in the U.S. Perceptions on instruction in the U.S. compared to the Philippines was not consistent among all participants.

The key theme of *resilience* is exemplified by the parents' perceptions of their familiarity of the U.S. education in comparison to the Philippine education. This theme supports Quezada and Alfaro's (2007) assertion that *resilience* happens when one is willing to shift from a notion of "risk" to a sense of "hope and change." In terms of the parents' level of involvement, parents had a clear understanding of the risks involved in terms of their varied limitations and/or benefits of the U.S. school instruction versus the Philippine education. Yet the parents chose to adapt to the mainstream schools in ways that may not be completely understood by the dominant culture. These parents resolved to gain a new sense of hope and change by getting fully involved in their children's education, even though they were not completely visible in the participation of the school activities.

The key theme of *resilience* supports Li's (2004) study on cultural integration of Eastern and Western culture. In discussing the strengths and weaknesses of the Philippine education and the U.S. education, Filipino immigrant parents believed that a cultural integration would help their children succeed in mainstream society and also enrich their lives. While maintaining high standards for academic standing, Filipino immigrant parents were making efforts to adjust to mainstream culture. Hence, the concept of *resilience* is exemplified among these immigrant parents.

The fact that some parents believed that the U.S. education is superior to the Philippine education while others believed otherwise proves that parents were acting and reflecting based on their specific situations and circumstances. For example, the educational background and/or the occupational status of the parents may or may not influence their level of involvement depending on their particular case. In essence, student engagement becomes increasingly evident when parents do their best to show an example of resiliency in their lives. This means that when parents (specifically immigrants) make efforts to adjust to the mainstream culture, students get more involved and engaged in their own learning.

Conclusion

Clearly, the current findings of this study provide U.S. teachers with some insights about the child-rearing styles and strategies of Filipino immigrant families. Similarly, as Bronfenbrenner (Xu & Filler, 2008) called attention to the role of the individual's microsystem (i.e., parents and siblings), mesosystem (peers and school), exosystem (community connection), and macrosystem (cultural influence), his ecological theory provided rationale for examining the effect of parental involvement and community context on student engagement. In the same way, Epstein's model (Beauregard, 2014) enabled us not only to articulate the different parental practices (i.e., parenting, communicating, volunteering, learning at home, decision-making, and collaborating), but it also helped us discover the reasons why parents used these practices. Understanding the underlying meaning of these parent practices will allow leaders to develop conditions that promote the development of effective partnerships between families and the school. Social and cultural capital are key elements to this study when utilizing the operationally developed framework for parental involvement. As seen in the data from this research, parents were highly involved in their children's lives regardless of whether they were formally involved in their children's school life. It is hoped that an understanding of how children of Filipino immigrant parents are reared helps American teachers to assess these children's learning needs and strengths and increase the parental involvement at the school level as well.

In addition, the current study contributed to the development of a model of parental involvement that takes into consideration the social and cultural practices among parents and children. The operationally created sociocultural dimension of parental involvement could be used in enhancing curriculum and policy-making in K-12 education. In summary, it was the intention of this research study to formalize a theoretical framework based on the social and cultural dimensions of parental involvement that could be useful across cultures and programs. With theory-building effort and support of the review of literature, the current study was able to conceptualize a model of parental involvement and categorize its social and cultural dimensions. This socially and culturally driven perspective provides an insightful guide for educators and parents to understand the whole notion of parental involvement that acknowledges parenting practices, resources, challenges and coping strategies, values and beliefs, expectations, and perceptions.

Applications of Parental Involvement and Student Engagement in Administration

- Help parents understand the decision-making process in schools in terms of educational goals that would best serve the students' needs.
- Obtain feedback from parents as to how educational priorities at schools should be addressed and dealt with.
- Join forces to bring about practical changes at school that will help motivate students to be engaged in every aspect of their learning.
- Create a parent advisory council for specific needs of diverse students.

Applications of Parental Involvement and Student Engagement in Teaching

- Collaborate with parents on how to develop effective study skills and good work ethics in students.
- Include parents in the discussion for transition to intermediate school, high school, and college.
- Collaborate with parents to help students enhance their communication skills and build self-confidence.
- Establish a system for communicating with parents via social media, print, or by phone to keep them engaged with activities happening at school and in the classroom.
- Provide regular opportunities for parents to engage in conversation regarding needs of students.

Applications of Parental Involvement and Student Engagement in Counseling

- Work collaboratively with parents to maximize the students' potential—their social, emotional, and personal growth at each stage of their development.
- Consult with parents in helping students understand themselves and develop a positive self-image.
- Work hand-in-hand with parents, showing students how to respect the feelings of others.
- Communicate with parents to understand parental involvement perspective (systems approach, cultural mismatch, etc.).
- Provide training opportunities on electronic portals to monitor students' academic progress.

Discussion Questions

1. What are some of the ways that teacher preparation programs can best train teachers to interact with parents in the context of the families' social and cultural resources?
2. How can school leaders, teachers, and counselors come together to develop a mind frame that emphasizes parental involvement as one of the critical predictors of student engagement?
3. How can colleagues and administrators help with the process of communicating with parents effectively?
4. What strategies have you found to be effective in engaging and communicating with parents?
5. In what ways do some programs (e.g., Mexican American Legal Defense and Education Fund, MALDF) inform parents about how the school system works and their rights in the system?
6. In what ways do parents interact in leadership classes that will enable them to act upon critical decisions regarding their children's academic success?
7. What collective actions do the parents engage in as a result of attending the leadership classes?

References

Arias, M.B., & Morillo-Campbell, M. (2008). Promoting ELL parental involvement: Challenges in contested times. The Great Lakes for Education Research and Practice.

APA Task Force (2008). Disseminating evidence-based practice for children and adolescents: A systems approach to enhancing care.

Beauregard, F., Petrakos, H., & Dupont, A. (2014). Family-school partnership: practices of immigrant parents in Quebec, Canada. *School Community Journal, 24*(1), 177–210.

Beynon, J., Larocque, L., Ilieva, R., & Dagenais, D. (2005). A sociocultural and critical analysis of educational policies and programs for minority youth in British Columbia. *Research on Immigration and Integration in the Metropolis.*

Bolivar, J., & Chrispeels, J. (2011). Enhancing parent leadership through building social and intellectual capital. *American Educational Research Journal, 48*(1), 4–38.

Carreon, G., Drake, C., & Barton, A. (2005). The importance of presence: Immigrant parents' school engagement. *American Educational Research Journal, 42*(3), 465–499.

Epstein, J. (2007). Improving family and community involvement in secondary schools. *Principal Leadership,* 8, 16–22.

Fan, X., & Chen, M. (2001). Parental involvement and students' academic achievement: A meta-analysis. *Educational Psychology Review, 13*(1), 1–23.

Freire, P. (1981). *Pedagogy of the oppressed.* New York: The Continuum Publishing Corporation.

Freire, P. (1987). *The politics of education: Culture, power and liberation.* South Hadley, MA: Bergin & Garvey.

Goldenberg, C., Gallimore, R., Reese, L., & Garnier, H. (2001). Cause or effect? Longitudinal study of immigrant Latino parents' aspirations and expectations, and their children's performance. *American Educational Research Journal, Washington, 38*(3), 547–583.

Gonzalez-Mena, J. (2009). *Child, family, and community: Family-centered early care and education.* Upper Saddle River, NJ: Merrill Pearson.

Gordon, M., & Cui, M. (2014). School-related parental involvement and adolescent academic achievement: The role of community poverty. *Family Relations Interdisciplinary Journal of Applied Family Studies, 63,* 616–626.

Gorinski, R., & Fraser, C. (2006). Literature review on the effective engagement of Pasifika parents & communities in education: Report to the ministry of education. Pacific Coast Applied Research Centre, New Zealand.

Guo, K. (2006). Raising children in Chinese immigrant families: Evidence from the research literature. *Asian Journal of Early Childhood, 31*(2), 7–13.

Henderson, A., Mapp, K., Johnson, V., & Davies, D. (2006). *Beyond the bake sale: The essential guide to family-school partnerships.* New York: The New Press.

Hidalgo, N., Siu, S., & Epstein, J. (2004). Research on families, schools, and communities: A multicultural perspective. In J. Banks & C. Banks (Eds.), *Handbook of research on multicultural education* (2nd ed.; pp. 631–655). San Francisco: Jossey-Bass.

Jennings, L. (2015). Jackson promotes parental involvement in schools. Education Week, Editorial Projects in Education.

Jeynes, William. (2011). *Parental involvement and academic success.* New York: Routledge.

Jeynes, William (ed.). (2012). *Family factors and the educational success of children.* London; New York: Routledge.

Kabir, A., & Akter, F. (2014). Parental involvement in the secondary schools in Bangladesh: Challenges and a way forward. *International Journal of Schooling, 10*(1), 1–19.

Kao, G. (2004). Social capital and its relevance to minority and immigrant populations. *Sociology of Education, 77,* 172–183.

Lopez, G. (2009). The value of hard work: Lessons on parent involvement from an (im)migrant household. *Harvard Educational Review, 71*(3), 416–438.

Lee, J., & Bowen, N. (2006). Parent involvement, cultural capital, and the achievement gap among elementary school children. *American Educational Research Journal, 43*(2), 193–218.

Li, G. (2006). What do parents think? Middle-class Chinese immigrant parents' perspectives on literacy learning, homework, and school-home communication. *The School Community Journal, 16*(2), 27–46.

Li, J. (2004). Parental expectations of Chinese immigrants: A folk theory about children's school achievement. *Race Ethnicity and Education, 7*(2), 167–183.

Ma, X., Jianping, S., & Krenn, H. (2014). The relationship between parental involvement and adequate yearly progress among urban, suburban, and rural schools. *School Effectiveness and School Improvement, 25*(4), 629–650.

Magno, C., Lynn, J., Lee, A., & Ko, R. (2008). *Parents' school-related behavior: Getting involved with a grade school and college child.* Manila, Philippines: De La Salle University.

McLaren, P. (2003). Critical pedagogy: A look at the major concepts. In A. Darder, M. Baltodano, & R. Torres (Eds.), *The critical pedagogy reader* (pp. 69–96). New York: Routledge.

Niehaus, K., & Adelson, J. School support, parental involvement, and social-emotional outcomes for English language learners. *American Educational Research Journal, 51*(4), 810–844.

Oglivie, A. (2008). Filipino-American K-12 public school students: A national survey. A national report from the National Federation of Filipino American Associations. Washington, D.C.

O'Sullivan, R., Chen, Y., & Fish, M. (2014). Parental mathematics homework involvement of low-income families with middle school students. *School Community Journal, 24*(2), 165–187.

Perez, M. (2009). Low-income Latina parents, school choice, and Pierre Bourdieu. In J. Anyon (Ed.), *Theory and educational research: Toward critical social explanation* (pp. 135–148). New York: Routledge.

Peterson, S., & Heywood, D. (2007). Contributions of families' linguistic, social, and cultural capital to minority-language children's literacy: Parents', teachers', and principals' perspectives. *The Canadian Modern Language Review, 63*(4), 517–538.

Quezada, R. (2014). Family, school, and community partnerships: working with culturally diverse families. Multicultural Education

Quezada, R., & Alfaro, C. (2007). Biliteracy teachers' self-reflections of their accounts while student teaching abroad: Speaking from "the other side." *Teacher Education Quarterly.*

Tan, E., & Goldberg, W. (2009). Parental school involvement in relation to children's grades and adaptation to school. *Journal of Applied Developmental Psychology, 30*, 442–453.

Wamba, N. (2006). Book review of culturally contested pedagogy: Battles of literacy and schooling between mainstream teachers and Asian immigrant parents. *Reading & Writing Quarterly, 22*, 299–304.

Wang, M., & Sheikh-Khalil, S. (2014). Does parental involvement matter for student achievement and mental health in high school? *Child Development, 85*(2), 610–625.

Whitaker, M., & Hoover-Dempsey, K. (2013). School influences on parents' role beliefs. *The Elementary School Journal, 114*(1), 73–99.

Whitmore, K., & Norton-Meier, L. (2008). Pearl and Ronda: Revaluing mothers' literate lives to imagine new relationships between homes and elementary schools. *Journal of Adolescent & Adult Literacy, 51*(6), 450–461.

Woo, E. (2005). Urie Bronfenbrenner; theories altered approach to child development; at 88. *Los Angeles Times*, September 29, 2005.

Worthy, J. (2006). *Como si le falta un brazo*: Latino immigrant parents and the costs of not knowing English. *Journal of Latinos and Education, 5*(2), 139–154.

Xu, Y, & Filler, J. (2008). Facilitating family involvement and support for inclusive education. *The School Community Journal, 18*(2), 53–71.

Ying, Y., & Han, M. (2008). Parental acculturation, parental involvement, intergenerational relationship and adolescent outcomes in immigrant Filipino American families. *Journal of Immigrant and Refugee Services, 6*(1), 112–131.

CHAPTER 5

Cultural Relevance and Responsiveness in Writing

A Tool to Engage Student Voice

The present reality for African American students in the American public school system continues to be a priority in educational research (Lewis, Hancock, James & Larke, 2008; Darling-Hammond, 2005; Noguera, 2008; Ladson-Billings, 1995). From the perspectives of Lewis et al. (2008), African American students have been "short-changed by elementary and secondary schools in the United States" (p. 10). Further, Darling-Hammond (2006) asserted that close to 40% of African American students attend schools that are more segregated and "significantly less well funded, with states like California and Massachusetts spending more on prisons than they spent on higher education" (p. 15). Ladson-Billings (1995) concluded that the majority of urban public schools serving African American students suffer from limited educational opportunities and resources and lack experienced teachers and administrators.

More significantly, literacy achievement is at the forefront of this non-achievement (Turner, 2005). A report completed by EdSource (2008) insisted that "African American student achievement in Language Arts is improving, but more slowly than for any other groups" (p. 6). Furthermore, statistics from the National Assessment of Educational Progress (NAEP) reported that in 2009, Black students had an average reading assessment score that was lower than that of white students by twenty-seven points (NAEP, 2009). Unfortunately, this gap was not significantly different from the thirty-point gap reported in 2007 (National Center for Educational Statistics, 2009). This particular chapter highlights the challenges faced by all students in writing, but especially African American students. The need for student engagement is imperative for future progression in education; therefore, culturally relevant and responsive strategies make liberatory practices a reality. Writing is the promising vehicle for student voice to be preserved.

The purpose of this chapter is to establish an understanding of how culturally relevant and responsive instruction (CRRI) impacts African American students and their engagement in their own learning. The chapter is divided into three major sections. First, you will explore the significance of CRRI and its development, followed by the significance of writing as a tool for engagement. Finally, the chapter ends with research on the importance of writing as a tool to engage students as sociocultural authors as well as embracing themselves as multiliterate beings.

What We Know about Literacy Achievement of African American Students

The NAEP assessment reports published by the National Center for Educational Statistics (NCES) have consistently illustrated the dire conditions of African American students concerning literacy. The latest results from NAEP (2011) reported that although the performance of all subgroups of students has moved many toward proficiency over the last two decades, the gap between African American students and their white counterparts still remains. The number of Black students who scored proficient or above in reading on the NAEP has increased from 9% in 1992 to 15% in 2011. Similarly, white students who scored proficient or advanced grew from 36% in 1992 to 43% in 2011 (NCES, 2011).

This imbalance can be seen in the NAEP writing assessment as well. As illustrated by the NCES report (2011), the struggle African American students face with writing is indicated by this subgroup having the highest number of students in the below basic category and the lowest number of students in the proficient/advanced category. The grim results reported for African American students' achievement will continue to be a problem for this subgroup without instructional strategies that target diverse learners.

Over the last decade, culturally responsive pedagogy has "gained increased attention" from researchers as the set of ideological and instructional practices that positively impact the outcomes of African American students (Howard & Terry, 2011, pg. 4). This chapter affirms the need of culturally relevant and responsive instruction (Balogun, 2011) as a viable pedagogy for African American students as it pertains to literacy and, in particular, writing.

The Need for Culturally Relevant and Responsive Instruction (CRRI)

Culturally responsive teaching is a pedagogy that requires teachers to acknowledge and understand students' realities, interests, and culture, and requires teachers to capitalize on this knowledge (Ladson-Billings, 1994; Gay, 2000; Villegas & Lucas, 2002). Howard and Terry (2011) assert,

The merger of culture and pedagogy represents a complex and intricate set of processes that many practitioners and researchers have suggested may improve student learning … the nexus of culture and pedagogy rests upon a comprehensive and informed set of knowledge and skills that many practitioners fail to possess in their attempts to engage diverse students in the teaching and learning process (p. 2).

The goal of culturally responsive teaching has been to celebrate underserved cultures while teaching the content. The theory of cultural responsiveness has affected many domains of education, including teaching, learning, curriculum, and the students involved in the instruction process (Gay, 2000).

Many researchers have studied the use of cultural inclusion and have referred to culturally relevant and responsive instruction as cultural congruence, cultural relevance, cultural competence, culturally sensitive pedagogy, cultural compatibility, cultural appropriateness, and culturally responsive pedagogy (Ladson-Billings, 1992; Gay, 2000; Au, 2008). Despite the various descriptors of the term, the intent has remained the same: to educate and empower children of color using a "socially just pedagogy" (Moje, 2007) that includes "funds of knowledge" (Moll, 1992) and the discourses they bring with them to school (Gee, 1996).

Bridging the gap between the home and school identities of African American students has been essential to their success in school (Clay, 2003). Culturally responsive instruction has enabled liberatory teaching practices to take place (Freire, 2000). Researchers such as Hale (1982) and Ladson-Billings (1994) referred to this type of liberatory pedagogy as relevant for the education of African American students. Hale (1982) first stated the purposes of liberatory pedagogy: "The educator advocating for liberation has parallel purposes for educating the oppressed: education for struggle and education for survival" (p. 154). She further contended that education for a struggle has been imperative for African Americans; it has made them more aware of their oppressive place in society in all its forms and disguises (Hale, 1982). Because education for survival has fostered a bridge-building, culturally inclusive schooling environment, it has complemented and reflected the culture of both the home and community. In doing so, the individual survival of African Americans has been "tied to the survival and development of Black people" (Hale, 1982, p. 157).

In terms of further defining the dual purposes of education, Hale (1982) maintained that the model has led to a reduction in individualism and competition and, more importantly, has promoted practices that have been pedagogically relevant. Some of the most relevant pedagogical practices that underscore this model of educating African American students have been inclusiveness, relevance, and academic rigor. Academic excellence, assistance in making learning enjoyable, and a strong emphasis on the importance of effective language and communication skills have also been core attitudes for educators. Hale's model (1982) for teaching African American students encompassed additional strategies such as the following: the effective use of body language, use of standard English, equal amounts of teacher and student talk time, encouragement of group learning, a variety of learning activities, and music in the classroom.

Following in the footsteps of Hale, Gloria Ladson-Billings continued the development of culturally relevant pedagogy. As early as 1992, Ladson-Billings explored the promise of culturally relevant pedagogy (CRP) with three overarching tenets. According to Ladson-Billings (1995), CRP is described as:

A pedagogy of oppression, not unlike critical pedagogy but specifically committed to collective, not merely individual, empowerment. Culturally relevant pedagogy rests on three criteria or propositions: a) students must experience academic success; b) students must develop and/or maintain cultural competence; and c) students must develop a critical consciousness through which they challenge the current status quo of the social order (p. 160).

The first characteristic of CRP was based on the notion that academic success should be the ultimate goal of instruction. The second characteristic was based on the premise that students need to develop and maintain their cultural competence. The third characteristic was established to ensure that students develop a socio-political critical consciousness "that allows them to critique the cultural norms, values, mores and institutions that produce and maintain social inequities" (Ladson-Billings, 1995, p. 476), which was similar to the concept of conscientization developed by Freire (2000).

After analyzing the results of interviews and the research on successful teachers of African American students, Ladson-Billings concluded that culturally relevant pedagogy has been the vehicle by which African American students have been able to achieve success within the education system. According to Ladson-Billings (1994), as culturally relevant teaching has evolved, many strategies that bridge students' home and school cultures have been implemented. In her book *Dreamkeepers*, based on Afrocentric Feminist Theory, she described the strategies of successful teachers of African American children. The strategy considered most important to the praxis of CRP was that of the teacher as facilitator. The premise was that all children could be successful when the teacher facilitated bridging the cultures between school and home.

Gay (2000) revealed further insights into effective strategies for teaching African American students when she wrote *Culturally Responsive Teaching* as a means to marry the theory with the research into the practice of cultural responsiveness. Her book highlighted several effective components of cultural responsiveness: caring, communication, curriculum, and instruction. This research contributed to the scholarship and theory of culturally responsive teaching in that it identified what is referred to as power pedagogy. Power pedagogy is the praxis of teaching that validates students' identities while simultaneously encouraging them to evolve as learners. Gay (2000) asserted the following:

> The individuality of students is deeply entwined with their ethnic identity and cultural socialization. Teachers need to understand very thoroughly both relationships and distinctions between these to avoid compromising the very thing they are most concerned about—the students. Inability to make distinctions among ethnicity, culture and individuality increases the risk that teachers will impose their notions on ethnically diverse students, insult their cultural heritages, or ignore them entirely in the instructional process. In reality, ethnicity and culture are significant filters through which one's individuality is made manifest. Yet individuality, culture and ethnicity are not synonymous (p. 23).

This "socioculturally centered teaching" has promoted students' academic achievement. It has done so by responding to the need for a bridge of discovery for students in the wholeness of their development. According to Gay (2000), culturally responsive pedagogy responded to the educational process by validating, facilitating, liberating, and empowering ethnically diverse students. Cultural responsiveness was founded on four premises: teachers' attitudes and expectations, cultural communication in the classroom, culturally

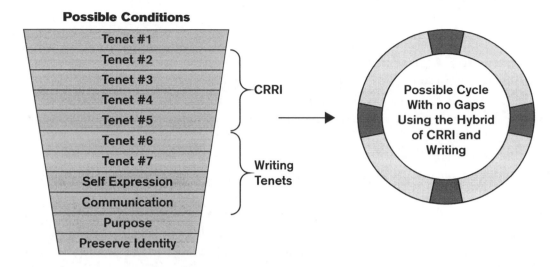

Figure 5–1. Conditions with CRRI Conceptual Framework

diverse content in the curriculum, and culturally congruent instructional strategies. It also has been multidimensional, transformative, and empowering while making learning a priority (Gay, 2000). This is similar to the research of both Hale (1982) and Ladson-Billings (1994), which found that this pedagogy made learning and academic success a non-negotiable while encouraging the notion of individual self-development and critique. Unfortunately, current practices of educators have been contrary to this development. Instead, educators have avoided the identities of students, therefore creating a "gap" in education (Delpit, 1995).

Culturally Relevant and Responsive Instruction (CRRI) is a theoretical model that places the learning of African American students at the forefront of instruction and provides a structure that educators can follow to develop the overall attitudes of African American students in a positive manner. Another goal of CRRI is to facilitate the learning process by providing an instructional practice that is liberating, invigorating, and promising (Hale, 1982; Ladson-Billings, 1994; Gay, 2000; Howard, 2008, 2010; Tatum, 2008). Under this model, teaching and learning can be more reciprocal, rewarding, and cyclical (Villegas & Lucas, 2002; Delpit, 2006; Freire, 2000). According to Howard and Terry (2011),

> Culturally responsive pedagogy is situated in a framework that recognizes the rich and varied cultural wealth, knowledge, and skills that diverse students bring to schools, and seeks to develop dynamic teaching practices, multicultural content, multiple means of assessment, and a philosophical view of teaching that is dedicated to nurturing student academic, social, emotional, cultural, psychological, and physiological wellbeing (p. 5).

Culturally Relevant and Responsive Instruction Tenets

Tenet #1: Culture is used as a vehicle to bridge the gap between content and instructional practices and the worldviews of students. Culture is multifaceted and includes descriptors such as family background, community, race and ethnicity, language, age and generational determinants, and geographic location (Freire, 2005; Hale, 1982; Ladson-Billings, 1994; Shade & Oberg, 1997; Gay, 2000; Lee, 2007; Irvine, 2003; Howard, 2008, 2010; Tatum, 2008; Tatum, 1997, 2007; Delpit, 1995, 2002; Au, 2008).

Tenet #2: Teachers, as masters of content, must demonstrate care and believe all students can learn, possess an affirming attitude toward students and learning, and demand excellence (Villegas & Lucas, 2002; Shade & Oberg, 1997; Gay, 2000; Lee, 2007; Irvine, 2003; Howard, 2008, 2010; Jeffy & Cooper, 2011; Morrison et al. 2008).

Tenet #3: Learning is shared between teacher and students and must scaffold what students already know. Knowledge is validating and empowering and demands that students become critically aware of their own learning processes (Freire, 2005; Hale, 1982; Ladson-Billings, 1994; Shade & Oberg, 1997; Gay, 2000; Lee, 2007; Irvine, 2003; Howard, 2008, 2010; Tatum, 2008; Tatum, 1997, 2007; Delpit, 1995, 2002).

Tenet #4: Instruction and environment must be inclusive of language, cultural practices, and learning styles, collaborative, and designed around a "community of learners." Students and teachers are responsible and accountable for each other's learning (Freire, 2005; Hale, 1982; Ladson-Billings, 1994; Shade & Oberg, 1997; Gay, 2000; Lee, 2007; Irvine, 2003; Howard, 2008, 2010; Tatum, 2008; Tatum, 1997, 2007; Delpit, 1995, 2002).

Tenet #5: Content and curriculum is examined and taught critically and strategically using a socio-political lens. Content, curriculum, and assessments must be age-appropriate and meet the needs of the individual learners (Freire, 2005; Hale, 1982; Ladson-Billings, 1994; Gay, 2000).

Tenet #6: Multiple literacies and multiple identities of students are embraced. Instruction must allow these identities to be expressed and expanded upon. Students should feel comfortable situating their socio-cultural identities in collaborative and individual settings (Freire, 2005; Kinloch, 2009; Moje, 2008; Moll, 1992: Lewis & Del Valle, 2009; Tatum, 2000).

Tenet #7: Literacy is highly respected and encouraged. According to Balogun (2011), CRRI engages in literary practices that benefit and position learners for optimal expression, empowerment, and validation. Multicultural literature should be used, and purposeful and reflective writing is essential for students to have maximum engagement in their education (Au, 2007; Busch & Ball, 2004; Lovejoy, 2009; Weinstein, 2007; Jocson, 2006; Malozzi & Malloy, 2007; Singer & Shagoury, 2006).

Tenets 1 through 6 in this research originated from several major researchers (Freire, 2005; Hale, 1982; Ladson-Billings, 1994; Shade & Oberg, 1997; Gay, 2000; Lee, 2007; Irvine, 2003; Howard, 2008, 2010; Tatum, 1997, 2007, 2008; Delpit, 1995, 2002; Au, 2008; Villegas & Lucas, 2002). Tenet 1 is the most overarching tenet. Tenets 2, 3, 4, and 5 are reviewed in clusters because they overlap. Tenet 6 addresses the need for educators to view, accept, celebrate, and include students in possession of multiple literacies and multiple identities.

Current research supports that CRRI is a powerful tool when addressing African American students in education. More specifically, the literature emphasizes writing as a staple in this theory instead of an option. In order to close the achievement gap, literacy instruction needs to include a balanced approach to relevant reading and writing. Writing permits students to apply the culturally responsive content and instruction in their daily lives and develop a non-negotiable identity complete with language and multiple literacies. A non-negotiable identity is a set of lived experiences from a socially and culturally defined family and community context. This occurs while students are situated in the cusp of their community, critiquing the world and knowledge around them.

Because the ability to write well has been directly linked to success in college, the significance of employing CRRI to increase literacy in African American students, particularly in writing, cannot be underestimated. In terms of responsive literacy teaching, Moje (2008) stated that "literacy pedagogy should account for and respond to the texts, and literacy practices of youths then connect those texts and practices to the disciplines"(p. 60). Some literacy practices Moje describes are out-of-school practices such as websites, emails, music lyrics, and magazines. Obviously, with the urgency of low writing scores and the value that writing has in constructing identity, this connection to home and personal life in writing is essential, particularly for African American students.

Writing as the Missing Piece in Education

From a sociocultural perspective, "literacy is something that one actively does" (Bartlett, 2007) in which identity construction is an ongoing process. Writing is the vehicle by which students communicate, express, and share these multiple identities in an effort to engage and build agency and relationships in the context of schooling. Smitherman (2007) asserts: "We must continue to be vigilant about language as an instrument of social transformation, not only for Black people but for all peoples everywhere... education must be about us and the language we use and understand" (p. 154). Strategies in CRRI include critical discussions and critical written reflections, which provide a platform in which multiple literacies may be accessed (Au, 2007; Street, 1995, 2005; Majiri & Godley, 1998; Stinson, 2008).

Street (2005) completed research on building writing communities to serve as a scaffold for conducting writing workshops that engage writers. As described by Street, writing communities provide an environment that allows students to write at their own pace about their own concerns. In his study, trust was created with reluctant writers by modeling the writing process with them. His research revealed that "the one key to transforming reluctant writers is to provide a social context that leads to identity transformation" (p. 641). Because writing is a social process, the community of writing in class allowed students to engage in the social act of writing. The students who participated in the study became engaged, confident, and more productive as they began to see themselves as a part of a community of writers.

Current research shows that effective writing strategies can be designed in a culturally relevant manner that requires teachers to provide support to students through a community of learning, which consists of written topics related to student interests. Writing instruction can be designed to preserve student identities, explore specific topics, or express ideas. Much of the current literature is centered on the significance of multiple identities and multiple literacies.

As of 2010, with the inception of Common Core, writing is now a required instructional practice across all disciplines as a fundamental component in the transmission of knowledge and the evidence of learning. Today's educational classrooms must allow space for students to develop their multiliterate selves (Street, 1995) as a means of engagement. Gee (2001) noted that as individuals emerge as literate persons, they develop and move in and out of various situations or discourses. They are challenged when their primary discourse or home language does not readily match literacy activities sponsored by schools and in many academic assessments. Davis (2013) asserts that teachers can use students' narratives to legitimize students' multiple perspectives, identities, and literacy histories.

With concerns and statistics for Hawaiian students congruent with those of African American children, Au (2007) also recognized the benefit of using writing to develop literacy in Hawaii. Her research led to positive achievements for native students (Au, 1995). She asserted that effective literacy instruction based on cultural responsiveness must bridge literacy of diverse backgrounds, and educators must embrace the broader concept of literacy, termed multiple literacies. Au's (2007) view of culturally responsive instruction added a new lens to the theory and praxis of literacy through writing. According to Au, educators need to first "help students acquire knowledge, strategies, and skills that will enable them to meet higher standards for literacy" and then "allow students to reach higher standards through culturally responsive instruction or ways of teaching and learning" (Au, 2007, p. 6). It is with this "hybridity" that cultural responsiveness has evolved in order to meet the needs of diverse learners.

Writing as a Multidimensional Tool

Under the CRRI model, the need for students to write for various purposes is evident. However, common practices for writing include writing as an assignment confined to a single genre, following a particular formulated structure. Despite this traditional view, current research implores that safe spaces be honored for writing and the requisite of writing being employed as a tool for expression, communication, personal purpose, and preservation of identity (Kinloch, 2010; Paris & Kirkland, 2011; Jocson, 2006; Smitherman, 2007; Majiri & Sablo, 1996). Writing is more than just responding to a specific writing prompt; it becomes a safe haven, as stated below by Ruben and Moll (2013):

> Many young adults feel powerless and trapped in adolescence; contrary to the central foci of authentic middle schools, their natural developmental needs to search for identity and meaning are not being met within the current school system (Erikson, 1968; Yost & Vogel, 2012). They need more than the basic academic skills so centrally characteristic of a junior high. True to the middle school model, young adolescents need a venue to try on identities, to explore who they are as people, and to figure out their place in the world. Writing is an appropriate, safe venue for that exploration (p. 17).

Multiple literacies refer to the varied literate behaviors inside and outside of school (Beaufort, 2009) and are specific to the social settings in which they occur. "Identity represents ways of being and performing as members of certain groups as well as the way our selfhood is recognized by others" (Lewis & Del Valle, p. 310, 2009). The significance of identity has emerged when marginalized students often have not fit the dominant mold within the education system. This alienation has transferred into a gap in learning that has resulted in a gap in achievement. The implementation of CRRI can fill these voids because the theory encourages making certain identities and literacies acceptable within the sociocultural contexts of schooling. As stated by Ladson-Billings (1995), Culturally Relevant Pedagogy "not only addresses student achievement, but also helps students accept and affirm their cultural identity while developing critical perspectives that challenge inequities that school perpetuate" (p. 469).

Teachers of African American students who have used CRRI effectively have capitalized on the many identities and literacies in an effort to teach content and further develop the whole child. According to Lewis & Del Valle (2009),

> Classrooms should offer a space to build on these out-of-school literacy practices to negotiate and critically examine systems and structures that students deal with in their everyday lives but that too often serve marginalize students at school and in other institutional contexts (p. 314).

Tatum (2000) has stated that African American students, in particular, have been forced to take on the identity of the dominant culture at the expense of their own. On the other hand, CRRI demands that the entire system of schooling accept, affirm, and validate all students. Students' sociocultural identities can bridge content and liberate marginalized students.

Freire (1970) expressed a similar theoretical concept in his idea of liberatory education, in which problem posing was at the heart of learning and a teacher was no longer "merely one who teaches, but one who is himself taught in dialogue with the students, who in turn is being taught to teach" (p. 80). Educators need to promote the development of students' multiple identities and multiple literacies in order for the students to become "critical co-investigators" of knowledge. This results in education becoming a practice of freedom as opposed to a practice of domination. This was further affirmed by Kinloch (2009), who suggested that educators should be very suspicious of pedagogical strategies that have separated community-based literacy from literacy events that have taken place in school. In other words, efficient literacy practices need to include the cultural and community contexts of students.

Singer and Shagoury's (2006) study is an example of how students can develop multiple out-of-school literacy practices. In their research, they tried to promote student agency through social justice issues. Students were given books based on social justice issues and were required to write and create projects. Students who participated in the study were passionate about their work and were able to grow as writers and activists. The foundation for educational justice allows students to have equitable learning experiences in the classroom. Writing can be a strong instrument for promoting social justice activism in the classroom and provide meaningful avenues for cultural relevance.

Current Research, Findings, and Implications

The current research was conducted in a large, urban, Southern California school district responsible for serving over 600,000 students. This case study investigated the influence of CRRI with the goal of informing instructional practices in the area of writing for African American students. Situated in two mini-cases, this case study aimed to comprehend the voices and perceptions of teachers and students in an effort to explain the various writing practices. The study was established in a mixed-methods design and triangulated with multiple collections of data, such as program information, questionnaires, interviews, and scored writing samples. Also, teachers were questioned for insight into their teaching practices, and students were questioned for their attitudes toward learning to write and on writing in general. This quantitative data was used to explore the results of this process (Stake, 2010, p. 125).

A comprehensive review of literature on culturally responsive pedagogy was synthesized to create the *Seven Cardinal Tenets of Culturally Relevant and Responsive Instruction* (CRRI). CRRI tenets emerged from the findings of pioneer researchers in the field such as Hale, Ladson-Billings, and Gay. In the current study, CRRI is described as a theoretical model that places African American students at the forefront of instruction and provides a structure that educators can follow to develop the overall attitudes of African American students in a positive manner. Tenets 1 through 6 developed as pedagogical practices that best facilitated learning for African American students and have been successfully implemented. Tenet 7 was developed to specifically address the multiple literacies needs of African American students, predominantly in the area of writing.

After an in-depth analysis of the findings from the current study, the need for writing to be the vehicle for student engagement was apparent. Research supports that when students write for multiple purposes, they become authors of their own identities and make meaning of their sociocultural spaces. Writing becomes more than a mundane task; it serves as an empowering, multifaceted tool for them to comprehend their multidimensional, multiliterate voice, thereby maximizing their level of engagement in the classroom.

The voices of the students in the current study revealed several reasons why writing engaged them as learners. The students spoke of the challenges with writing, the enhancement of writing through technology, and the significance of teacher interaction throughout the writing process, but they mainly focused on the customary practices in which writing can be meaningful. Student expression (identity, empowerment, and validation), writing as a refuge, writing as a personal task, along with writing being a tool for communication were the most profound of the themes.

Engaging Student Voice: Writing as Student Expression

As a tool, students use writing to express themselves and develop who they are as individuals. Nearly 40% of the student questionnaire responses reflected the students' desire to write as a means of expressing themselves. For students, expression serves a deeper purpose beyond the academic. According to the voices of the students, expression can symbolize a manifestation of self, an articulation of multiple identities, and a demonstration of creativity. Through writing as a tool for expression, students have a voice, therefore feeling validated. The voice of students through written expression facilitates healing, empowerment, and self-restoration. Writing as a tool for expression through voice was described by one student, who wrote, "I love writing because I get to express a whole different me. Also I get to write about anything that is true or not true and different kinds of genres."

Engaging Student Voice: Writing for Refuge

Writing as a tool for expressing student voice allows students to express their feelings and gives them a sense of empowerment. This sense of empowerment provides healing and enhances the purposes of writing to include writing as a refuge (Majari, 1998). Writing is understood as a safe place for pain to be stored, and the act of writing is viewed as therapeutic and engaging. Hill (2009) coined this sociocultural, meaning-making action of literacy practices as "wounded healing." He articulates that even in the absence of explicit focus on wounded healing, the effective use of culturally relevant curriculum and pedagogy inevitably creates new relationships among teachers, students, and the classroom context.

Students in the current research study agreed with the act of writing being a tool to release and process emotions. The following student remarks exemplify healing and refuge through writing:

"I write to communicate in letters or poems to myself to, like, encourage me to do stuff that I say I can't do."

"I think writing is important because sometimes there is something going on in your life and the way you can express it is with writing. It helps!"

"It helps you feel better."

"Well, I write songs because it helps me … it just helps me for my mind so whatever just comes. I write it down and I end up making me like a song."

"If nobody wants to listen to me, I just write. I just write and I write a letter and just give it to somebody then and then they can help me solve my problem."

Through remarks that allude to writing as a tool for expression, student creativity can be observed. Students expressed a desire to be heard on their terms and with their guidelines; they wanted to choose the topics and genres for their writing. Consistent with Callins (2006), students expressed the need for freedom in creativity and choice in topics. As students discussed their perception of writing, they disclosed their view of writing as a personal task that they wanted to complete. Students commented:

"I usually write letters to my friends, my cousin, she lives far away so I mainly write lots of letters and send her pictures."

"Ok, like when I don't use the computer to communicate with writing, sometimes I do, but it's just like things I write just to myself to keep [my writing] personal."

"I write because my mom has diabetes and she's blind."

In this way, students in the CRRI groups wrote for many purposes, which demonstrates their understanding of the complex nature of writing. They shared their teachers' view of writing as the gatekeeper to success. They wrote,

"Uh, I think I like the process because writing gets you to places, like you can be famous for just writing a story."

"Just a little writing can get you anywhere you wanna go."

In all, students perceived writing as a necessary task that served multiple purposes. They used writing as a tool for expression, which gave them a *voice* that established them within society. Writing as a tool for expression also allowed students to use writing to complete personal tasks, such as sending emails or other forms of communication. Students vocalized the task of writing as a multifaceted practice. They were operationally equipped to navigate academic and cultural spaces. This made them personally inspired and able to find a place of refuge for their multiple selves.

Engaging Student Voice: Writing for Personal Task and Communication

Students instructed by teachers trained in CRRI believed that their writing served multiple purposes, as evidenced by their questionnaires and focus groups. Students recorded that their writing relieved them of stress, the ability to write freed them to be anything they wanted to be in life, and writing was a private and personal task. CRRI students shared that writing allowed them to be creative and voice their own thoughts. These comments are in direct correlation with CRRI Tenet 7, which posits that writing is utilized by students for optimal expression.

Students instructed by teachers trained in CRRI liked writing as a communication tool and as a vehicle for expressing themselves. However, they felt the tedious tasks of writing presented many challenges for them. One of the challenges was the writing process itself. Students commented that it took too long and often caused their hands to hurt, which is why they liked texting and typing. Students shared that writing essays with a word limit was a challenge, but typing on a computer was easier, as the computer counted the words for them. Grammar, spelling, and punctuation kept emerging as a challenge for students.

The African American students commented on how their teacher taught them about appropriate times to use their home language. They mentioned that when they wrote poems, songs, or raps, they could use their home language, but when they turned in their assignments, it was their responsibility to switch to academic English. African American students also perceived writing as a tool for personal encouragement and a source of healing.

African American boys consistently shared that they liked writing and liked having the freedom to choose their topics. Some of the writing topics mentioned were video games, non-fiction, wildlife, sports, and fiction. Throughout their three-page transcript, the mention of free writing appeared five times. One little boy commented, "By me being able to express my feelings, you don't have to worry about anyone else's opinion, you can just be in your zone and [that's] the reason I like to write."

In essence, students instructed by teachers trained in CRRI liked writing for many different purposes. They were aware of the appropriateness of their home language, but they also viewed it as a valuable asset, as it served several purposes. African American students enjoyed writing for personal and creative tasks, and they said that they liked it when teachers allowed them to choose their own topics.

Student Engagement with Teachers and Technology

Ultimately, students from CRRI classrooms illuminated some of the problems encountered in writing through their transcripts and questionnaires. Throughout the data, CRRI students openly shared the challenges they experienced with writing. Some students expressed concerns about teachers who failed to provide clear prompts or explanation of assignments. Students shared,

> " … sometime[s] I write the wrong word and sometime[s] I don't get what the teacher is telling me. Sometime[s] I get nervous and put the same words again."

> "I don't like writing because I think it's boring and I don't know what to write. I feel uncomfortable because then I get confuse[d] in writing because instead of writing a paragraph I write a summary."

> "I feel nervous about the writing process because I am scared to do something wrong."

For these students, the most prominent challenge was their insecurity with writing. They highlighted their concerns using words such as nervous, uncomfortable, and scared, which indicates a lack of confidence or security in their writing skills. Other areas of concern included the length of the process, writing essays, grammar and spelling, and the lack of choice or ideas. Further, many students thought that the length of the process was too long, saying, "I don't like it (the writing process) because it takes too long, and I think it takes forever to finish." One student lamented,

> "I'm mad cuz I have to go all the way through that just to get this, then I have to rewrite it, prewrite it, and then get it edited and proof read it, and all of that, type it. Yeah, we have to type our papers. If we don't type our papers we get like Cs on our work. And she says we have to have at least one typed paper a month and that's only a C."

Not only were students unhappy with the length of the process, they translated the lengthiness into boredom with writing. Several other students in the study expressed similar frustrations.

Many students in the study also expressed unease with the technical aspects of the writing experience. Their concerns centered on spelling and grammar in their writing, with statements like, "I get frustrated with the spelling … and my challenge was grammar." Another concern for students was the negative stigma associated with being corrected by the teacher; one student said,

> "We always do our best but she [was] always correcting us, and she doesn't tell us why … she doesn't explain she just says do this over, and then like every time we write something, it's like she's professional at all kinds of stuff, but we're like amateurs, and she corrects our papers, and we end up getting like Ds and Fs on it because we do what we write and she does not write. Some people they write how they talk, and we write how we talk, in that area, that's how we talk."

For these sixth-grade students, the joy in writing was overrun with the technicalities about their use of language. These students felt frustrated with the process and overwhelmed with the task of academic writing. For them, the teacher focused on their errors without an explanation and did not allow for spaces to include students' home languages or other literacies, which is why the interaction with the teacher is so significant. Student success was commonly tied to teachers' involvement and when teachers publicly recognized their work. Students shared:

> "Mrs. Washington helped. She made me a better writer because she made me understand the processing of writing. She helped me get it like understand it more instead of just like putting stuff down on a piece of paper and saying oh I'm done. She actually made it easy for me to understand writing."

> "To make it 'click' for me, she actually made essays for us to do so she actually like explained what to do for writing. She actually made it kinda easy by explaining and showing us and like letting us to get ready. So she's actually preparing us for higher grades and stuff. So she mainly helped me 'click' by just explaining it then, if we need help she explains it over in a simpler way."

In spite of this individual success, students were most proud when their teachers acknowledged their writing and rewarded them in some way. Some of the students testified to being rewarded ice cream shakes and classroom recognition. Through the teachers' acts of kindness, these successful moments were crystallized in the eyes of the students as being great.

> "The most successful was with USC readers I made a story and did a play of it. My teacher loved it and kept a copy and sometime later, I got a note from the principal saying it was great and displayed it in the main office."

Writing with Technology

Students repeatedly mentioned their use of technology, an exciting and important factor in the lives of nearly all students. As a result, students stressed that technology was important for practical purposes. African American girls in the focus groups shared that they enjoyed texting and social networking because it allowed them to use their home language without being corrected. They also stated that it was fun to text because they could receive instant feedback and it was sort of like a game to them. They commented that their teachers allowed them to choose pieces of their writing to type and turn in once a month. This point is in alignment with CRRI Tenet 4, which addresses instruction and environment being inclusive of the learner. Some of the students' comments include:

"I usually get on email and text and stuff. But I think computers are better to write with to communicate with because it's faster. You don't really have to try to write all faster you can just type what you need."

"I like typing better than writing cuz when I type like ideas come to me and I just type and then I'm happy, when I'm writing, I'm getting hand cramps and then I have to stop and then I forget what I was gonna say. But when I'm typing, it's better. I get kind of bored when I write, like hand write, but when I'm typing it's kind of fun to me."

"Yeah it's better for you to type it cuz sometimes it tells you how many words you have, then like if you're writing you're supposed to go back and count a thousand words, and that is dumb."

These students used technology for the ease and efficiency, communicating through email or text messaging. For the CRRI students, technology was a necessary part of life. The use of technology allowed them to be curious and expressive. One student commented, "You have to use hash tag with everything, that tells people you serious about the topic." With the fast-growing development of social media, students have begun to define their own literacy practices with their own rules for their own purposes. It is the obligation of the teacher to participate and use this knowledge as an empowering and relevant tool in our curriculum.

In all, students perceived writing as a necessary task that served multiple purposes. Students vocalized the task of writing as a multifaceted practice, were operationally equipped to navigate academic and cultural spaces, were personally inspired, and were able to find a place of refuge for their multiple selves. Writing was the manifestation of empowerment, validation, liberation, and, finally, the crux of engagement.

Implications of Culturally Relevant and Responsive Instruction

Future research needs to be explored to include African American students and other students of color in a much larger sample. It would be fitting to examine the practices of state and local school districts in an effort to gain insight into the present condition of writing in America. If teachers do not use CRRI in the classroom, achievement gaps may continue to increase. Additionally, teachers must be equipped to teach the twenty-first century learner in the area of writing and include cultural identities and multiple literacies. With the advancement of technology, teachers also need to be trained on instructing students who come with digital literacies. The issue of teachers not being administered pre-service writing training in order to effectively educate students of color is worth examining. Darling-Hammond (2006) avows, "Inequalities in spending, class sizes, textbooks, computers, facilities, curriculum offerings and access to qualified teachers contributes to disparate achievement by races and class, which increasingly feeds the 'school to prison pipeline'" (p. 13).

In essence, teachers need to be provided with strategic writing training to meet the needs of diverse learners. The intent of this study was to explore how CRRI and non-CRRI teachers and students experience writing to inform writing instruction. Even though both types of teachers were novice writing teachers, their care was demonstrated through the findings of the study. However, some of the successes mentioned throughout the study reflect students overcoming these challenges with the help of their teachers. Students constantly shared that their individual successes were connected to a teacher assisting them in their writing process or from teachers acknowledging their work. Teachers' acknowledgement of student work came in the form of public praising, writing publicly posted, or treats rewarded for writing well.

According to Cholewa, Amatea, West-Olatunji, and Wright (2012), school administrators should advocate for hiring an extra staff member, perhaps a former master teacher, who could serve as a consultant regarding the culturally responsive pedagogical practices and lesson plans. This person could work alongside the school counselor, who collaboratively consults with teachers concerning culturally responsive relationship development.

Proper writing training and culturally relevant and responsive instruction training should be staples within teacher education programs. The classes need to center around practice that encourages the cultural identities of students. Teachers who are bound to programs or formulaic teaching do a disservice to students of color. Students should be exposed to and trained in the many purposes of writing. Teachers should be flexible in providing options for students to demonstrate writing for these multiple purposes. Students possessing multiple literacies and identities should employ writing to articulate these characteristics.

Further research and interpretation is needed, but with students feeling like their success is linked with teacher approval, the obvious questions are: Can there ever be an autonomous feeling toward writing for diverse students? Did students seek the approval of their writing from teachers as a result of the teachers' expectations? Were the students' "words in bondage"? In other words, since African American and Latino students stressed the importance of "free writing," could their cry be representative of their place in the school setting? Do students feel like their voices are being held captive? Teachers and teacher educators need to focus on using writing as an instrument that hears these silenced voices. Lastly, further research is needed in the area of the instructional writing practices of successful teachers who balance teaching writing that empowers students and maintaining their identities and high standardized test scores. As educationally just educators, it is our responsibility to provide spaces for students to be liberated, celebrated, and empowered through CRRI and writing. Hill (2009) asserts that we must

> … reimagine the classroom as a space in which teachers and students can "risk the self" through individual and collective storytelling. Although scholarship in fields such as composition theory and critical race theory advocate the use of storytelling, there remains a need to develop educational theory and practice that prepares us for the benefits, challenges, and consequences of enabling personal disclosures within the classroom … . the failure to take such considerations seriously severely undermines our ability to transform the classroom into a more safe, democratic, productive, and culturally responsive space.#woundedhealing

Writing instruction must provide a balanced space for these sociocultural situated identities to be expressed and expanded upon, and it should be seen as an academic tool for many purposes. Teachers need to embrace students' home languages while also being experts on writing strategies for diverse youth. Students should feel encouraged and comfortable situating their sociocultural identities in collaborative and individual settings.

Applications for Teachers

- Understand the importance of the relevance of "student voice" in writing
- Incorporate CRRI strategies in all of their lessons
- Create lesson plans inclusive of CRRI writing topics
- Attend professional learning communities (PLCs) focused on writing calibration
- Allow students time and space to write for personal gains

Counselors

- Utilize writing as a liberatory tool allowing students to express themselves within a counseling session
- Assist students in building self-efficacy by seeking out writing opportunities for non-traditional writing (across the campus, district, community)

Administrators

- Provide staff development focused on CRRI and writing
- Add an accountability measure for writing and CRRI within professional learning communities
- Assess lesson plans for components of CRRI
- Allow teachers time to calibrate and establish a plan for writing
- Use instructional rounds to monitor the progress of CRRI and writing
- Identify effective, culturally responsive teachers and compensate them to mentor new teachers
- Create opportunities for collaborations between counselors and teachers in an effort to provide a cultural climate that is welcoming to all students

Discussion Questions/Activities

1. Foster a conversation with students about the relevance of "student voice."
2. Describe several culturally relevant and responsive activities in a classroom.
3. Outline the significance of CRRI and writing in a classroom fully immersed in Common Core State Standards.
4. In a small group, create a list of activities present in a CRRI school-wide culture.

References

Au, K. (2007).Culturally responsive instruction: Application to multiethnic classrooms. *Pedagogies: An International Journal, 2*(1), pp.1–18.

Ball, A. (1996). Expository writing patterns of African American students. *National Council of Teachers of English, 85*(1), p. 27–38.

Beaufort, A. (2009). Preparing adolescents for the literacy demands of the 21st century workplace. In Christenbury, L., Bomer, R., & Smagoriskiy, P. (Eds.), *Handbook of adolescent literacy research* (pp. 239–253). New York: Guildford Press.

Beachum, F., & Lewis, C. (2008). Educational quagmires: Balancing excellence and equity for African American students in the 21st century. *Multicultural Learning and Teaching, 3*(2), pp. 1–8.

Brown-Jeffy, S., & Cooper, J. (2011). Toward a conceptual framework of culturally relevant pedagogy: An overview of the conceptual and theoretical literature. *Teacher Education Quarterly*, Winter, pp. 65–84.

Callins, T. (2006).Culturally responsive literacy instruction. *Teaching Exceptional Children, 39*(2), pp. 62–65.

Cholewa, B., Amatea, E., West-Olatunji, C., & Wright, A. (2012). Examining the relational processes of a highly successful teacher of African American children. *Urban Education 47*(1), 250–279.

Lewis, C., Hancock, S., James, M., & Larke, P. (2008). African American students and No Child Left Behind Legislation: Progression or digression in educational attainment. *Multicultural Learning and Teaching, 3*(2), 9–29.

Clay, A.(2003). Keepin' it real: Black youth, hip-hop culture, and Black identity. *American Behavior Scientist 46* (10), 1346–1358.

Darling-Hammond, L. (2000). New standards and old inequalities: School reform and African American students. *Journal of Negro Education, 69*(4), 263–287.

Davis, D. (2013). Fifth-grade students reveal about their literacies by writing and telling narratives. *Writing and Telling Narratives, 52*(2), 121–141.

Elbow, P. (2004). Write first: putting writing before reading is an effective approach to teaching and learning. *Educational Leadership*, October 2004, 8–14.

Elbow, P. (2007). Voice in writing again: Embracing contraries. *In College English, 70*(2), 168–188.

Florez, I. R., Mccaslin, M. (2008). Student perceptions of small-group learning. *Teacher College Record, 110*(11), 2438–2451.

Foster, M. (1997). *Black teachers on teaching.* New York: New Press.

Geisler, J., Hessler, T., Gardner, R., & Lovelace, T. (2009). Differentiated writing interventions for high-achieving urban African American elementary students. *Journal of Advanced Academics, 20*(2), 214–247.

Grant, C. (2008). An essay on searching for curriculum and pedagogy for African American students: Highlights and remarks regarding the role of gender. *American Behaviorist Scientist, 51*(7), 885–906.

Hill, M. L. (2008). Toward a pedagogy of the popular: Bourdieu, hip-hop, and out-of-school literacies. In A. Luke & J. Albright (Eds.), *Bourdieu and literacy education* (136–161). New York: Routledge.

Hill, D. K. (2009) Code switching pedagogies and African American student voices: Acceptance and resistance. *Journal of Adolescent and Adult Literacy, 53*(2), 120–131.

Howard, T. (2001). Telling their side of the story: African American student perceptions of culturally relevant teaching. *The Urban Review, 33*(2), 132–149.

Howard, T. (2008). Who really cares? The disenfranchisement of African American males in PreK-12 schools: A critical race theory perspective. *Teachers College Record, 110*, p. 954–985.

Howard, T., & Terry, C. (2011). Culturally responsive pedagogy for African American students. *Teaching Education, 22*(4), 345–364.

Hull, G., & Schultz, K. (2001). Literacy and learning out of school: A review of theory and research. *Review of Educational Research, 71*(4), 575–611.

Jackson, J., & Moore, J. (2006). African American males in education: Endangered or ignored. *Teachers College Record, 108*, p. 201–205.

Jeffy, S., & Cooper, J. (2011), Toward a conceptual framework of culturally relevant pedagogy: An overview of the theoretical and conceptual literature. *Teacher Education Quarterly,* Winter, 65–84.

Jocson, K. (2006). Bob Dylan and hip hop: Intersecting literacy practices in youth poetry communities. *Written Communication 23*(3), p. 231–259.

Kinloch, V. (2010). "To be a traitor of Black English": Youth perceptions of language rights in an urban context. *Teachers College Record, 112*(1), 1–18.

Ladson-Billings, G. (1994). *Dreamkeepers.* San Francisco, California: Jossey Bass.

Ladson-Billings, G. (1995). But that's just good teaching! The case for culturally relevant pedagogy. *Theory into Practice, 34*(3), 159–165.

Ladson-Billings, G. (1992). Reading between the lines and beyond the pages: A culturally relevant approach to literacy teaching. *Theory into Practice, 31*(4), 312–320.

Lee, C. (2008) as cited in Green, S. (Ed.) *Literacy is a Civil Right.* New York: Peter Lang Publishing.

Lewis, J., & Kim, E. (2008). A desire to learn: African American children's positive attitudes toward learning within schools cultures of low expectations. *Teachers College Record, 110*, p. 1304–1329.

Lewis, C., & Del Valle, A. (2009). Literacy and Identity: Implications for research and practice. In Christenbury, L., Bomer, R., & Smagoriskiy, P. (Eds.), *Handbook of adolescent literacy research* (239–253). New York: Guildford Press

Lovejoy, B. (2009). Self-directed writing: Giving voice to student writers. *English Journal, 98*(6), 79–86.

Majiri, J. (1991). Discourse in sports: Language and literacy features of preadolescent African American males in a youth basketball program. *Journal of Negro Education, 60*(3).

Majiri, J., & Sablo, S. (1996). Writing for their lives: The non-school literacy of California's urban youth. *Journal of Negro Education, 65*, p. 164–180.

Majiri, J., & Godley, A. (1998). Rewriting identity: Social meanings of literacy and "re-visions" of self. *International Reading Association, 33,*(4), p. 416–433.

Mitra, D. (2004). The significance of students: Can increasing "student voice" in schools lead to gains in youth development? *Teachers College Record, 106*, p. 651–688.

Moje, E. (2008). Responsive literacy teaching in secondary school content areas. In Conley, M., Freidhoff, J., Sherry, M., & Tuckey, S. (Eds.), *Meeting the challenge of adolescent literacy: Research we have and research we need* (58–87). New York: The Guildford Press.

Moll, L. C., Amanti, C., Neff, D., & Gonzalez, N. (1992). Funds of knowledge for teaching: Using a qualitative approach to connect homes and classroom. *Theory to Practice, 31*(2), p. 132–141.

Morrison, K., Robbins, H., & Rose, D. (2008). Operationalizing culturally relevant pedagogy: A synthesis of classroom based research. *Equity & Excellence in Education, 41*(4), 433–452.

National Center for Education Statistics (2012). The Nation's Report Card: Writing 2011(NCES 2012–470). Institute of Education Sciences, U.S. Department of Education, Washington, D.C.

Neito, S. (1999). *The light in their eyes: Creating multicultural learning communities.* New York: Teachers College Press.

Norment, N. (1995). Discourse features of African American student writings. *Journal of Black Studies*, *25*(5), p. 558–576.

Ruben, B., & Moll, L. (2013). Putting the heart back into writing: Nurturing voice in middle school students. *Middle School Journal*, 45(2), p.12–18.

Tatum, A. (2005). *Teaching reading to Black adolescent males: Closing the achievement gap.* Portland, ME: Steinhouse Publishers.

Tatum, A. (2008). The literacy development of African American male adolescents: The influence of contexts and text. In Conley, M., Freidhoff, J., Sherry, M., & Tuckey, S. (Eds.), *Meeting the challenge of adolescent literacy: Research we have and research we need* (36–57). New York: The Guilford Press.

Shade, B., Kelly, C., & Oberg, M. (1997). *Culturally responsive classrooms.* Washington, DC: American Psychological Association.

Singer, J., & Shagoury, R. (2006). Stirring up justice: Adolescents reading and writing and changing the world. *Journal of Adolescent Literacy, 49*(4), 318–339.

Sleeter, C. (2012). Confronting the marginalization of culturally responsive pedagogy. *Urban Education, 47*(3), 562–584.

Smitherman, G. (2007). Afterward. In Alim, S., & Baugh, J. (Eds.), *Talkin Black talk: Language, education, and social change.* New York: Teachers College.

Solorzano, D., & Yosso, T. (2000). Towards a critical race theory of Chicano and education. In C. Tejada, C. Martinez, & Z. Leonardo (Eds.), *Charting new terrains in Chicana(o)/Latina(o) education* (35–66). Cresskill, NJ: Hampton Press.

Sperling, M., & Appleman, D. (2011). Voice in the context of literacy studies. *Reading Research Quarterly, 46*(1), 70–84.

Street, C. (2005). A reluctant writer's entry into a community of writers. *Journal of Adolescent & Adult Literacy, 48*(8), 636–641.

Stuart, D., & Volk, D. (2002). Collaboration in a culturally responsive literacy pedagogy: Educating teachers and Latino students. *Reading literacy and language*, November, 2002.

U.S. Department of Education, Institute of Education Sciences, National Center for Education Statistics, National Assessment of Educational Progress (NAEP), 2011 Writing Assessment.

Villegas, A., & Lucas, T. (2002). Preparing culturally responsive teachers: Rethinking the Curriculum. *Journal of Teacher Education*, 53(1), 20–32.

Villegas, A., & Lucas, T. (2002). *Educating culturally responsive teachers: A coherent approach.* Albany: State University of New York Press.

CHAPTER 6

Social and Cultural Capital

A Story of Successful Parent Involvement

by Pearl Vongprateep

What We Know About Student Engagement

Education in America is in a state of change, trying to better prepare students for their adult lives. Policies in place have the intention of increasing student achievement. Schools want students to achieve, whether it is for global competition, to close achievement gaps, or simply to receive funding. Student engagement has become one platform for school reform (Reschly & Christenson, 2012). Many studies have associated academic achievement with student engagement (Finn & Zimmer, 2012; Fredricks, Blumenfeld & Paris, 2004; Mahatmya, Lohman, Matjasko & Farb, 2012; Reschly & Christenson, 2012; Skinner & Pitzer, 2012). Student engagement is integral for student learning and academic achievement. Despite the best efforts made by educators, if a student is not engaged at school, he or she will feel disconnected from his or her learning, which often manifests itself in poor progress academically or socially. It is the "outward manifestation of motivation" (Eccles & Wang, 2012, p. 135).

Student engagement is multifaceted, and often, many factors are considered when measuring it. Although factors for measuring student engagement among researchers vary, Fredrick et al.'s (2004) three components for measurement are often referenced. The three areas of student engagement are behavioral, cognitive, and emotional engagement. Behavioral engagement can be associated with participation and effort, which can often be reflected in students' grades or involvement in clubs and sports and non-involvement in behaviors like skipping school. Emotional engagement speaks more to the affective component of student engagement and pertains to students' feelings toward school—do they find it interesting or boring? Does it make them happy, sad, or anxious? Cognitive engagement has more to do with students' long-term investment in learning—are they willing to stick it out to master those complex ideas or skills? One approach for students to be more engaged and connected to school is by having their parents involved and become active partners in their education. Several studies highlight parent involvement as a role in student engagement (Bempechat & Shernoff, 2012; Mahatmya, Lohman, Matjasko & Farb, 2012; Skinner & Pitzer, 2012). Oftentimes, parents' interest in student progress is enough to keep a student engaged at school and results in positive gains in achievement.

What We Know About Parent Involvement

Parents play a large role in student engagement. It has been "identified as a way to close gaps in achievement between more and less advantaged children and minority and majority youth" (Raftery, Grolnick & Flamm, 2012). Parent involvement has been shown to affect student engagement and achievement positively when all other factors are removed. One meta-analysis that studied the effect of parental involvement on the achievement of minority students found that the academic achievement of all minority groups was significantly impacted by parent involvement (Jeynes, 2003). Jeynes (2003) asserted that parent involvement might have the greatest impact on student achievement if cultural factors were removed. For these beneficial reasons, schools are constantly seeking ways for parents to be more involved with their children's education.

Current education policy mirrors the belief that parent involvement is important to student achievement. No Child Left Behind (NCLB), Blueprint for Reform, and even the new Local Control Funding Formula (LCFF) and Local Control Accountability Plans (LCAP) in California accentuate the importance of parental involvement (Epstein, 2005; Taylor, 2013; U.S. Department of Education, Office of Planning, Evaluation, and Policy Development, 2010). These policies mandate districts to regularly communicate with parents about the state of the schools and student achievement and to keep goals in the area of parent involvement a consideration as they develop their funding and accountability plans.

The Factors that Affect Parents' Decision to be Involved

Grolnick et al. (1997) identified three sets of factors that influenced parent involvement. The three factors were parent and child characteristics, family context, and teacher behavior and attitudes. They studied these three factors while focusing on three types of involvement: behavior (involvement in school), cognitive (participating in cognitively stimulating activities), and personal (being informed about what was going on with their child). They asserted that personal involvement, which was being informed about the happenings of their child, is evident for parents of all occupations and education levels. However, socioeconomic status (SES) could often help predict parents' level of involvement at school and participation in cognitively stimulating activities with their children at home.

Parents' life contexts influenced their level of involvement because the contexts often determined the capacity in which they could be involved or if they had the time or skills needed to do so (Hoover-Dempsey et al., 2005; Hornby & Lafaele, 2011). Grolnick et al. (1997) theorized that single mothers probably had a hard time actually participating at school during the school day and suggested that schools look for other types of involvement that do not require parents to be available during the day.

They found that parents are more willing to engage in cognitively stimulating activities with their child when they themselves felt confident that they could be successful at playing the role of teacher. Two different studies, one focusing on why parents become involved and another focusing on the reasons that prevent parents from being involved, had similar findings in that they both found that parent beliefs were a significant factor when parents chose whether to be involved or not (Hoover-Dempsey, Walker & Sandler, 2005; Hornby & Lafaele, 2011). Parents were more likely to play an active role in their child's education if they believed that it was their responsibility to be involved and they felt confident in their ability to help. When parents found the context difficult or felt they were not well-supported in their efforts, they were less likely to participate in cognitive forms of involvement. Support often came in the form of the networks that parents might have with other parents. Sheldon (2002) asserted that the more networks parents had, the more likely they were to be involved; if parents believed that all parents should be involved, they were more likely to be involved themselves.

Studies have found that teacher practices significantly affected parents' desire to be involved. Teachers needed to make concerted efforts to involve parents, and parents needed teachers to make apparent that they had a role in their child's education (Epstein, 1992; Grolnick et al., 1997; Hoover-Dempsey, Walker & Sandler, 2005; Hornby & Lafaele, 2011). Grolnick et al. (1997) asserted that even though teachers may find success in their efforts to include parents, "these attempts may not reach those most in need" (Grolnick et al., 1997, p. 547). Parents want to know exactly how they can help, and they want to feel welcomed and invited to participate and be at school.

The Varying Levels of Involvement

Levels of parental involvement vary considerably. The ways in which parents can be considered involved range from the parent who simply asks their child about their school day to the parent who ensures that their child has the proper breakfast before going to school, all the way to the parent who is actually at school volunteering to head up a committee. Some see parents being directly involved in their children's learning, while others see parents as motivation facilitators for children (Raftery, Grolnick & Flamm, 2012).

All students benefit from any form of parental involvement, and most families are actually involved with their student to some extent (Lee & Bowen, 2006). Lee and Bowen (2006) noted that while everyone may practice forms of involvement, some forms of parent involvement are more readily recognized by schools than others. European American middle-class families tend to see their efforts more acknowledged than those made by parents of more diverse economic and racial/ethnic backgrounds. Epstein (1992) found that parent involvement at school is highly associated with academic achievement, implying that parent involvement outside of school is not perceived to have the same effect. So although some parents are involved with their children's education, they practice it in a form outside of school that goes unrecognized by educators and, furthermore, is mistakenly seen by teachers as a lack of caring for their child's education. Many times,

COPYRIGHTED MATERIAL — DO NOT DUPLICATE, DISTRIBUTE, OR POST

108 | Who We Are and How We Learn

parents' level of involvement is often a result of the amount and types of social and cultural capitals parents possess. Social and cultural capitals act as access points for parents.

What We Know About Social And Cultural Capitals

Social and cultural capitals are abstract ideas that stem from the theoretical concepts of Pierre Bourdieu. Capital, much like money, can be exchanged for goods. Capital can offer an individual privileges and advantages that others may not have. Goods can be more than material things, and particularly with this form of symbolic capital, goods often come in the form of services or access points. Social capital is defined by Bourdieu as the

> aggregate of the actual or potential resources which are linked to possession of a durable network of more or less institutionalized relationships of mutual acquaintance and recognition—or in other words, to membership in a group—which provides each of its members with the backing of the collectively-owned capital" (1986, p. 21).

Social capital is the networks individuals have and the privileges that come along with being a part of those groups. Cultural capital can be defined as "the knowledge, skills, education, experiences, and/or connections one has had through the course of his or her life that do or do not enable success" (Howard, 2010, p. 55). Cultural capital exists in three states: embodied, having to do with one's dispositions; objectified, having to do with culturally related material objects; and institutionalized, having to do with the degrees and certificates one lacks or possesses (Bourdieu, 1986; Winkle-Wagner, 2010).

Social and cultural capitals are smaller pieces of Bourdieu's larger theory on social reproduction. A more in-depth exploration of the ideas of habitus, field, and capital and their interactions will help to gain a better understanding of how social and cultural capitals contribute to the continuing perpetuation of inequalities found in education.

Habitus refers to an individual's way of being and how he or she perceives cultural norms as a result of his or her life experiences. "Habitus refers to categories of perception and appreciation in the social realm" (Winkle-Wagner, 2010). Field refers to the space where particular norms, dispositions, or capital exist and may be recognized to be more valuable over other forms of dispositions, norms, or capital. When fields change, what is recognized as valued also changes. Bourdieu often associated the field to a game. Capital, as mentioned earlier, can be seen as assets or advantages that an individual possesses, but it draws its value from social recognition in the appropriate field.

The three components interact to provide some individuals with advantages over others. This can be better understood by the following card-game analogy adapted from Winkle-Wagner (2010): Think of the card game being played as the field. The cards in the game represent cultural capital. The cards were either dealt to you (the capital you received from your family) or exchanged or picked up during the game (what you acquired through education). Some of the cards you hold are more valuable in the particular game you are playing at the moment; however, if the game were to change, those same cards may not have any value at all.

COPYRIGHTED MATERIAL — DO NOT DUPLICATE, DISTRIBUTE, OR POST

So if you possessed the valued cards in the game being played, you had an advantage over other players who did not hold those cards in said game. You have a better chance of winning. The strategy you chose to employ while playing the game, your habitus, was dependent on your understanding of the game and its rules. Social capital acts as an added advantage if the individual had a connection with the dealer or if the individual had an insider tip from someone he or she knew. When the game, or field, changes, all the rules change, and the cards you held and people you knew, your capital in the previous game, which may have been valuable before could no longer be valued in the new game. If the field changed, so the rules change, and so your approach will also change. So in every game, there are those who are in a better position to win and those who are more inclined to lose. All players, however, approached the game in ways they felt would put them in the winning circle. Bourdieu saw this constant battle to be on top as the power struggle found in every field.

Theory of Social Reproduction

Bourdieu and Passeron's (1977) theory of social reproduction supposed that those who made up the majority, or dominant group, possessed the power to decide what forms of capital would be most valuable. It would make sense that these groups would give value to capital that they themselves already possessed. By doing this, they are rewarding themselves while also building upon their already existing supply of capital. This only serves to keep them in the advantageous position of power—in the winning circle. These individuals with power ensure that they continue to be the ones with the advantages over those individuals who, although not lacking capital, happen to lack the capital that has been deemed worth having. "The structure of the distribution of the different types and subtypes of capital at a given moment in time represents the immanent structure of the social world" (Bourdieu, 1986, p. 15) and is an example of what Bourdieu referred to as symbolic violence and serves to reproduce the social structures and inequalities that are found in society (Anyon, 1980; Bourdieu & Passeron, 1977; Nolan, 2009; Schubert, 2012; Swartz, 1945; Winkle-Wagner, 2010). Those who are at the top dictate what is valued in society, and by doing so, they serve to keep themselves at the top, and so the social structure with all its inequalities continues to reproduce itself.

Schools and Social Reproduction

Schools, like any other field, have their own set of rules and their own way of doing things. As in any field, there are individuals who have advantages over others. Schools, in essence, have their own habitus. This habitus imitates the habitus of white, middle-class norms and traditions. In other words, schools as institutions tend to teach, recognize, and/or value the norms that middle-class families find significant; they are the place where middle-class dispositions are nurtured (Schutz, 2008). Schools teach students that white, middle-class norms are normal and that anything different is less valuable. This serves to help perpetuate the social stratifications that are found in society.

Symbolic Violence

Bourdieu saw schools as an aid in perpetuating and reproducing the power relations found in society. Those who are dominant continue to dominate while continuing to keep those who are disadvantaged at a disadvantage. Symbolic power, as asserted by Bourdieu (1979), was a power privileged individuals used to impose their idea of social reality onto others, even if it was subjective in nature. Bourdieu found this relationship to be oppressive. Unfortunately, the oppressors as well as the oppressed often do not realize that they play these roles because this relationship has become an accepted norm or reality. Bourdieu felt this was an act of symbolic violence. It was within the walls of schools that these power relations were reproduced, and although it is not equitable, schools legitimize the act of symbolic violence upon students due to the fact that they rely on these power relations in order to serve the structured purpose of socialization. Schools repeatedly socialize children of different classes differently (DiMaggio, 1979); Anyon (1980) referred to this as the hidden curriculum. Symbolic violence therefore occurs in schools when we indoctrinate students with the dominant hegemonic culture or award and recognize students only on the capital that is valued by the dominant group (Vongprateep, 2014). As mentioned earlier, researchers found that most families are involved with their children's education in some form or another, but oftentimes, teachers or schools do not recognize everyone's efforts. Many times, it is the families who do not practice parent involvement as defined by white, middle-class norms that are seen as lacking care for their child's education. Schools reward those families who practice the "right" forms of involvement while not acknowledging those families whose efforts do not seem familiar. By doing this, schools continue to help those advantaged individuals remain privileged because these individuals are good at school—the habitus of these individuals and the habitus of the school match. On the other hand, those students whose habitus do not match up as well to the habitus of school have a difficult time succeeding at school and remain at a disadvantage to those who understand and practice white, middle-class norms, thereby continuing the cycle of violence.

Current Research Findings, and Implications

Summary of Research Methodology

The conceptual framework in Figure 6.1 guided the theoretical approach and methodology of the current study and provided the snapshot summary of the framework and the study's findings at the completion of the study. The figure illustrates the social and cultural aspects of parental involvement, with its expressed manifestations gathered from interviews of the participants in the study. The figure also shows how student engagement was manifested behaviorally, cognitively, and emotionally.

The study presented in this chapter utilized the qualitative research approach of narrative inquiry. Narrative inquiry uses the method of storytelling to make meaning out of life experiences. This approach allowed researchers to discover, by way of listening to the authentic voices of the fifteen participants, how one parent group in a high school located in an upper-middle class community in Southern California was able to positively influence academic success for students and significantly narrow the achievement gap for African American students. The fifteen participants in this study included administrators, teachers, parents, students, and community members. The interview questions were open-ended and semi-structured. The instrumentation used in this study had been field tested on over one hundred participants in various other studies. The interviews were recorded and then transcribed before being imported into NVivo software.

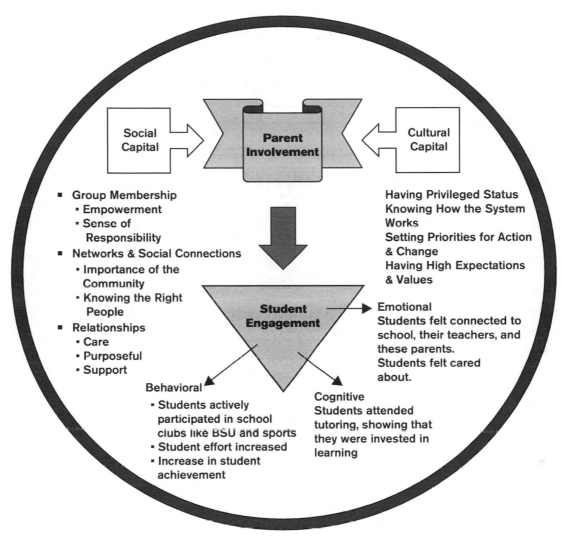

Figure 6–1. Parental Involvement and Student Engagement Conceptual Framework

Approximately forty initial codes were created using the nodes feature in NVivo. Reliability was ensured for the coded data through consensus reached by three researchers. The initial codes were collapsed until twelve themes emerged in the areas of social and cultural capitals.

Findings

While observing and listening to the voices of teachers, administrators, parents, students, and community members, twelve themes emerged related to the influence of parents' social and cultural capital on parent involvement and student engagement. Four of these themes fell under the category of cultural capital, while the other eight themes pertained to the social capital of parents.

Themes in the Area of Cultural Capital

Bourdieu defined cultural capital as the "knowledge, skills, education, experiences, and/or connections one has had through the course of his or her life that do or do not enable success" (Howard, 2010, p. 55). The members of the parent group in this study had a rich supply of cultural capital that allowed them privileges to help advance their goals.

Table 6–1. Cultural Capital Themes

Notable Quotes Pertaining to Cultural Capital Themes

Knowing How the System Works	Setting Priorities for Action & Change	Having Privileged Status	Having High Expectations & Values
"In institutions, there are so many rules and hierarchy of things that they don't know because they're parents. Someone who is within the system has to help them navigate that system." ~Administrator "We made it a point to understand what she needed to take in order to be eligible to be able to go to college." ~Parent	"As I got older, I realized I am where I am today because people took the time to give me guidance, give me some information, show me some things, exposure to a better way of life. And I guess as I got older, I made a promise that if I ever got to a position where I could do that, I would reciprocate that to the best of my ability by giving back to my community, to make life a better place, the world a better place, … and I figured what better place but the students, whose lives you can get them on the right path and get them going" ~Parent	"Everybody's got really nice homes over there, it's not ghetto … they will come to school with parents, well-paid, you know, great jobs … " ~Parent "I got the chance to meet some pretty influential black men, upstanding good fathers. They set a good example for me … for my kids too" ~Administrator	"My dad always told me that education was the key to choices" ~Community Member "My family cared about education … that I got a good education, so that was always paramount … To learn. To get an education and to do well. Not just to take the class, but to, you know, to do well" ~Parent

There were four themes that emerged in the area of cultural capital:

1. **Having privileged status.** First, the community in which this study took place was fairly affluent. Being in a community that had an upper-middle class status afforded privileges and advantages for these men and the students they provided services to. The members of the parent group themselves were well-educated professionals. The men that made up the parent group included a judge, an AP teacher, a regional manager for a Fortune 500 company, a regional director for a major corporation, and a retired firefighter and entrepreneur. One of the administrators in the study

described these men as being "very professional" and as "influential black men, upstanding good fathers." Their privileged identities allowed them to be viewed seriously by the school and school district. The respect their statuses earned them allowed them to gain access to the school and the opportunity to work closely with students. Their statuses also enabled them to secure speakers who would serve as positive role models for students. Their affluence allowed them to hold the first annual banquet for academic achievement without help from the community; they were able to pay for the banquet out of their own pockets. Not all parent groups are that fortunate; being privileged was beneficial in helping to boost student engagement.

2. **Knowing how the system works.** Even if parents want to make changes, not all parents know how to go about doing so. Many parents are not familiar with how school works or what channels would be necessary to take in order to do the things these men were doing. Knowing how to navigate the system aids parents in holding their students accountable while also helping their students be more successful at school. The parents in this study were familiar with the way the school system was run, and their privileged status allowed them to go into the schools and speak to the people they needed to speak to. These men knew that if parents were more informed about how things worked, they would be in a place to better provide their students with help; they even went as far as trying to provide parents with workshops so they would be more informed.

3. **Setting priorities for action and change.** Although the members of the parent group were working professionals busy with their own lives, they made the active decision to enact change. Their priority was to change the attitudes of students as well as the culture of the school to one where academics superseded everything else. They saw this opportunity and made sure they did not pass it up. They did not simply sit and contemplate the situation, but rather took action to try to amend the situation. All the members of this parent group were passionately dedicated to giving back. They all felt someone in their past had taken a chance on them, and they wanted to provide these students with a similar experience. Students reacted positively to the fact that these men had made them a priority. This was evident in their increased efforts at school and the increase in student engagement.

4. **Having high expectations and values.** The members of the parent group truly believed that low scores and failure were not an option. They believed in setting expectations and holding students, as well as parents, accountable. During the interviews, the word "expectation(s)" was mentioned nearly sixty times by eight different participants. It was clear that the parent group had high expectations for all students at the school and that they felt it was integral to academic success and student engagement. Education held a high value for these parents, and it was a value that they wanted to instill in all students. This was something they truly believed; it was a part of their habitus. Students knew what was expected and how hard this parent group worked to help them, and so they worked hard to meet these expectations. It was evident in the actions of the parent group that obtaining a good education was important; they worked with students, teachers, and community members for countless hours to try to make students see the relevance of having a successful academic career. The annual banquet centered around recognizing academic achievement. Students were proud to share their accomplishments here, and at the least, their parents, who might not have been as involved as these men, would come out and honor their students. The expectations showed once again how much they cared for student success, and these students responded to the attention in a positive manner.

Themes in the Area of Social Capital

Social capital, as defined earlier, is the networks, relationships, and social connections that serve to increase opportunities and resources for members in a group. Themes that emerged in the area of social capital fell under three different categories.

Table 6–2. Social Capital Themes

Notable Quotes Pertaining to Social Capital Themes

Responsibility to Others	Empowerment	Importance of the Community	Knowing the Right People
"We decided it is our responsibility, not the schools. I mean we're the primary [ones] responsible for the education of our kids." ~Teacher/Parent "We wouldn't have BSU without [parent group]" ~ Student	"They feel empowered to go to the school. Because a lot of times it's that empowerment feeling, feeling welcome." ~Administrator "We want to create this bubble of influence … " ~Teacher/Parent	"So the mayor comes every year. The superintendent is always there. So it's just really meaningful, to have the city leadership be there … .I think especially to the students when they have exposure to people like that … it makes them think, OK, I did something important and people care about me. I'm not just invisible to the community." ~Community Member	"You need somebody on the inside, somebody on the inside who's familiar with the campus and who has access to the school district." ~Parent "I was part of the district so I knew who to go to." ~Administrator
Purposeful Relationships	Caring Relationships	Supportive Relationships	Trusting Relationships
"I found [the other members of the parent group] because we were talking about it in the stands at the basketball game. And we said this is my problem too." ~Community Member "As parents they were seeing, well … they weren't eligible. They're not making the grades. So they started out asking questions." ~Administrator	"They committed themselves to being the village elders despite the fact that they no longer have a personal investment in the program, which tells the student they do care about you. It's not about them anymore. Their kids aren't here. They're not gaining anything. They're a non-profit. They don't get paid. It's solely for the good of these students." ~ Student	" … to be successful … surround themselves with successful people and have a good attitude. I think that would be a big boost in being successful academically or wherever they're headed to, even at home. Like if they have a good support system at home, parents or whoever is raising them. That will, that helps a lot … .my parents, my mom and dad are really supportive in what I do … I think that's an important factor, one of the most important factors in being successful in high school." ~Student	"Once we help them to understand the probability of them making the NFL, the NBA, becoming a rapper or Beyoncé, is slim to none, they kinda sort of start to listen." ~Parent "We're breaking down suspicion and building bridges." ~Administrator

A. Group Membership
 1. **Empowerment.** Being a part of this parent group empowered these men to actively seek change for their students. Working together, these parents felt they were a part of something bigger. This allowed them to actively advocate for students. They were not afraid to approach the school or the school board about their concerns and felt comfortable enough to have a hand in helping to alleviate the situations. They also sought ways to educate other parents about how to be better involved with their students' educational progress through workshops that they led for parents. These men were able to reach out to the community in order to secure lunchtime speakers for students. Students attended the lunchtime meetings voluntarily, showing that they were engaged behaviorally.
 2. **Sense of responsibility.** The parent group felt it was their responsibility to care for students. They did not look for someone to point fingers at, but instead wished to take action to help students. They sought out things they could do as parents to turn things around. Although initially, the parent group felt their responsibility was only their own kids, they expanded their zone of accountability to include Black Student Union (BSU) students and, eventually, all students. Not only did these parents feel responsible for the students, they also felt a sense of accountability to each of the other members of the group. They were truly committed to each other, and the group sought out only members who were serious about helping students. It was not only the parent group that felt a sense of responsibility, but also the students who were under their care. Students felt the sense of membership and the need to be accountable to themselves and others. These aspects of being responsible to a group contributed to increased levels of engagement for students.

B. Networks and Social Connections

Many of the actions taken by the parent group would not have been possible without these parents tapping into their networks and social connections. These networks and connections allowed these men to access support that might not have been readily available to everyone.
 3. **Importance of the community.** The motto of the parent group in the study was "It takes a village to raise a child," and they made sure to make use of the members in the surrounding "village." The ties these parents had in the community allowed them to take advantage of resource opportunities. Community members and local businesses donated various things like cases of water for meetings, money, prizes, and even their time. Some community members donated their time through awarding students with coupons for services like haircuts and salon services, while others went into the school to be guest speakers at lunchtime meetings. The parent group felt the ties to the community were important to bridge school to the real world to make things more relevant to students. They wanted students to redefine what it meant to be successful because many students saw success as being an athlete or celebrity. The guest speakers coming from the community served as positive role models for the students. Furthermore, community involvement expanded the realm of care for students; students

saw that many different people cared about their success, pushing them to work harder and achieve more.

4. **Knowing the right people.** The success of this parent group would not be possible if the right relationships had not been formed. The parent group itself started out with a connection made by a few parents who had common concerns for the failure of African American students and wanted to make the changes necessary to fix that. One of those parents connected with a teacher at the school, who became a founding member of the parent group. This teacher served as an insider who was able to make connections with the administration in the building. Members of administration became allies to this group. These administrators knew the proper channels that were needed to implement a project like this and helped to support and guide the parent group through them. Knowing the right people helped the parent group gain access to the school, which provided them with pertinent information and, more importantly, allowed them access to the students they would directly serve.

C. Relationships

Due to this parent advisory group's goal to impact student achievement, many relationships were formed and/or strengthened. These relationships were essential to the success of the group's mission. Relationships found in this study included those between school/administration and parents, parents and parents, and parents and students. All of these relationships were marked by the following characteristics:

5. **Care.** The ethic of care was evident in all relationships found in this study. The men in the parent group cared deeply for the group and the members of the group. This was evident in their commitment to the group and their sense of accountability to each other. These parents cared for the success of ALL students. In fact, none of the parents in the parent group had students at the high school; they simply wanted to see all students do well. Students appreciated knowing that there was a group of parents, even if it wasn't their own, watching out for them. Part of caring for the students was making the students feel valued. These parents did this by pulling individuals aside and letting them know that they cared about them, that they would be monitoring them, and, most importantly, that they believed that the students could do it. Furthermore, the parent group showed they cared by hosting an annual awards banquet at the end of each academic year, recognizing the achievements students had made that year. These caring relationships served as an impetus for students to work hard to achieve and make their parents and the parents of the advisory group proud.

6. **Purpose**. All the relationships formed or strengthened in this study appeared to have a purpose. Every relationship was intentional in order to advance the goals of the parent group. The members of the parent group formed relationships so that they could gain access to the school, tap into resources, communicate information effectively, and create overall change. The initial reason for forming the group was because a group of parents shared a common concern for a problem and wanted to contribute to possible solutions. Parents formed relationships with the students at school purposefully to help those particular individuals

they felt would benefit from their help. The relationships were targeted so that they would successfully increase student engagement and achievement.

7. **Support.** Supportive relationships in this study were integral to the success of the parent group. On multiple occasions, participants stressed the need to have top-down support from school personnel. This parent group had the support of the school system from district personnel down to the classroom teacher. Without these support measures in place, it would've been difficult for these parents to erect change. The group needed the support of school personnel in order to gain access to the school itself. The school showed its support by welcoming these parents onto campus, while the parent group returned the hospitality by helping to support and work directly with the at-risk population. The parent group also felt the support of other parents who were not a part of the group in the sense that they liked what these men were doing and sometimes requested that their child be a part of it, even if they themselves did not seek an active role to help. Regardless, the members of the parent group still tried to support outside parents by holding workshops to provide parents with information that would help them to support their students at home. One of the most important supportive relationships was that formed between the parent group and students. The parent group sponsored BSU activities, provided lunch for students during speaker presentations, and encouraged students to be the best they could be. The support in the form of encouragement provided many students with the motivation to work harder and be academically successful.

8. **Trust.** Trusting relationships were integral to the success of the parent group's goals and was found throughout the stories shared. Without trust from the administration, this parent group would never have gained access to the school. Administrators showed they trusted these men by allowing them onto campus to work with students and giving them access to things like student grades. Without this access and the information these parents were able to gain, their work may not have yielded such successful results. Trust was evident in other relationships as well. It was clear that outside parents trusted the parent group members to help their students, many calling upon the group when they needed guidance in matters pertaining to their child. As one administrator in the study said, they were "breaking down bridges of suspicion and then building positive relationships." One of the most important trusting relationships was that formed between students and the men of the parent group. The students trusted that these men truly cared that they did well, and this was evident in the students' actions and aspirations to succeed.

The increased levels of student engagement in this study were marked by purposely formed supportive and caring relationships built upon trust.

Conclusions and Implications

This study found that social and cultural capital influenced how parents were involved, and their involvement positively affected student engagement. Some forms of capital that parents possessed did directly help to increase student engagement by way of guest speakers and prizes, which were a direct result of the networks and privileged status these parents had; however, social and cultural capital more indirectly affected student engagement by their influences on the form that involvement came in. Parents who possessed the social and cultural capitals that best fit that of the school's habitus were at an advantage over those parents who lacked those forms of capital. These parents were able to better navigate the correct channels of the schooling system to yield results for their students. Students' increased engagement with school was evident in their improved grades and increased efforts. It was clear that the more students felt cared for by these parents, the more engaged they became with school. The parent group in the study demonstrated that it is more about quality than quantity. A small group of dedicated parents was capable of making a significant difference; it was not necessary to have a large group of parents. However, the key word is "dedicated." Overall, students wanted to know that their parents, or any parental figures, cared enough about their successes in education to hold them accountable and set high expectations for them.

What administrators can do

- Involve parents in decision-making bodies
- Attend school functions—be present to make the home-school connections
- Recognize parents for the things they do
- Ask for help—set up a panel to find out the needs of parents and how parents can help the school
- Make the school a welcoming place—establish a school culture that is inviting for all stakeholders
- Arm parents with the appropriate forms of capital—informing parents about how school "works"

What teachers can do

- Learn about student cultures and recognize all forms of participation
- Keep families informed
- Explicitly tell parents how they can help
- Make parents feel welcome

What counselors can do

- Provide families with information
- Provide teachers with information about students and their families
- Be conscientious of capitals that students and their families possess, and use this information when providing students with guidance and/or advising students for academic growth, college, and careers

References

Anyon, J. (1980). Social class and the hidden curriculum of work. *Journal of Education, 162*(1), Retrieved from http://www-scf.usc.edu/~clarkjen/Jean%20Anyon.htm.

Bempechat, J., & Shernoff, D. J. (2012). Parental influences on achievement motivation and student engage-ment. In S. L. Christenson, A. L. Reschly, & C. Wylie (Eds.), *Handbook of research on student engagement* (pp. 315–342). New York: Springer.

Bourdieu, P. (1979). Symbolic power. *Critique of Anthropology, 4,* 77–85.

Bourdieu, P. (1986). The forms of capital. In J. Richardson, *Handbook of theory and research for the sociology of education* (pp. 241–258). Westport, CT: Greenwood.

Bourdieu, P., & Passeron, J. C. (1977). *Reproduction in education, society and culture.* (R. Nice, Trans.) London: Sage Publications.

DiMaggio, P. (1979). Review essay: On Pierre Bourdieu. *American Journal of Sociology, 84*(6), 1460–1474.

Eccles, J., & Wang, M. T. (2012). Part I commentary: So what is student engagmment anyway? In S. L. Christenson, A. L. Reschly, & C. Wylie (Eds.), *Handbook of research on student engagement* (pp. 133–145). New York: Springer.

Epstein, J. L. (1992). School and family partnerships. In M. Alkin (Ed.), *Encyclopedia of educational research* (pp. 1139–1151). New York: Macmillan.

Epstein, J. L. (2005). Attainable goals? The spirit and letter of the No Child Left Behind Act on parental involvement. *Sociology of Education, 78*(2), 179–182.

Finn, J. D., & Zimmer, K. S. (2012). Student engagement: What is it? Why does it matter? In S. L. Christenson, A. L. Reschly, & C. Wylie (Eds.), *Handbook of research on student engagement* (pp. 97–131). New York: Springer.

Fredricks, J. A., Blumenfeld, P. C., & Paris, A. H. (2004). School engagement: Potential of the concept, state of the evidence. *Review of Educational Research, 74*(1), 59–109.

Grolnick, W. S., Benjet, C., Kurowski, C. O., & Apostoleris, N. H. (1997). Predictors of parent involvement in children's schooling. *Journal of Educational Psychology, 89*(3), 538–548.

Hoover-Dempsey, K. V., Walker, J. M., & Sandler, H. M. (2005). Why do parents become involved? Research findings and implications. *The Elementary School Journal, 106*(2), 105–130.

Hornby, G., & Lafaele, R. (2011). Barriers to parental involvement in education: An explanatory model. *Educational Review, 63*(1), 37–52.

Howard, T. C. (2010). Achievement Gap: Contextualizing the Problem. In T. C. Howard, *Why Race and Culture Matter in Schools* (pp. 9–34). New York: Teachers College, Columbia University.

Jeynes, W. H. (2003). A meta-analysis: The effects of parental involvement on minority children's academic achievement. *Education and Urban Society, 35*(2), 202–218.

Lee, J. S., & Bowen, N. K. (2006). Parent involvement, cultural capital, and the achievement gap among elementary school children. *American Educational Research Journal, 43*(2), 193–218.

Mahatmya, D., Lohman, B. J., Matjasko, J. L., & Farb, A. F. (2012). Engagement across developmental peri-ods. In S. L. Christenson, A. L. Reschly, & C. Wylie (Eds.), *Handbook of research on student engagement* (pp. 45–63). New York: Springer.

Nolan, K. (2009). Critical social theory and the study of urban school discipline: The culture of control in a Bronx high school. In J. Anyon (Ed.), *Theory and educational research: Toward critical social explanation* (pp. 27–54). New York and London: Routledge.

Raftery, J. N., Grolnick, W. S., & Flamm, E. S. (2012). Families as facilitators of student engagement: Toward a home-school partnership model. In S. L. Christenson, A. L. Reschly, & C. Wylie (Eds.), *Handbook of research on student engagement* (pp. 343–364). New York: Springer.

Reschly, A. L., & Christenson, S. L. (2012). Jingle, jangle, and conceptual haziness: Evolution and future directions of the engagement construct. In S. L. Christenson, A. L. Reschly, & C. Wylie (Eds.), *Handbook of research on student engagement* (pp. 3–19). New York: Springer.

Schubert, J. D. (2012). Suffering/symbolic violence. In M. Grenfell (Ed.), *Pierre Bourdieu* (pp. 179–194). Durham: Acumen Publishing.

Schutz, A. (2008). Social class and social action: The middle-class bias of democratic theory in education. *Teacher College Record, 110*(2), 405–442.

Sheldon, S. B. (2002). Parents' social networks and beliefs as predictors of parent involvement. *The Elementary School Journal, 102*(4), 301–316.

Skinner, E. A., & Pitzer, J. R. (2012). Developmental dynamics of student engagement, coping, and everyday resilience. In S. L. Christenson, A. L. Reschly, & C. Wylie (Eds.), *Handbook of research on student engagement* (pp. 21–44). New York: Springer.

Swartz, D. (1945). *Culture and power: The sociology of Pierre Bourdieu.* Chicago: The University of Chicago Press.

Taylor, M. (2013). *An Overview of the Local Control Funding Formula.* Sacramento, CA: The Legislative Analyst's Office. Retrieved May 3, 2014 from http://www.lao.ca.gov/reports/2013/edu/lcff/lcff-072913.pdf.

U.S. Department of Education, Office of Planning, Evaluation, and Policy Development. (2010). *ESEA Blueprint for Reform.* Washington, D.C.: ED Pubs.

Vongprateep, K. P. (2014). *Parents' social and cultural capital: One parent group's influence on student engagement in an upper middle class high school.* University Of Redlands: Doctoral dissertation.

Winkle-Wagner, R. (2010). Cultural capital: The promises and pitfalls in educational research. *ASHE Higher Education Report, 36*(1), 1–144.

CHAPTER 7

Student Engagement through Social and Cultural Capital

A Guide for School Counselors

by Joanna Dorado

I n a secondary setting, school counselors are usually on the frontlines of guiding course selection and informing and preparing students to become college- and career-ready in a changing job market. Counselors are in an ideal position to engage students and shepherd them toward graduation and keep students engaged in furthering their career preparation. Unfortunately, there is an ongoing issue with the lack of understanding by educators, national leaders, and policy-makers as to what a school counselor does to impact student educational outcomes (McGannon, *Carey & Dimmitt*, 2005).

Historically, Hispanic students have been the least represented in higher education institutions, although they continue to be among the fastest-growing population in the nation (U.S. Census Bureau, 2012). According to Howard (2010), "The Latino population will triple in size over the next several decades and will account for most of the nation's population growth between 2005 and 2050" (p. 37). This creates an opportunity for school counselors to intentionally focus their efforts on student engagement when working with Hispanic students.

According to Shields (2013), educators must attend to the social and cultural contexts within education in order to address the issues of oppressed and marginalized groups in wider society. Therefore, the research presented in this chapter describes a social and cultural capital theory and its relation to first-generation Mexican American students' engagement. The data is analyzed through the lens of Bourdieu's full social reproduction theory from its social and cultural capital theoretical framework. Furthermore, the conclusive framework guides the understanding of counselors when interacting with low-income students of color.

Social and Cultural Capital

Hispanic students are often marginalized and perceived as deficient in cultural and social capital compared to their white counterparts, which are considered as holders of dominant cultural capital. Shields (2013) found that many educators are conditioned and socialized to understand the status quo as the way to succeed academically. Dominant culture is represented by what knowledge, social skills, or cultural capital is valued and privileged in certain environments, causing marginalization to those who do not possess it (Winkle-Wagner, 2010). In addition, the lack of research that focuses on these issues is a problem for states such as California, which consistently records growth in its Hispanic student population. Therefore, this creates the opportunity for educators to better understand how social and cultural capital can be utilized during counseling sessions to improve the educational outcomes for students of color.

Cultural capital is a set of knowledge, skills, abilities, tastes, preferences, norms, or traditions that act as a form of currency in social settings (Bourdieu, 1984). Involvement in certain cultural activities through education or family origins results in the possession of knowledge, skills, abilities, norms, preferences, or mannerisms that are basically habituated and can grant social privilege, "acceptance, recognition, inclusion, or even social mobility" to some students over others (Winkle-Wagner, 2010, p. 5). The research in this chapter will explain what cultural capital is being recorded as having an influence on student engagement. This is specific to Hispanic students, who often do not fit into the traditional, mainstream way of viewing cultural capital in America.

Social capital is having a connection to a network based on a group membership that serves as an enrichment of knowledge, support, and resources, such as the relationship between a student and counselor, which can contribute to the student's social welfare—a connection that can later be rewarded or recognized in educational realms or other social settings (Bourdieu, 1986). The research in this chapter will also be covering what specific social capital is recorded to be most beneficial when working with students of color.

The study from Ishimaru (2013) offers an example of principals who have attempted to share leadership by *bonding* social capital and *bridging* social capital, taken from the conceptual framework of social capital theory. "*Bonding* social capital" (Ishimaru, 2013, p. 9) was demonstrated by low-income Latino families engaged in relationships of mutual trust and support in order to work together toward a common goal of change to support their children's success. In efforts to better navigate the school system, the educators and low-income families engaged in "*bridging* social capital" (p. 9)—creating a network built on trust, reciprocity, support, and a common interest—thus affording the Latino parents access to institutional knowledge and resources (Ishimaru, 2013). Ishimaru's study contributed to the theory of social capital by demonstrating that educators who have valuable social capital are able to bridge between themselves and the students and parents that need it.

A study by Saunders and Serna (2004) reported the experience of first-generation Latino students who enrolled in a four-year university immediately after graduating from high school. The findings indicate "Hispanics are as likely as whites to enroll in a 4-year college or university after adding measurements of social and cultural capital to control for gender, costs, benefits, financial recourses, and ability" (p. 148). The study pointed out those Hispanic students with limited access to cultural capital benefit most from developing relationships with teachers, counselors, and other school mentors, thus increasing the sort of capital that will be beneficial for college enrollment (Saunders & Serna, 2004). This chapter will help to explain the different types of cultural capital that contribute to student engagement when working with Hispanic students.

Lareau and Weininger (2003) argued for a different use of Bourdieu's cultural capital after critically assessing several studies that explicitly measured for "highbrow" (p. 568) cultural participation. These scholars have found this approach inadequate as a measure for educational settings because it focuses mainly on competence and knowledge of high-status or dominant culture. Lareau and Weininger (2003) concluded by suggesting: "Cultural capital in school settings must identify the particular expectations–both formal and, especially, informal–by means of which school personnel appraise students" (p. 588). The research in this chapter uses Lareau and Weininger's (2003) perspective of revealing the potential cultural capital that may often go unnoticed by educators when working with a specific ethnic group and during the analysis of the data.

According to Winkle-Wagner (2010), "Educational institutions present an excellent location to understand the way cultural capital is reinforced, rewarded, and acquired," as students who acquire "forms of cultural capital valued by the dominant groups will be more highly rewarded" (pp. 17–18). Therefore, the research presented in this chapter focuses on taking findings from previous research and understanding the "cultural capital" that contributes to Hispanic student engagement, which allows them to do well academically.

Current Research, Findings, and Implications

This research was accomplished by investigating the unique perception of four school counselors, two administrators, three students, and three parents of an urban school district located in Southern California. The researcher used a qualitative narrative inquiry, semi-structured protocol to interview the participants face-to-face. Once analyzed, the results allowed for deeper insight into the different dynamics of cultural and social capital acquired by Hispanic families and how they are reinforced and rewarded in a unique, urban home and school setting.

The process of data analysis for this study began with transcribing each of the twelve digitally recorded interviews. The next step was to listen to the recordings while paying close attention to how each participant (i.e., administrator, counselor, parent, or student) answered a variation of the same question through each participant's unique perspective. "Triangulation" helps validate the thematic process and is defined as the ability to use multiple data sets to corroborate the evidence, thus validating the researcher's findings (Creswell, 2013, p. 251).

Narrative inquiry methodology has usually been used to understand cultural experiences, historical events, and social processes while acknowledging each individual circumstance in an organizational or social membership, setting, or location (Chase, 2005, 2011). This is why "narrative inquiry is increasingly used in studies of educational experience" (Clandinin & Connelly, 1990, p. 2) as qualitative research and the research being presented in this chapter.

In the current study, social capital and cultural capital were used in defining and interpreting the types of relationships and teachings school counselors share with their students. These relationships would ideally allow school counselors to embed students from minority groups—many of whom normally do not have access to networks with experience in realizing higher education attainment—in an exchange of resources and information. According to the work of Sauder and Serna (2004), access to social and cultural capital through social connection in first-generation Hispanic students can begin to disrupt social reproduction while creating a college attainment mentality. The research of Moll, Amanti, Neff, and Gonzalez (1992) confirmed that a teacher's desire to learn about his or her student's domestic situation can be useful in the classroom and lead to more meaningful relationships. The research in this chapter used a similar approach in determining specific relationships, resources, and memberships that allowed for the sharing of knowledge and resources that supports the common goal of student success.

Research findings

The following figures illustrate the basic concepts that emerged from the data analysis. These are the primary factors that provide evidence for the themes regarding social and cultural capital theory. All the themes allow a deeper understanding and description of the lives that Hispanic students specifically live. The themes are summarized in charts that illustrate the factors that are most influential in the academic achievements of Mexican American students.

The four themes that emerged from the data provided answers to the research questions about how student engagement can be supported with social and cultural capital to improve outcomes for Hispanic students. Furthermore, the findings allowed for an understanding of how four valuable themes elucidate the process of social reproduction for young, first-generation Mexican American students. By listening to the

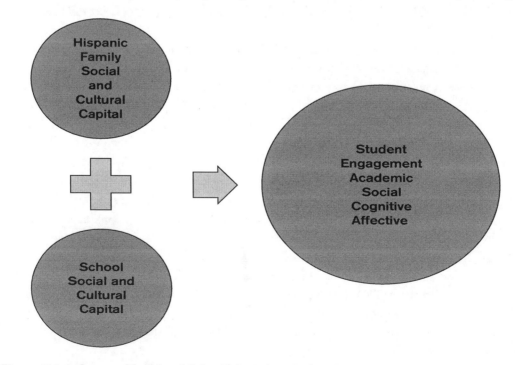

Figure 7–1. Influence of Social and Cultural Capital on Student Engagement.

authentic voices of the participants, looking at Bourdieu's form of capital, and considering how low-income Hispanic families interacted with available resources, the researcher gained an understanding of why these students seemed to be more engaged. The themes that emerged from the data are as follows:

1. Theme 1: Becoming Academically Engaged (Family Cultural Capital)
2. Theme 2: Meaningful Relationships Found Outside of School (Family Social Capital)
3. Theme 3: Specific Networks Most Useful in Schools (School Social Capital)
4. Theme 4: Influential Educational Habitus on Students' Engagement (School Cultural Capital)

Theme 1 allowed the researcher to gain a unique perspective on the lived experiences of Mexican American students whose parents are working class and have never attended higher education. The students' narrated experiences demonstrated very unique forms of capital not typically derived from the same experiences of the elite dominant culture in America. These narratives provided insight into how certain traits, norms, abilities, preferences, traditions, and knowledge have influenced their decisions to become academically and socially engaged as high school students. In other words, the *students' cultural capital* supports the family cultural expectations for Hispanic students to work hard and to seize their opportunities, which some families take to mean graduating from high school with the requirements to pursue a four-year university education and others take to mean entering the work force as soon as possible.

Theme 2 outlined meaningful narratives that demonstrated how Mexican American students were supported by meaningful relationships they made outside of school. The study found these connections to be a form of social capital that the students accrued outside of school hours. Contrary to the kind of deficit-thinking assumptions that are made about working-class Hispanics, the Mexican American narratives demonstrated how important their group memberships outside of school were for them. Such memberships were influential in their motivation to remain engaged with their graduation plans and college goals.

Theme 3 explored how the most relevant programs, individuals, and activities found in schools assisted Mexican American students to stay informed and motivated in their aspirations to be the first in their family to attend a four-year university. According to Coleman (1988), different channels of information exist. He has defined social capital as a social relationship that acts as a beneficial resource to people. The results of this study demonstrated that counselors are a beneficial source of information if and when the relationship is built during high school. Theme 3 contributed to the idea that school counselors are a source of social capital that work to help students develop additional skills, knowledge, and norms. It was found in the study that the counselors who built strong and consistent relationships with students provided social capital that led to greater development of cultural capital and school habitus.

Finally, Theme 4 explored how *habitus* (or the student's cultural habits) is an important factor in developing cultural capital at school. The cultural capital explored in Theme 4 can be seen as currency in higher education systems or other dominant *fields*. It is about developing both the students and their families so they can successfully manage the bureaucratic systems that are often too complicated for many Hispanic families. Such examples include educating families in making formal requests in the school office for academic support and informing students and parents about seeking accurate information about financial aid, college applications, and the necessity of taking rigorous courses (House & Hayes, 2002).

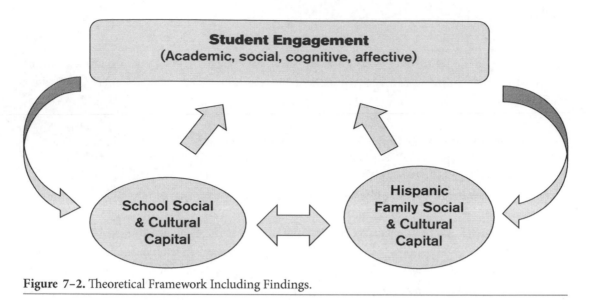

Figure 7–2. Theoretical Framework Including Findings.

Figure 7.2 applies the findings from this research to the conclusive theoretical framework. The following conclusions can be posited: (a) social capital influencing student engagement existed both in and out of school; (b) family cultural capital as well as the school's cultural capital contributed to the student's level of academic engagement; (c) the greater the level of student engagement, the more it influenced the sources of social and cultural capital found both in school and home; (d) educators' and families' levels of engagement and the exchange of information about each other's capital allowed for better decisions that positively impacted student engagement. Understanding this conclusive theoretical framework allows for critical conversations that can contribute to the construction of knowledge and empower other educational leaders to assist marginalized individuals—specifically students of color—in having better social outcomes.

Summary of Findings

Table 7.1 shows the aspirations of students who wish to be the first in their families to go to a university. It is apparent that their unique lived experiences contributed to their desire for a higher education. When listening to the authentic voices of Mexican American students, one can clearly see that their family and cultural backgrounds were large contributors to forming their goals. Three out of the three student participants explained that they would be the first in their family to attend a university with the hope of pursuing a higher degree. The abilities and commitments that these students had in order to do well academically relate to the set of skills found under the indicators for *family cultural capital.* While it may be realistic that many students find themselves in a situation of "cultural reproduction" that perpetuates the inequalities of their parents' generation, the students who were interviewed in the current study were willing to take all they had learned from their families—and from other available community resources—to change their circumstances. This is where educators, counselors, and administrators, to a certain extent, influence student engagement by recognizing and emphasizing the positive impact of family cultural capital. Statements such as "I don't want you to live the way we live. I want you to do better"; "You need to go to college, you don't

Table 7–1. Summary of Cultural Capital Found in Hispanic Families

Family Cultural Capital			
Becoming Academically Engaged	The rationale for why students continue in their pursuit of academic success and the contributing factors associated with their family environment.	Family Hardships Financial Struggle Emotional Support Familial Skills Responsibility Good Work Ethic	"I don't want you to live the way we live. I want you to do better." "You need to go to college, you don't want to be like me." "I work hard with my back, so you can work hard with your brain."

want to be like me"; and "I work hard with my back, so you can work hard with your brain" were reminders to participants of how important being academically engaged was to their family.

Table 7.2 summarizes the findings gathered from participants' comments that identified the indicators that result in the development of a meaningful social capital. The results from this section demonstrate the importance of social capital found outside of school. It implied that students' involvement in community activities not only increased their networks with knowledgeable individuals, but also fostered their cultural capital. Positive social networks contributed to positive student engagement. Meaningful relationships found through family connections to community activities, church, sports, friends, membership to organizations, and museum visits were also significant contributors to cultural capital. The availability of networks or relationships functions to build cultural capital for students to aspire for a higher education and greater academic success. Participants made comments related to the importance of social capital such as "The team is and it's another family to me and it pushes me to be better not only in my sport" and "Friends and family that have older siblings that have are going through college." These findings are similar to the study by Martinez and Ulanoff (2013), who demonstrated how community organizations create social and cultural capital opportunities that "increase student achievement and promote social justice" in East Los Angeles (Martinez & Ulanoff, 2013, p. 196).

Table 7.3 shows the social connections that proved to be the most helpful for students and most utilized in the school district to encourage student engagement. Programs such as Upward Bound, IB, Academy Pathways, AVID, school counselors, career center, and cultural clubs were places where students could become connected. Students gained access to resources and knowledge specific to higher education needed to navigate toward their goals. Participants made comments such as "I feel like our school has a bunch of clubs that offer you all these opportunities and chance to learn more about college and how you can get there" and "I can go to the school counselor that might know more about it and they can help me more," signifying that these relationships were of importance to them and helped them to remain focused on their goal of academic success. The students who were interviewed felt that their family cultural capital was rewarded and reinforced through their social interactions and participation in many school-sponsored activities. The interviews implied that school administrators and counselors work directly with the city's

Table 7–2. Summary of Social Capital Found Outside of School

Family Social Capital			
Meaningful Relationships Found Outside of School	The availability of community networks or relationships that are most significant contributors in the students' lives, which function as social capital for students found outside of the educational institution	Community Activities/Church Sport Coaches Family Members Friends Digital Community Museum Membership	"The team is and it's another family to me and it pushes me to be better not only in my sport" "Friends and family that have older siblings that have or going through college"

resources and local universities, and that this interaction expands their capability in connecting students to more information, networks, and resources. Different school programs improve student engagement through the relationships created during their participation.

Table 7.4 summarizes the available cultural capital in school, which contributes to the identity development of students related to their acquired and learned knowledge, abilities, skills, and disposition. This identity development is one of the significant roles and responsibilities facilitated by informed and caring school counselors. House and Hayes (2002) have suggested that school counselors have influence in promoting equity for students of color—who traditionally have been the least served—by helping students gain access to more rigorous courses, college preparatory courses, tutoring, and academic enrichment opportunities.

Few studies have specifically considered the notion of Bourdieu's social and cultural capital in relation to the roles of a school counselor. The current research presents an opportunity to inform counselors about how providing access to rigorous courses, college preparatory programs, and school activities is an effective way of building the students' social and cultural capital. The study also shared the reality that different ethnic groups often have unique and valuable traditions, abilities, and forms of expressing culture that are not even recognized in the context of the dominant culture's norms (Yosso, 2005). The data gathered from the current research supports the idea that Mexican American students have a wealth of cultural capital that often requires recognition from an educational institution to more fully engage students in a way that results in better outcomes.

This study had a strong focus on cultural and social capital and is concerned specifically with the school counselors' ability to recognize the quantity and quality of this capital possessed by students of color, in addition to the capital that can be shared through bridging and bonding, as mentioned in Ishimaru (2013).

Furthermore, school counselors who teach students and their families how to successfully manage the bureaucratic system by teaching them how to make formal requests in school offices—for information about such things as financial aid and additional academic support (House & Hayes, 2002)—offer an example of Bourdieu's cultural and social capital being transmitted to a non-dominant group. The research concluded

Table 7–3. Summary of Social Capital Found in School

School Social Capital			
Specific Networks Most Useful in Schools	The social capital most regarded as social connections in helping students become connected to new resources or knowledge, specifically about higher education found in schools	Upward Bound IB Academy Pathways AVID School Counselors Career Center Cultural Clubs	"I feel like our school has a bunch of clubs and that offer you all these opportunities and chance to learn more about college and how you can get there" "I can go to the school counselor that might know more about it and they can help me more"

that capital circulates between schools and homes, and that the differences in student engagement and outcomes depend on how this capital is utilized and recognized.

Implications for Practice

Although the sample studied here represented a small group of Mexican American students and families and a small number of educators from an urban high school setting, it has provided useful insight about the importance of cultural and social capital in developing college aspirations and student engagement. The current study was purposefully limited to college-bound high school Hispanic students who had already shown great academic progress. Such selection allowed further understanding about non-dominant cultural capital and its effect on Hispanic students' ability to succeed in high school.

The research focused on cultural and social capital and the way they functioned in educational settings. When school agents cease to overlook the abilities and skills that these students and families have—skills that have made their families resilient and strong—the students and families will find their stories recognized and shared rather than continuing to be marginalized. It is worth it to determine and share the implications of the current research findings in other educational settings, particularly with Hispanic students who are not engaged so that they may develop a college aspirational culture. Understanding the marginalized cultural and social backgrounds of Hispanic students also suggests more exploration of different ethnic groups in order to understand the different nuances that make each ethic group unique and rich in social and cultural capital.

The results here showed the lack of understanding of the parents and teachers about the important influence of social and cultural capital for improving student engagement. If parents do not understand how to use their cultural capital to appropriately motivate their children academically, then the students may not see the value in pursuing higher education. The result is lower student engagement and the social reproduction of

Table 7–4. Summary of Cultural Capital Found in School

School Cultural Capital			
Influential Educational Habitus on Student Engagement	The habits most utilized from their participation in relationships that allows for the students' development, and acquiring, of a different set of skills, knowledge, and abilities that contribute to student engagement. More specifically, the impact of counselors' cultural capital	Exploration Access Navigation Rigor	"Being involved and go ask your counselor or ask the AVID teacher or any teacher because they had to have gone somewhere to be a teacher." "Maneuver through the system, because a lot of times it's not set up to be very easy for them to navigate."

existing inequalities. According to some of the students and counselors, teachers have different expectations of students. They either have positive or negative expectations of their Hispanic students. These expectations vary depending on how well the teachers understand Hispanic cultural capital or non-dominant cultural capital. Not being aware of the students' cultural capital could affect the ability and intention of teachers to build a meaningful relationship with their students. Often, teachers have different ethnic, social, and economic backgrounds, making it more difficult to stay in touch with non-dominant values.

In one of the themes that emerged from the interview (Theme 2: Meaningful Relationships Found Outside of School—Family Social Capital), the accuracy of the information gathered by students from outside networks was seen as a limitation because people and outside agencies might not have college expertise. Counselors and other school agents believe that students can misunderstand some of the college and financial aid information when someone other than a school official is presenting the information to students who have not attended college yet. In Theme 3: Specific Networks Most Useful in Schools—School Social Capital, the discussion of social capital relates to how the social relationship with a school counselor can be a stumbling block to a student's engagement. This concern can manifest in diverse ways, such as insufficient time to know students individually or few numbers of counselors with whom to develop meaningful relationships. It has been written that school counselors in higher poverty schools with higher minority demographics are more likely to have non-counseling responsibilities, or clerical work, which does not allow them time to adequately provide college information to all students (Brigman & Campbell, 2003; Bryan et al., 2009). The students interviewed in this study perceived their counselors as having limited time to see all students more than once a year (Theme 3). This arrangement limits not only each student's opportunity to successfully build a social connection, but also the opportunity to see school counselors as more approachable. In Theme 4: Influential Educational Habitus on Students' Engagement—School Cultural Capital, access to certain college-prep classes was covered. Students may be easily taken out of rigorous courses without first exploring optional interventions to keep them there. In the process, they may lose a chance to develop skills needed for the future, such as those that might help them with college and career readiness. This concern touches on whether the interests of the teachers surpass the interests of the students. Educational leaders must pay close attention to whose needs are being served—non-dominant or dominant groups—and who is being impacted by the decisions being made in school districts.

This study seeks to make clear that people of color are able to network with those in their own community by working together to achieve a shared goal or vision, thus demonstrating the transferability of social capital between or among individuals. In doing so, people show the potential for social change. The present research suggests that school counselors can initiate meaningful and equitable change by simply providing valuable information or building the students' and parents' social and cultural capital about school and schooling. As such, they can promote equity and a socially just education for all students by building and advancing strong relationships, examining inequalities, and acknowledging differences in one's lived experiences—especially for those currently not being adequately served (Shields, 2004). These are all important reasons to consider viewing the school counselors in high school as agents of social and cultural capital, especially for students of color.

School Counselor's Guide

- School counselors can promote equity by affording access to more rigorous courses, college preparatory programs, tutoring, workshops, and academic enrichment opportunities for students of color who traditionally have been the least served.
- Create an opportunity to start addressing concerns of lack of understanding of how social capital and cultural capital are developed through participation in cultural groups and clubs at school.
- Administrators, counselors, teachers, and parents must work collaboratively toward implementing programs, curriculum, and instruction that value social and cultural capital development opportunities within classroom projects, assignments, and lessons.
- Provide students of color access and more opportunities for developing student-counselor relationships, which allow for an exchange of cultural capital and enrichment of social capital.
- Communicate more effectively with parents and students of color in urban schools regarding preparation for graduation, college, and career choices regardless of perceived resources, including the students' or families' social or cultural backgrounds.
- School counselors should be more intentional when offering academic course planning, encouraging extracurricular involvement (social capital), and offering guidance about college and career assessments/exploration, the college admissions process, and college affordability when speaking to first-generation college students of color.
- Finally, school counselors should work closely with their school community to identify and understand the family social and cultural capital resources

References

Bourdieu, P. (1984). *Distinction: A social critique of the judgment of taste.* Cambridge, MA: Harvard University Press.

Bourdieu, P. (1986). The forms of capital. In J. G. Richardson (Ed.), *Handbook of theory and research for the sociology of education* (pp. 241–258). New York, NY: Greenwood Press.

Brigman, G., & Campbell, C. (2003). Helping students improve academic achievement and school success behavior. *Professional School Counseling, 7*(2), 91–98.

Bryan, J., Holcomb-McCoy, C., Moore-Thomas, C., & Day-Vines, N. L. (2009). Who sees the school counselor for college information? A national study. *Professional School Counseling, 12*(4), 280–291.

Chase, S. E. (2005). Narrative inquiry: Multiple lenses, approaches, voices. In N. Denzin & Y. Lincoln (Eds.), *The Sage handbook of qualitative research* (3rd ed.) (pp. 651–674). Thousand Oaks, CA: Sage Publications.

Coleman, J. S. (1988). Social capital in the creation of human capital. *American Journal of Sociology, 94*, 95–121.

Connelly, F. M., & Clandini, D. J. (1990). Stories of experience and narrative inquiry. *Educational Research, 19*(5), 2–14.

Creswell, J.W. (2013). *Qualitative inquiry and research design: Choosing among five approaches* (3rd ed). Thousand Oaks, CA: Sage Publications.

House, R. M., & Hayes, R. L. (2002). School Counselors: Becoming key players in school reform. *Professional School Counseling, 5*(4), 249.

Howard, T. C. (2010). *Why race and culture matters in schools: Closing the achievement gap in American's classrooms.* New York, NY: Teachers College Press.

Ishimaru, A. (2013). From heroes to organizers principals and education organizing in urban school reform. *Educational Administration Quarterly, 49*(1), 3–51.

Lareau, A., & Weininger, E. B. (2003). Cultural capital in educational research: A critical assessment. *Theory and society, 32*(5–6), 567–606.

Martinez, E., & Ulanoff, S. H. (2013). Latino parents and teachers: Key players building neighborhood social capital. *Teaching Education, 24*(2), 195–208.

McGannon, W., Carey, J., & Dimmitt, C. (2005). The current status of school counseling outcome research. Retrieved from http://www.spu.edu/orgs/schoolcounseling/OutcomeStudyMonograph.pdf.

Moll, L. C., Amanti, C., Neff, D., & Gonzalez, N. (1992). Funds of knowledge for teaching: Using a qualitative approach to connect homes and classrooms. *Theory into Practice, 31*(2), 132–141.

Saunders, M., & Serna, I. (2004). Making college happen: The college experiences of first-generation Latino students. *Journal of Hispanic Higher Education, 3*(2), 146–163.

Shields, C. M. (2004). Dialogic leadership for social justice: Overcoming pathologies of silence. *Educational Administration Quarterly, 40*(1), 109–132

Shields, C. M. (2013). *Transformative leadership in education: Equitable change in an uncertain and complex world.* New York, NY: Routledge.

U. S. Census Bureau. (2012). *Statistical abstract of the United States: 2012.* Washington, DC. Retrieved from http://www.census.gov/compendia/statab/2012edition.html.

Winkle-Wagner, R. (2010). Cultural capital: The promises and pitfalls in educational research. *ASHE Higher Education Report, 36*(1), 1–132.

Yosso, T. J. (2005). Whose culture has capital? A critical race theory discussion of community cultural wealth. *Race Ethnicity and Education, 8*(1), 69–91.

CHAPTER 8

Leadership for Developing a Learning School Culture that Maximizes Student Engagement

by Margaret Solomon

Introduction

"If only schools could become better at educating children" is a common phrase we hear people saying. In this statement of blame, there is also a sense of hope expressed. "If only schools could become better" implies that school can become better and children can be educated for success. Much of that depends on school leadership and the culture of learning that exists in the school. It is not a secret that the leadership style of a school is a determinant factor on student achievement. A school leader, by the nature of his job, exerts influence on teachers' attitudes toward students and their learning. This happens in a school culture that reflects learning, exchange of ideas, respect for each other, and total commitment to educating all the children equally.

This book emphasizes student engagement as an essential component for effective learning, and this chapter contends that school leaders must take the responsibility to bring a learning culture in the school to support total student engagement. Infusing a vision for student engagement, passion, and purpose for achieving that goal can create an influential culture to accomplish the desired outcome. Therefore, the responsibility of a school leader is not only to manage the instructional program in the school, but also to provide an effective leadership to create a culture for learning and student engagement.

The next questions we have to ask are, "What type of leaders do we need for that to happen?" and "What dispositions, knowledge, and skills should they demonstrate to effect student engagement in learning?"

Contemporary Schools and Their Diverse Student Body

Due to rapid demographic changes in the U.S. society, the schools are filled with students coming from different regions of the world, speaking multiple languages and exhibiting different cultures. The twenty-first century schools are unlike those from recent years. Students in these schools come with their unique strengths and weaknesses, challenging the current school system to cater to their needs. They bring rich funds of knowledge from their home cultures that are not recognized or tapped by the school personnel. It is the responsibility of the schools to provide an education that takes into consideration the cultural and linguistic gifts they bring. The purpose of this chapter is to discuss what type of leadership would be effective in making student engagement become an essential part of a learning culture in a school that validates student identity and differences. It will also discuss how a principal could develop a learning culture in the school that provides opportunities for engaging students in the total learning process.

Student engagement in the learning process has been accepted as an important step, and without that quality, learning cannot take place. Research on this topic indicates that student engagement is more than students simply engaging in an academic task. Fredricks et al. (2004) say that it is multidimensional and involves students' emotions, their participation in academic tasks, and cognition that takes place in the cortex of their brain. Completing a learning assignment is important, but for accomplishing student engagement in the total learning process, it must go "across academic, social, emotional and behavioral domains" (p. 3). In this case, student engagement refers to students engaging in the learning that takes place in the classroom, school, and community.

The task of a school administrator is to make sure that student engagement for all students with all their differences is a reality in his/her school. Therefore, bringing an inclusive environment in the school is an important step. Many studies have been done on the topic of diversity, providing some light on what conditions are necessary for principals to work effectively with their diverse students and teachers. For too long, mainstream theories basically looked at how leaders managed diversity and how they used their abilities to influence their employees. This view mainly depended on the ability of a leader and his/her skills in building positive relationships with everyone regardless of his/her ethnic or social identity. This has been described as the color-blind theory and was dominantly practiced by principals and teachers, who began to think of themselves as racially neutral and not responsible for excluding others who were different. This caused them to ignore the cultural identities of students by expecting those differences to slowly assimilate with the mainstream culture.

Contrary to this perspective, the diversity research looks at how social, cultural, and racial issues that arose from outside influenced leader-member relationships and interactions in an organization. Here, principals who worked with diverse students recognized and validated the cultural identities the students brought, building a relationship with them became the main task in this context. Accepting ethnically and linguistically different students as valuable members will create an inclusive environment in the school.

Components of Student Engagement

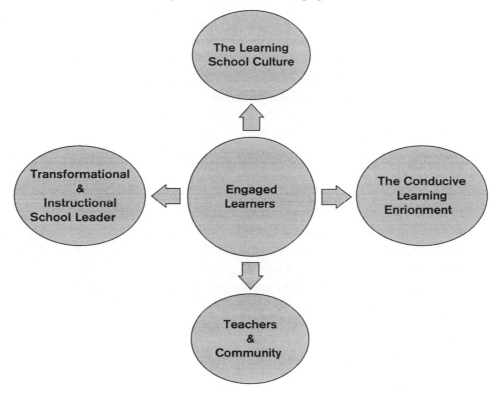

Figure 8–1. Components of Student Engagement

Recognizing the importance of social group identity and leading a diverse group within an organization is emphasized as a positive step (Madson & Mbokela, 2002). It is desirable that school leaders have qualities that bring people together regardless of their differences and develop a school environment that supports all children excelling in their academic work.

Leadership for Developing a Learning Culture for Student Engaged Learning

The leadership literature shows that school leadership and its relationship to student achievement cannot be ignored. Engaging students as active participants in the learning process is not only an essential task of a teacher, but also of the principal. A school leader creates a learning culture that is not only limited to classroom learning, but also is ingrained in all the activities of the school. He/she also makes sure that student engagement goes across social, cultural, and linguistic differences.

There are many types of leadership theories emphasizing how one must lead an organization. In the early part of the twentieth century, leadership was viewed as control and centralization of power with a common theme of domination. Later, leadership was viewed as influencing the members with a specific personality trait the leader exhibited. Currently, the literature organizes the leadership concepts within the themes of traits and process approaches with multiple dimensions and brings out over ten different leadership theories. Under the traits approach, leadership is viewed as an assigned entity, whereas in the process approach, it is seen as an emergent factor. In this chapter, process approach to leadership is preferred because leadership is seen as an emerging entity here. Leaders come to the leadership context and develop themselves as leaders with special qualities appropriate for their school context. It also teaches what type of leadership supports the administrator bringing student engagement as an important feature of the school. Of all the leadership theories, transformational and instructional leadership styles seem to be the most appropriate leadership models.

Transformational and instructional leaderships are the two preferred models that would transform the school's instructional culture to bring student engagement with socially and culturally situated perspectives in the classrooms. There are enough evidences in the literature favoring the characteristics highlighted in these two school leadership models (Shatzer et al., 2013). However, many have preferred transformational leadership to instructional leadership because it is an overall leadership principle that guides leadership practice and does not have a uniform conceptual model. The abilities that spring from practicing transformational leadership match the current demands from educational reforms for change in schools (Leithwood et al., 2006; Murphy et al., 1983). Nevertheless, in the context of this chapter, both instructional and transformational leadership are encouraged.

Transformational Leadership

In the literature on leadership theories, transformational leadership is popular because of its many positive characteristics. Burns (1978) came up with the term *transformation* to describe leadership. He saw leadership as a transformational process "when one or more persons engage with others in such a way that leaders and followers raise one another to higher levels of motivation and morality" (Northouse, 2013, p. 4). According to him, transformational leadership has to do with empowering and enabling the followers.

> Transformational leadership, while more complex, is more potent. The transforming leader recognizes and exploits an existing need or demand of a potential follower. But, beyond that, he/she also looks for potential motives in followers, seeking to satisfy higher needs, and engaging the full person of the follower. The result of transforming leadership is a relationship of mutual stimulation and elevation that converts followers into leaders and may convert leaders into moral agents (Hickman, 2010, p. 66).

Four different practices are addressed in transformational leadership theory: (1) inspirational motivation, (2) individualized consideration, (3) idealized influence (charisma), and (4) intellectual stimulation (Avolio et al., 1991; Bass & Avolio, 1994). First, he/she provides motivation, then recognizes the needs of the followers and seeks to satisfy them. Then, he/she pursues to understand their motives and helps them grow higher in their thinking and doing and engages the followers to achieve their full development. Bass and Riggo (2006) give an excellent description of a transformational leader that is relevant to this discussion. "The leadership inspires followers with challenge and persuasion, providing both meaning and understanding … is intellectually stimulating, expanding the followers' use of their abilities. Finally it is considerate, providing the follower with support, mentoring, and coaching" (p. 78). The transformational leader demonstrates extraordinary capabilities in interacting with his followers and helps them to have a collective sense of mission. In addition, they have a great deal of idealized influence and are ready to take risks and exhibit a high level of ethical and moral conduct (Hickman, 2010).

The positive impact of the principal's leadership on teacher behaviors and student achievement is certainly an enviable matter. In order for school leaders to make lasting impact on teachers and students, they have to be leaders with a moral purpose for improving teaching and learning in their schools. A transformational leader acts with great moral strength coming from within. "Moral purpose is about both ends and means" (Fullan, 2001, p. 13). In a school, an important end is making a difference in the lives of students by assuring them success in their learning. A transformational leader is one who has a moral purpose to make teaching and learning in his/her school vibrant and meaningful for all students, especially to those who are culturally and socially different from the mainstream.

Transformational leadership has been suggested as the ideal leadership style for principals of schools considering substantial reform because change management has been recognized as an attribute of transformational leaders. (Leithwood & Jantzi, 2006). A principal who follows the transformational leadership also has the capacity to bring the changes that are necessary to bring an inclusive environment in a school and empower its teachers to change the traditional paradigm of teaching. He/She will assist teachers in bringing student centered instruction and provide the support for learning new teaching techniques and methods. He/she will be very much interested to bring a student-centered instruction and will also provide the support teachers need to learn new techniques and methods in their teaching. He/she also will make the school a learning organization for teachers by providing professional learning experiences that will bring intellectual stimulation and change in their instructional practice.

In addition, a transformational leader also assists in the followers' growth and serves as a coach or mentor. "Principals who are transformational leaders are able to identify and articulate a school vision, motivate others through example, support a culture of intellectual stimulation, and provide support and development to individual staff members" (Robinson et al., 2008, p. 635). It can be summarized that transformational principals are those who are able to provide inspirational motivation, individualized consideration, idealized influence (charisma), and intellectual stimulation to their teachers and staff (Shatzer et al., 2013).

It is well-supported in the literature that transformation leadership is associated with substantial reform, positive school environment, and good teacher and staff relations (Bogler, 2005; Griffith, 2004). It was also found that transformative leadership showed strong, direct effects on teachers' motivation, teacher commitment, teacher self-efficacy, and the school environment (Leithwood & Jantzi, 2006; Ross & Gray, 2006).

Instructional Leadership

Next, a transformational leader also should be an instructional leader in schools where student engagement becomes an important feature of the school's culture. An instructional leader not only knows the curriculum, but also is familiar with effective pedagogy. Research from the past shows that instructional leadership results in higher student academic achievement than transformational leadership.

The literature on instructional leadership is extensive, and Shatzer et al. (2013), who compiled a set of studies on instructional leadership, came to the following conclusions.

> … that school principals who employ an instructional leadership style have some influence over student outcomes … had an indirect effect on student reading achievement and direct effects on school climate variables in elementary schools. Van de Grift and Houtveen examined instructional leadership in elementary schools and found that leadership had a small but significant effect on student achievement scores. In a study in which O'Donnell and White surveyed 250 middle-level educators, perceptions of principal instructional leadership behaviors that focused on improving school learning climate were identified as predictors of student achievement. The relationship between instructional leadership and student achievement is often mediated by school-level factors such as school climate or classroom-level factors such as teacher efficacy and job satisfaction (p. 2).

According to Hallinger (2003), instructional leadership consists of three goals: (1) defining the mission of the school, (2) managing the instructional program, and (3) promoting a positive school climate. The first goal is achieved by working with teachers and staff in establishing clear and measurable goals. The principal and teachers develop a shared mission that is well-monitored by them. Together, they clarify to themselves how their work is tied to achieving the mission of the school and then come up with specific goals that will shape their work. They make sure that the goals are primarily concerned with the academic growth of the students and can be achieved efficiently. Next, they regularly communicate to the school community about how the school mission is being achieved.

First, an instructional leader manages the instructional program by having much influence over the curriculum of the school. He/she also has content expertise and is knowledgeable in relevant pedagogy; therefore, he/she is able to supervise instruction in the classrooms effectively and also provide the necessary support for teachers when they need help. In managing and supervising instruction, instructional leaders make sure students are making progress in their education and develop a school climate that reflects a high standard of excellence. Besides providing incentives for teachers and students, being visible and making sure classroom instruction is vibrant in each classroom are qualities an instructional leader exhibits. He/she also protects his/her time from being overloaded with managerial duties and makes sure that there is enough time to visit classrooms and monitor the teaching and learning in the school.

There are many evidences in the literature to support that there is a high correlation between instructional leadership and student achievement. Hallinger and Heck (1998) noted that schools where the principals followed instructional leadership style had small but significant student outcomes and a school climate that supported efficient learning. A study by O'Donnell and White (2005) on instructional leadership found that "perceptions of principal instructional leadership behaviors that focused on improving school learning climate were identified as predictors of student achievement. The relationship between instructional leadership and student achievement is often mediated by school-level factors such as school climate, teacher efficacy and job satisfaction" (p. 56).

Further research in recent years has shed more light on the characteristics of instructional leadership. It has been documented that when the principal is an instructional leader, he/she first seeks collaboration among teachers for improving instruction and creates several opportunities for growth in professional practice through professional learning. In many cases, professional learning communities (PLC) were established to carry out the professional learning purposes. Here, the instructional leader uses shared or distributed leadership, invoking the commitment of all teachers to bring the expected academic achievement for all learners in the school. There are enough evidences to support the theory that instructional leadership practices of a principal impact student achievement positively (Nettles & Herrington, 2007; Silva et al., 2011).

In this great task of moving a school from a traditional instructional system to one that is receptive to the cultural, social, and linguistic needs of students, the principal must truly be an instructional leader. He/she also will be providing the students opportunities for academic, social, emotional, and cultural engagement. As an instructional leader, the principal is knowledgeable in the subject matter and the pedagogy that goes along with it. The administrators will not be able to support the instructional practices of teachers unless they understand how teachers can make their classrooms not only inclusive, but also where student engagement is at its highest. "Good instructional leaders praise effective teaching and encourage change when needed, rather than criticizing practices without providing support. An effective instructional leader will find ways to extend autonomy to their teachers in a way that allows teachers to gain control over their professional responsibilities" (Blasé & Blasé, 1999, p. 349).

There is certainly a shortage of principals who are truly instructional leaders and lean toward transformational leadership and bring a school culture where all the students are engaged in the total learning process.

Understanding an Organization's Culture

The first challenge of a school leader who wants to bring change in the traditional learning culture is to take charge of the school environment for student engagement in the classroom, school, and community. He/she develops a phenomenon that shows how things are done and how people are supposed to behave and act. In this process, he/she develops a culture with some specific characteristics. Schein (2010) defines culture as " ... a pattern of shared basic assumptions learned by a group as it solved its problems of external adaptation and internal integration ... " (p. 18). For the purpose of improving schools for better student academic engagement, the leader first must gain a valuable insight into its existing culture and see how he/she can impact it to bring the desirable student outcomes.

Levels of Culture

According to Schein (2010) and agreed by Deal and Patterson (2009), the culture in an organization is demonstrated in the artifacts of the school, espoused values of the people, and the assumptions they hold. First, it is exhibited at the surface level in its artifacts, which refers to the architecture of its physical environment, "its language; its technology and products; its artistic creations; its style, as embodied in clothing, manners of dress, and emotional displays; its myths and stories told about the organization; its published lists of values and its observable rituals and ceremonies" (Schein, 2010, p. 23).

These elements are easy to recognize, but it is difficult to interpret their symbolism and associate meanings. For example, when you want to go into a school, you have to first sign in at a counter, and once you go in, you will face the school's layout, the organization of the classrooms and the administrative offices, and so on. As you walk through the school, it becomes clear that individuals who occupy the offices and the classrooms all have ranks assigned to them. The furniture in the classrooms, the playground, and the offices are of different types and quality. As you observe these artifacts, you get a glimpse of the school and also gain a sense of its total environment. Then there are also other artifacts such as symbols, traditions, and routines, stories that are part of the culture and allow one to get a peek into the school's existing culture.

The next level of the culture is the espoused beliefs and values of the people in the organization. It is by understanding the espoused beliefs and values of everyone in the school that one can sense and experience its culture and find meanings to the artifacts observed. People, by nature, hold their worldviews, which are made up of beliefs and values that are core to them, as filters. In any organization, as people interact with each other doing their work, they act from their personal values and beliefs, but while working together as a group, they may face situations where they have to negotiate their values and beliefs with others and develop shared values and beliefs. This process continuously goes on in all functional organizations. In order for a school to function efficiently, there has to be congruence in espoused beliefs and values of individuals who work there. That is when a school leader becomes involved to guide and shape peoples' thinking and actions. A school culture is certainly determined by the beliefs and values people hold about their work and how they work with each other in achieving the organization's goal.

The third level of a school culture is the basic underlying assumptions of everyone in the school. This is a very important level of the culture because as human beings, we function from the basic assumptions that guide our beliefs and values. Theories are used in an organization to guide behavior, indicating how members in an organization think and behave, but it cannot be refuted because it has rooted itself within the organization (Schein, 2010).

In order to understand the culture of an organization, one needs to look at the basic assumptions that drive all the actions. If one does not figure out the pattern of assumptions that are operating in a school, he/she may not know how to interpret the artifacts clearly and figure out how much the espoused values influenced the actions of teachers and staff. "To understand a group's culture, you must attempt to get at its shared basic assumptions and understand the learning process by which such basic assumptions evolve" (Schein, 2010, p. 32) as well as how they can be changed. However, the principal who wants to bring change in the established assumptions of the people in the school must first assess how the activities of the school are influenced by those assumptions and take steps to gradually influence them for change.

Shaping and Developing a Learning Culture

The first responsibility of a principal who wants to make student engagement his/her school's priority goal is to assess the existing culture and identify areas where changes would be needed in the three levels of culture. He/she puts forth proactive efforts to make the school a real learning organization. Teachers and the principal here first become learners and then problem solvers. This learning leader will also have faith in people and empower them to manage their learning environment. These leaders also will have a positive orientation toward the future and will put forth effort to inquire what the best way to accomplish a task is. They will also be committed to cultural learning, think systemically, and support cultural diversity (Schein, 2010).

The principal's first task in bringing a learning culture that emphasizes student engagement in the classrooms is to create structures for the learning activities. For example, teachers need more knowledge and skills in bringing in student engagement as part of their teaching. In order to accomplish that, they need many professional learning opportunities that include not only learning, but also coaching. A learning leader implements professional learning sessions for all teachers on topics related to student engagement and includes coaching as part of the learning. Then, professional guidance is provided for teachers as they implement different activities for student engagement. This is done frequently until students engaging in the learning activities of the classrooms, the school, and the community becomes a regular learning feature of the school.

Transformational leaders who demonstrate instructional leadership skills first create a vision for the school and adopt a collaborative approach to create a culture that supports all students becoming engaged learners in the classrooms, the school, and the community. The leaders' mission for bringing student engagement in the school must be infused with a moral purpose. All their work toward that is driven by a strong moral commitment they have within themselves to develop a learning culture to facilitate engaged learning for all students.

In order to bring the changes in the culture, the leader creates new systems and structures to facilitate the desired changes. For example, if teachers require more time to plan their instruction for student engagement, the principal and teachers work out a special time for that. They might introduce weekly team planning sessions by making time adjustments in the daily schedule. The principals empower their teachers and staff by providing learning opportunities to explore new ways of gaining information through technology on innovative teaching. A school leader needs to have extraordinary skills to accomplish such a culture in a school.

Conclusion

A transformational leader not only develops and shapes a new culture for student engagement, but also builds the capacity for sustaining the student-engaged learning culture that is emerging in the school. "More recently, the literature has focused on social-cultural norms, including collaborative problem-solving, shared commitment, the development of collaborative cultures, mutual values and goals, and social norms that sustain more satisfying work environments" (Gloria, 1995, p. 22). He/she distributes the responsibilities among his/her teachers and staff and holds them accountable in a positive way. The instructional culture of the school is supported through various kinds of activities and a wider alliance among teachers, staff, and community.

Implications for Developing a Learning Culture for Student Engagement

Bringing student engagement in the classrooms, school, and community involves the school leaders, teachers, counselors, staff, and community members. Each group has specific responsibilities in impacting the school culture to become a learning culture that is continually emerging and is not static.

Applications for School Administrators

1. Set goals for becoming a leader who will bring change in the school's culture for student engagement
2. Learn the process of educational change and try simple change initiatives first
3. Create a clear vision for change and communicate that in different ways continuously
4. Create a sense of urgency for change among the teachers, staff, and community members
5. Establish different coalitions of teachers, staff, and community members who will be active in guiding the change efforts
6. Plan change efforts systemically: first at the artifact level, then impact the espoused values and beliefs, and finally work on changing the deep-rooted assumptions of the people
7. Communicate results of each effort to all the members in the school community
8. Celebrate short-term and long-term wins
9. Remember building positive relationships within the school and the community will be the key to your success in this endeavor
10. Make bringing in student engagement a moral purpose of your leadership

Applications for Teachers

1. Understand the vision your administrator has set for student engagement
2. Set high goals for yourself and your students in implementing student engagement in the learning process
3. Create a learning environment in the classroom to support student engagement
4. Engage in continuous learning for improving your teaching that engages students not only in the learning process, but also in the school and community issues
5. Collaborate with colleagues in setting up goals toward the expected outcome and planning actions to achieve the goals
6. Plan and implement different learning activities related to student engagement becoming part of the total learning experience
7. Establish coalitions with community agencies to extend student engagement in community issues

Applications for Counselors

1. Work closely with teachers and the administrators in helping student engagement become part of the school's learning
2. Plan activities that touch the emotional and behavioral sides of student engagement
3. Establish a positive relationship with students in guiding them to become engaged learners
4. Provide positive reinforcements for students who overcome difficulties in this process
5. Make yourself available for students to come to you with their challenges
6. Always be prepared to tackle problems at the "bud"
7. Collaborate with teachers in offering lessons on student engagement

Applications for Community Members

1. Have a positive approach to your involvement in the school
2. Become part of the school team through active engagement
3. Always look for opportunities for bringing community resources to support the school initiatives
4. Initiate community alliances
5. Organize community volunteers to assist in different activities of the school

Discussion Questions

1. How do you envision student engagement in the classroom, school, and community?
2. What are the responsibilities of a school leader in making student engagement a part of the school's learning culture?
3. What are the levels of a school culture?
4. How would you bring urgency for change in the school in making student engagement a number-one priority?
5. How can a school leader change the deep-rooted assumptions of teachers regarding student engagement?
6. What would socially and culturally engaged learning look like?
7. What challenges would a school leader face in bringing change in the learning culture to incorporate student engagement?
8. How could a leader incorporate funds of knowledge and the cultural capital of students in student engagement?

A School Case for Analysis
A Principal Who Changes Long-Held Values

Martin Luther Elementary was one of the three oldest schools in the San Pedro school district in California. It was located in a neighborhood that was of low economic status. The houses around the school were old and deteriorating in their appearance. The sidewalks around the school were cracked and filled with graffiti with English and Spanish words in bright colors. The demography of the school was similar to many of the urban schools in California. Hispanics were 65%, African Americans 30%, Asians 3%, and others 2%. The playground also reflected the waning environment with litter and broken swings and strewn slides. However, in the morning when school began, children came dressed in their best with excitement. Teachers stood at the class entrance and welcomed them with open arms. Although the school environment looked bleak, the spirit of a learning community expressed by the principal, teachers, students, and parents was exemplary. The principal, Mr. Lattimore, was at the school entrance and greeted the students and their parents. He exhibited a friendly demeanor, and his charismatic appearance and commanding voice set a very positive tone.

The academic achievement in the school improved in the past year. A high percentage of students achieved above the proficient level in the state assessment, and the school was not an improvement school any longer. However, Mr. Lattimore wanted to take the school to the next level. He envisioned the student engagement becoming a major characteristic of his school. He organized his core team to begin this work, and they are looking for a consultant to guide them every step of the way to make student engagement a reality in the classroom, the school, and the community. If you are that consultant, where would your guidance begin? What would be your follow-up steps to accomplish the school's expected outcome?

References

Avolio et al. (1991). Leading in the 1990's: The four I's of transformational leadership. *Journal of European Industrial Training, 15,* 9–16.

Bass, B., & Avolio, B. (1994). Transformational leadership: Industrial military and educational impact. Mahwah, NJ: Lawrence Erlbaum Associates.

Bass, B., & Riggo, R. (2006). *Transformational Leadership* (2nd ed.), Mahwah, NJ: Lawrence Erlbaum.

Blase, J., & Blase, J. (1999). Principals' instructional leadership and teacher development: Teachers' perspectives. *Educational Administration Quarterly, 35*(3), 349–378

Blase, J., & Blase, J. (2001). The teacher's principal. *Journal of Staff Development, 22*(1), 22–25.

Blase, J., & Blase, J. (2004). *Handbook of instructional leadership.* Thousand Oaks, CA: Corwin Press.

Bogler, R. (2005). Satisfaction of Jewish and Arab teachers in Israel. *Journal of Social Psychology, 145,* 19–33.

Burns, J. (1978). *Leadership.* New York, NY: Free Press. Christenson, S. et al. (Eds.). (2012). *Handbook of Research on Student Engagement.* New York, NY: Springer.

Deal, T., & Patterson, K. (2009). *Shaping School Culture.* San Francisco, CA: Jossey Bass.

Gloria, A. (1995). Shaping your school's culture. *Thrust for Educational Leadership, 24*(7), 22–25.

Griffith, J. (2004). Relation of principal transformational leadership to school staff job satisfaction staff turnover and school performance. *Journal of Educational Administration, 42,* 335–356.

Fredricks, J. et al. (2004). Student engagement: Potential of the concept state of evidence. *Review of Educational Research, 74*(1), 59–109.

Fullan, M. (2001). *Leading in a Culture of Change.* San Francisco, CA: Jossey-Bass, p. 13.

Hallinger, P. (2003). *Instructional Management Rating Scale: Resource manual.* Bangkok, Thailand: Mahidol University.

Hallinger, P., & Heck, R. (1998). Exploring the principal's role in school effectiveness: 1980–1995. *School Effectiveness and School Improvement, 9,*157.

Hickman, G. 2010. *Leading organizations: Perspectives for a new era.* Thousand Oaks, CA: Sage Publications, Inc.

Kotter, J. (2012). *Leading Change.* (2nd Ed). Boston, MA: Harvard Business Review Press.

Leithwood, K. et al. (2006). The development and testing of a school improvement model. *School Effectiveness and School Improvement, 17,* 441–464.

Leithwood, K., & Jantzi, D. (2006). The effects of transformational leadership for large-scale reform: Effects on students, teachers and their classroom practice. *School Effectiveness and School Improvement, 17,* 201–227; *29,* 798–822.

Murphy, J. et al. (1983). Problems with research on educational leadership: Issues to be addressed. *Educational Evaluation and Policy Analysis, 5,* 297–305.

Madson, J., & Mbokela, R. (2002). Introduction: Leadership and diversity: Creating inclusive schools. *Peabody Journal of Education, 77*(1), 1–6.

Nettles, S., & Herrington, C. (2007). Revising the importance of the direct effects of school leadership on student achievement: The implications for school improvement policy. *Peabody Journal of Education, 82,* 724–736.

Northouse, P. (2013). *Leadership: Theory and practice* (5th ed.). Thousand Oaks, CA: Sage, p. 4.

Robinson, V. et al. (2008). The impact of leadership on student outcomes: An analysis of the differential effects of leadership types. *Educational Administration Quarterly, 44,* 635–674.

Ross, J., & Gray, P. (2006). School leadership and student achievement: The mediating effects of teacher beliefs. *Canadian Journal of Education*, 29, (3), 798–822.

Schein, E. (2010). *Organizational culture and leadership.* San Francisco, CA: Jossey-Bass.

Shatzer, R. et al. (2013). Comparing the effects of instructional and transformational leadership on student achievement. *Educational Management Administration & Leadership*, October 29, 2013.

Silva, J. et al. (2011). The direct effects of principal-student discussion on eighth grade students' gains in reading achievement: An experimental study. *Educational Administration Quarterly, 47,* 772–793.

CHAPTER 9

Adaptation Pedagogy for English Learners in Multicultural Contexts

by Jose Lalas and Marie Therese A. P. Bustos

The *process of integrating* what individuals know into a unified whole (Ziegler and Alibali, 2005) and the "internal balancing between assimilation and accommodation" (Meadows, 2006, p. 263) spurs development in human beings.

However, we submit that this paper is different because not only is it practical and research-based, it also raises the issues of equity, social and cultural factors, ethic of care, and social justice as theoretical underpinnings and practical considerations in planning for instruction for English learners in multicultural contexts. It also implies working with English learners as a social and cultural obligation, not just pedagogical, to facilitate access to academic content across subject matter areas. It emphasizes the notion that effective teachers "make adaptation" all the time to provide comprehensible information and ensure student engagement. More importantly, this paper revisits the contributions of developmental theorists such as Piaget and Vygotsky but goes beyond to complement them by stressing the importance of social and cultural factors in cognitive development and language learning.

In addition, this paper suggests a structured strategy for making instructional adaptation that could facilitate the subject matter content understanding and classroom engagement of English learners. Through making academic content adaptation, we describe as "adaptation

Jose W. Lalas and Therese M. Bustos, "Adaptation Pedagogy for English Learners in Multicultural Contexts," Perspectives, vol. 34, no. 2, pp. 5-11. Copyright © 2012 by National Association for Bilingual Education. Reprinted with permission.

pedagogy," cognitive and educationally-just solutions are created to meet the instructional needs of English learners and facilitate greater access for academic achievement in various "politically, socially-situated contexts" (Faltis, 2011; Lalas, 2007). Multicultural settings may empower or disadvantage group of learners due to their race, ethnicity, socioeconomic status, gender, sexual orientation, exceptionality, handicapping conditions, geography, and other "politically, socially-situated contexts" (Faltis, 2011; Gollnick & Chinn, 2009).

We commit that adaptation pedagogy goes beyond "recipes," "quick-fixes," or "add-ons" in providing the English learners access to academic content. It is an epistemological perspective, a "system of knowing," (Ladson-Billings, 2000) and a reflective decision-making event that a teacher employs in working with diverse students. Therefore, this paper presents the notion of "adaptation pedagogy" as a practical solution to making academic content comprehensible to English learners through the integration of cognitive development and contemporary social justice perspectives.

Cognitive Development and Adaptation Pedagogy

Although Piaget did not endorse any specific educational practices, schools have emerged following a pedagogy that centers on the development of cognition, interaction between children, coordination of physical actions, respect for the child as a constructor of knowledge, play as a method of learning (Boyle, 1982) and the teaching of mathematical and scientific concepts following the thought structures (Demetriou, Shayer and Efklides, 1992).

Piagetian theory is premised on the study of intelligence and cognitive developmental processes. Piaget (1952, 1975) considered intelligence as an adaptation. Intelligence is man's ability to adapt to his environment. Adaptation requires a balance of two processes, namely assimilation and accommodation. Assimilation is the initial process of receiving stimuli from the environment and incorporating these into one's schema. New elements are incorporated in existing schemata, which are constantly modified to adjust to these new elements. The reciprocal process is called accommodation, which refers to the "ways in which people adapt their thinking to new experience" (Siegler & Alibali, 2005, p. 31). Adjusting to these new experiences or new information involve developing new mental structures. Piaget (1975) mentioned that such changes may be internal within the schemata, or external as a response to an object or reality in the environment. He described the process as follows, "The organism adapts itself by materially constructing new forms to fit them into those of the universe, whereas intelligence extends this creation by constructing mentally structures which can be applied to those of the environment" (Piaget, 1952, p. 5).

Inconsistency between existing schemata and incoming stimuli produce disequilibrium in an individual. When stimuli are different from existing structures, difficulty in assimilating and accommodating new concepts will be experienced. "The mind can only be adapted to a reality if perfect accommodation exists, that is, to say if nothing, in that reality intervenes to modify the subject's schemata. But, inversely, adaptation does not exist if the new reality has imposed motor or mental attitudes contrary to those which were adopted on contact with other earlier given data: adaptation only exists if there is coherence, hence assimilation" (Piaget, 1952, p. 7).

The process of integrating what individuals know into a unified whole (Ziegler and Alibali, 2005) and the "internal balancing between assimilation and accommodation" (Meadows, 2006, p. 263) spurs development in human beings. *Equilibration* or the balance between the two processes stimulates cognitive growth especially when resolutions are found and new knowledge is accommodated and applied. Human growth, from infancy to adulthood, is a series of adaptations.

Vygotsky (1978) focuses on the importance of social interaction in cognitive development. Like Piaget, he believed that learning occurs through the interaction of the learners with the world around them. He formulated the zone of proximal development that he defined as "the distance between the actual developmental level as determined by independent problem solving and the level of potential development as determined through problem solving under adult guidance or in collaboration with more capable peers" (p. 84). This definition is key in understanding how adaptation pedagogy facilitates learning at the zone of proximal development as the English learner attempts to understand concepts with support from a capable peer or adult.

Consequently, English learners gain access to academic content with support from teachers who make instructional adaptations. Adaptation pedagogy considers what the English learners bring in the instructional contexts and provides productive opportunities to engage them actively with the curriculum, instructional delivery, classroom assessment, and overall academic content. Making instructional adaptation can be viewed as an example of Vygotsky's concept of scaffolding that a teacher provides to allow English learners the opportunity to function on a higher level.

According to Gunning (2010), the instructional implications of integrating the theories of Piaget and Vygotsky in facilitating literacy include the use of hands-on experiences, recognition of individual differences that explain the development of learning of children at different rates, use of developmentally appropriate activities, and the fostering of learning through interaction of the learners with the teacher and peers. These implications are intricately embedded in making instructional adaptations for English learners.

Complementary Theoretical Frameworks and Adaptation Pedagogy

Demetriou, Shayer and Efklides (1992) and Guvain (2001) indicated the limitations of the Piagetian theory and cognitive development in explaining learning. Noteworthy is the lack of focus on the socio-cultural nature of learning and its effect on how children perform on cognitive tasks. Cognitive development theories emphasize more on the interaction between human beings and the physical world than human interaction. Neo-Piagetians recognize the involvement of the social environment in the construction of meaning and the reality of intra- and interpersonal differences in learning. Siegel and Hodkin (1982) aptly argued the need for other theoretical frameworks to understand and address human differences.

Other theoretical frameworks that complement cognitive development theories that may serve as pedagogical support for making instructional adaptations for English learners include "ethic of caring" (Collier, 2005; Noddings, 1992), teacher learning (Darling-Hammond & McLaughlin, 1999; Elmore & Burney, 1999), working with diverse learners (Valenzuela, 1999; Nieto, 2000, 2003; Trueba, 1999; Stanton-Salazar, 2001;

Moll & Gonzalez, 2001), teaching for social justice (Michelli & Keiser, 2005; Cochran-Smith, 2004; Brown, 2004; Marshall & Oliva, 2006; Rodgers, 2006; Adams, Bell & Griffin, 1997), and language, literacy, and academic language development (Echevarria, Vogt, & Short, 2008;). These frameworks imply the influence of social and cultural factors in planning for instruction and making appropriate and relevant instructional adaptations for English learners. They also reflect the dynamic interaction among the learner, the teacher, and the classroom context as described by Ruddell and Unrau (2004). In addition, there is an opportunity for teacher reflection to take place in utilizing these theoretical frameworks for making instructional decisions (Tremmel, 1993; Schon, 1987).

Collier (2005) stresses the importance of the "ethic of caring" as a motivating force for teacher efficacy—teacher's belief in his/her ability to make a difference in student learning—as well as the purposeful instructional decisions teachers make in their classrooms. The caring roles of a teacher is similar to that of "mothering" which include the protection, nurturing, and shaping of the growth of the child. Good caring teacher s are committed to their students, improve their pedagogical skills and content knowledge to meet the needs of their students, establish trusts with their students, and model how to care for the well being of all students (Noddings, 1992). These are "caring" characteristics that teachers need to possess when working with English learners.

Figure 9–1. Special Education Teachers/Volunteers Enriching the Lives of Bilingual Students with Special Needs Through Community Activities.

Similarly, Darling-Hammond and Bartz-Snowden (2005 p. 5) explain that a good teacher in every classroom must have knowledge of who their learners are and how they learn within social contexts, understanding of the subject matter and skills to be taught, and understanding of teaching in light of the content and learners to be taught, as informed by assessment and supported by a productive environment. These essential areas of knowledge provide teachers with a framework for understanding teaching and learning and inform teachers in making learning accessible to English language learners.

It is also important for teachers of English learners to understand the interactive connection between a teacher's set of knowledge, skills, abilities, and disposition and the students' prior knowledge, academic, literacy, and language skills, and their overall personal abilities. This dynamic teacher-learner interactive relationship within a diverse classroom context is vital to learning including the acquisition of academic content knowledge and student engagement (Ruddell and Unrau, 2004). The dynamic interaction between what experiences and academic capabilities English learners bring to the classroom and what backgrounds a teacher has plays significant roles in facilitating access to academic subject matter content, development of language, and the construction of meaningful and purposeful knowledge.

The cognitive process of teacher reflection includes problem solving, inference, activation of prior knowledge and beliefs, and decision making. It is this thoughtful reflective process that allows both the teacher and the learner to intentionally connect ideas based on their beliefs and knowledge to classroom context, evaluate past classroom interaction or practice, assess weaknesses and strengths, and create an atmosphere of openness for instructional adaptation. Reflection plays a very important role in making adaptation that facilitates access to academic content, comprehension, and language development (Tremmel, 1993; Schon, 1987).

Contemporary Educational Justice Lenses and Adaptation Pedagogy

Figure 9–2. A Parent/Volunteer Reading Aloud with Bilingual Children Using a Big Book.

Adaptation pedagogy reflects a social and educational justice instructional agenda. It honors diversity, equity, openness, and individual voice and unique expression (Brooks & Thompson, 2005). Teachers need to understand, value, and advocate for diversity and educational justice because they are the foundations for providing ALL students with equitable learning environments (Brooks & Thompson, 2005). It is personal commitment, passion, care, and virtue for equity and educational justice that drive teachers to engage in adaptation pedagogy for English language learners. Cochran-Smith (2004, p. 159) asserts that teaching from a social justice perspective, is not a matter simply of transmitting knowledge and equating pupil learning to higher scores on high-stakes tests but rather engaging pupils in "developing critical habits of mind, understanding and sorting out multiple perspectives, and learning to participate in and contribute to a democratic society by developing both the skill and the inclination for civic engagement."

Making instructional adaptation starts with the recognition that there are specific cultural characteristics that all students, including the English learners, bring to the learning process. Howard (2010) asserts that "culture is not bound by exclusively by one's race, ethnicity, or place of origin, but is shaped by a myriad of factors" (p. 53) such as social class, gender, family history, religion, geography, migration status, and language. He explains that these factors or cultural characteristics influence student learning. As we view culture as socially-situated contexts, it is imperative that we share relevant research that implies the strong influence of social and cultural factors on building resiliency, character, and self-identity for academic success of the English learners. Several related "social justice lenses" such as politics of caring, social networking, and funds of knowledge (Lalas & Valle, 2007) provide teachers a framework for advocating for effective schooling for English learners.

Diverse students have to be cared for, respected, and valued by their peers, teachers, and administrators before they can care about school. It is important for the English learners to feel connected and comfortable in the classroom.

Valenzuela (1999) describes "politics of caring" as the reciprocal relations of respect and support that need to be established between students and educators. She believes that students and teachers need to nurture meaningful relationships to foster learning and enhance academic success. She asserts that diverse students have to be *cared for*, respected, and valued by their peers, teachers, and administrators before they can *care about* school. It is important for the English learners to feel connected and comfortable in the classroom. Nieto (2003; 2000) cites studies that linked supportive networks of teachers and friends to academic success of Hispanic students. Personal relationships that developed between teachers and minority students serve as "protective networks" that strengthen and motivate students to achieve.

Stanton-Salazar (2001) explains the need for diverse students to create social connections with "institutional agents" such as teachers, counselors, and mentors who can provide them career and academic guidance, defend their interests, and advocate for their success. While student motivation and talents are important, the assistance provided by these institutional agents is important and can guide the students' overall progress in the highly competitive and complex learning environments. Stanton-Salazar (2001) also recognizes the valuable role of parents in inspiring their bilingual children to strengthen their bilingual-bicultural forms identity that can serve to develop their self-esteem and allow them to perform at a higher level academically.

The term "funds of knowledge" refers to students' lived experiences in their homes, schools, and communities including the variety of multiple identities students have, their social backgrounds, and their overall experiences. These are practices that are embedded in the labor, domestic, family, and community affairs of Mexican American families as shown in research studies by Luis Moll and other colleagues (Moll & Gonzalez, 2001; Moll, Amanti, Neff, & Gonzalez, 1992). The notion of funds of knowledge is a recognition of the set of knowledge, experiences, abilities, practices, resources, and dispositions at homes and communities where students live including the English learners. It fosters positive social identities for English learners and informs teachers about the harmful ways in which the school curriculum may exclude some and privilege others. Teachers should learn how to build from the "funds of knowledge" diverse students already have by openly acknowledging diversity in language, culture, gender, ethnicity, sexual orientation, and class backgrounds as valuable points of reference.

Similarly, Trueba (1999) explains the notion of cultural resiliency as a process by which immigrant children and their families learn to rely upon their culture, family, friends, and ethnic community as sources of support. Teachers should recognize the notion of resiliency as they build the students' positive personal traits, self-esteem, and dispositions through their classroom interaction with students. Generally, students who maintain a strong self-identity with their social and cultural community are able to do well in school in spite of social inequities.

Adaptation Pedagogy: What is it?

Current approaches to teaching English as a second language take the form of sheltered instruction in which English learners are taught subject matter concepts while developing proficiency in English. The SIOP (Sheltered Instruction Observation Protocol) Model, for example, outlines a comprehensive set of components in facilitating language and content that includes lesson preparation, building background, comprehensible input, strategies, interaction, practice/application, lesson delivery, and review/assessment (Echevarria, Vogt, & Short, 2008). Other current studies focus on teaching academic language, content, and vocabulary as well as equip students with thinking strategies and critical literacy they need to be active learners (Luke & Dooley, 2011; Echevarria, Richards-Tutor, Chinn, & Ratleff, 2011; Kieffer & Lesaux, 2010).

However, the growing concern of many teachers is how to teach language and content to a few English learners in class while also teaching a whole class of mainstream native-English speaking students in a multicultural classroom. Making instructional adaptation is imperative in order to provide English learners access to academic curriculum and instruction. In this situation, teachers are not only teaching the English learners academic content and language, they are also serving as advocates for equity, positive behavior, caring connections, resiliency, and students' race and culture. Subsequently, through teachers' careful attention to their linguistic, cultural, social, and academic needs, English learners become connected participants to the classroom culture and active users and consumers of the curriculum. Teachers have the ultimate opportunity to involve English learners in worthy comprehensible activities that promote the recognition of the value of each individual in the classroom and create learning environments that are democratic, just, equitable, and caring.

As can be gathered at this point, adaptation pedagogy is not just a process of knowing and making relevant and appropriate plans for English learners to make subject matter comprehensible, engage and support students in learning, and create effective environments for learning. It is influenced by an informed decision to create a relevant and appropriate yet challenging learning experience where all students feel safe, comfortable, trusted, confident, and respected for who they are, what identity they take on, what level of academic proficiency they bring, and the cultural beliefs and traditions they uphold. The teacher engaged in adaptation pedagogy is not only knowledgeable of subject matter content and aware of the social, economic, linguistic, and cultural factors that affect learning; he/she also recognizes the need for students to acquire a deeper understanding of the instructional material in order to make it relevant to their lives.

Adaptation Pedagogy: Start with Reflection

To begin with, pre-service or in-service teachers need to reflect on their own experiential backgrounds, their students' identities and levels of academic and language proficiency, and the classroom contexts and tasks or assignments. Reflection helps teachers to look at instructional dilemmas carefully and think about what the English learners bring to the learning tasks.

Here are some **reflective questions** using Gordon, Lalas, and McDermott's learning and teaching framework (2006): Does your student work comfortably by her/himself? Does your student enjoy working with others? Do you think he or she can work productively with another student? Do you think he or she can thrive in group work situations? Does your student show eagerness in solving problems and thinking critically for solutions? Do you think he or she is a risk-taker? Does your student demonstrate independence in applying the concepts learned in the various subject matter areas? Does your student think about consequences of their actions? Do you think he or she is able to identify the strengths and weaknesses of his or her performance?

Knowledge about the students also include specific information related to their linguistic and cultural backgrounds, academic language abilities and content knowledge related to subject matter, interests, and other relevant physical, social, and emotional development information. It is important that pre-service and in-service teachers identify the necessary formal and informal assessment tools that they can use to know who their students are and what knowledge, skills, and abilities they bring in the classroom.

Research-based Adaptation Categories and Procedures

Adaptations are alternative means for English learners to acquire and demonstrate their content knowledge and must compensate for the students' learning needs. A colleague and I from previous studies identified three categories of instructional adaptations based on the responses of preservice teachers on their teaching performance assessment tasks that include instructional planning and teaching: classroom organization adaptation, instructional presentation adaptation, and activating student motivation and response adaptation (Lalas & Solomon, 2007). Using the list of adaptation activities, several experienced inservice teachers implemented lesson plans with adaptation activities.

Some examples of **instructional presentation adaptations** are activating prior knowledge, building background knowledge of content, relating to personal experiences, previewing information, using advance organizers, preteaching vocabulary, using K-W-L strategies, questioning strategies, activate recall, summarize, outlines, cue cards, vocabulary glossary, simplifying abstract concepts, dramatization, music, guest speakers, interactive writing, drawing or painting, journal entries, student "think-alouds," self-monitoring checklists, and many others. Some examples of **classroom organization adaptations** are peer partners, cooperative learning groups, physical room arrangement, seating arrangements or seat assignments, lighting, material accessibility, work space, prompting and gesturing, and many other classroom adaptive equipment and materials such as lapboard, personal computers, enlarged print, maps, and many others. Some examples of **activating student response and motivation adaptations** that relate to response format and response procedures are completing information organizers, data chart, illustrations through posters, collages, or murals, journal entries, songs, poems, and raps, bulletin board displays, extended time, practice exercises, use of an interpreter, shorter or more frequent assessments, creating more interest, activity choice, personally meaningful activities, doable tasks, choice to work with others, student involvement in assessment activities, and many other activities that foster confidence and comfort.

Table 1 on the next page identifies the three categories of adaptation activities with examples of adaptation strategies (Lalas & Solomon, 2007).1

Adaptations can be planned before the presentation of the lesson, during the lesson, and after the completion of the lesson. A simple adaptation planning grid that can be used to lay out the adaptation activities before, during, and after the lesson can be seen below.

Adaptation Pedagogy: A Conscious Decision-Making Process

Adaptation pedagogy is a conscious effort on the part of the pre-service or in-service teachers to be explicit in the academic content standards that their instructional plan is covering, specific learning goals addressing the standards, assessment, and sequence of activities including the different categories of adaptation strategies and student activities. Teacher's instructional strategies are the set of activities a teacher does that focuses on input presentation and the instructional presentation and classroom organization categories of adaptation. Student activities are the set of activities students do that activate student response and motivation adaptations.

Teacher reflection on what English learners can do, the academic content curriculum, his or her own pedagogical skills, abilities, and dispositions, categories of appropriate adaptations, and how to manage instruction and monitor students progress plays a valuable role in making purposeful and intentional instructional decisions. It is not a mechanical but an intentional process that involves a deep understanding of the societal factors that influence academic achievement and the dynamic interaction among the teacher, the student, and the classroom context in the learning process. It involves figuring out what the students can and cannot do and their level of comfort in recognizing their individuality, working with others, problem-solving, demonstrating knowledge, and reflecting on their own learning. Adaptation pedagogy drives teachers' advocacy for the English learners, commitment to their learning, and respect for their well-being.*

Adaptation Planning Grid

Adaptations	Classroom Organization Instructional Presentation Adaptations	Activating Student Motivation and Response Adaptations
Before instruction		
During instruction		
After instruction		

Table 9–1. Types of Adaptation Strategies for the English Language Learners

Classroom Organization	Instructional Presentation	Activating Student Motivation & Response	
• After school/before school tutoring, • Work one on one in class when time is available • Provide additional time • EL Paraprofessional assistance for one on one instruction • Sit with a translator • Elicit Parental support and cooperation • Place the ELL closer to the teacher to make sure the materials are clear and directions are heard • Recognize cultural characteristics and validate them—like the accent and ways of interaction • Pre-lesson assignment	• Pre-teach & re-teach • Make learning goals specific • Focus on content and meaning instead of grammar and spelling in the written work • The assessment stresses vocabulary • Daily journals • Modeling • Graphic Organizers • Bubble Cluster • KWL Chart • Provide Spanish vocabulary list • Vocabulary wall in English • Use illustrations to teach science concepts • Include English development standards in the content • In an assignment that required written description the ELL just labels the pictures and orally • Slow down the pace of teaching to accommodate the ELL • Make adjustments in journaling activities • Provide visuals and examples before and during lesson	• Include the EL in student presentations to encourage her develop confidence, oral and language skills. • Accept oral answers vs. written answers • Use dialogue and other forms of oral expression to process content ideas and concepts • Write directions on the board • Allow to do research in Spanish • Student draws a picture to illustrate her learning and her thoughts • Student re-writes rules and explain them in own words • Allowing student to finish a written report with pictures to represent the learning • Provide guided practice • Portfolio to record student learning and monitor progress • Make adjustment in the assessment cueing to the student's level of understanding	• Alternative assignment • Personally meaningful group work • Omit singling out in front of • Reduce number of paragraphs to a few sentences • Reduce writing requirement • Provide glossary of words taken from the content to be discussed ahead of time • Showing samples of assignments—A simple paragraph • Reduce writing requirement • Less quantity in assignment • Peer Tutoring • Pairing with bilingual student • Assign homework before and after a lesson • Provide positive feedback on written or spoken answers • Teacher as editing service • Translated materials • Modified assignments in writing • Positive feedback

References

Adams, M., Bell, L., & Griffin, P. (Eds.) (1997). *Teaching for diversity and social Justice*. New York: Routledge.

Bailey, A. (Ed.), (2007). The language demands of school: Putting academic English to *the test*. New Haven and London: Yale University Press.

Boyle, D. (1982) Piaget and education: a negative evaluation. In S. and C. Modgil, (Eds.) *Jean Piaget: Consensus and Controversy* (pp. 291–308). London: Holt, Rinehart and Winston.

Brooks, J., & Thompson, E. (2005). Social justice in the classroom. *Educational Leadership*, September 2005, 48–52.

Brown, K. (2004). Leadership for social justice and equity: Weaving a transformative framework and pedagogy. *Educational Administration Quarterly*, 40(1), 77–108.

Cochran-Smith, M. (2004). Walking the road: Race, diversity, and social justice. New York: Teachers College Press.

Collier, M. (2005). An ethic of caring: The fuel for high teacher efficacy. *The Urban Review*, 37(4), 351–359.

Darling-Hammond, L. & Baratz-Snowden, J. (Eds.) (2005). *A good teacher in every classroom: Preparing the highly qualified teachers our children deserve.* San Francisco, CA: Jossey-Bass Publishers.

Darling-Hammond, L. & McLaughlin, M. (1999). Investing in teaching as a learning profession: Policy problems and prospects. In L. Darling-Hammond & G. Sykes (Eds.), *Teaching as the learning profession.* San Francisco, CA: Jossey-Bass Publishers.

Demetriou, A., Shayer, M. and Efklides, A. (Eds.). (1992). Introduction. In *Neo-Piagetian theories of cognitive development* (pp. 1–7). London: Routledge.

Echevarria, J., Richards-Tutor, Chinn, V. & Ratleff, P. (2011). Did they get it? The role of fidelity in teaching English learners. *Journal of Adolescent & Adult Literacy*, 54 (6), 425–434.

Echevarria, J., Vogt, M. & Short, D. (2008). *Making content comprehensible for English learners.* Boston, MA: Allyn and Bacon.

Elmore, R.F. & Burney, D. (1999). Investing in teacher learning: Staff development and instructional improvement. In L. Darling-Hammond & G. Sykes (Eds.), *Teaching as the learning profession: Handbook of policy and practice.* San Francisco, CA: Jossey-Bass Publishers.

Faltis, C. (Ed.) (2011). Introduction: teaching in politically, socially-situated contexts. Teacher Education Quarterly, 38 (1), 3–5.

Gollnick, D. & Chinn, P. (2009). Multicultural education in a pluralistic society. Columbus, OH: Merrill.

Gordon, R., Lalas, J., & Mcdermott, J. C. (2006). *Omni-education: A teaching and* learning framework for social justice in urban classrooms. Dubuque, IA: Kendall/Hunt Publishing Company.

Gunning, T. (2010). Creating literacy instruction for all students (7th ed.). Boston, MA: Allyn and Bacon.

Guvain, M. (2001). *The social context of cognitive development.* New York, NY: The Guilford Press.

Hinkel, E. (Ed.) (2011). *Handbook of research in second language teaching and learning volume II.* New York and London: Routledge.

Howard, T. (2010). *Why race and culture matter in schools: Closing the achievement gap in America's classrooms.* New York and London: Teachers College Press.

Kieffer, M. & Lesaux, N. (2010). Morphing into adolescents: Active word learning for English-language learners and their classmates in middle school. *Journal of Adolescent & Adult Literacy*, 54(1), 47–56.

Ladson-Billings, G. (2000). Racialized discourses and ethnic epistemologies. In N. Denzin & Y. Lincoln (Eds.), *Handbook of qualitative research* (2nd ed., pp. 257–277). Thousand Oaks, CA: Sage.

Lalas, J. & Solomon. M. (2007). Instructional Adaptation as an equity solution for the English learners and special needs students: Practicing educational justice in the mainstream classroom. Dubuque, IA: Kendall/Hunt Publishing Company.

Lalas, J. & Valle, M. (2007). Social justice lenses and authentic student voices: Enhancing leadership for educational justice. Educational Leadership and Administration: Teaching and Program Development, Fall 2007.

Luke, A. & Dooley, K. (2011). Critical literacy and second language learning. In E. Hinkel (Ed.), Handbook of research in second language teaching and learning volume II. New York and London: Routledge.

Marshall, C., & Oliva, M. (2010). Leadership for social justice: Making revolutions in *education*. Boston, MA: Pearson Allyn & Bacon.

Meadows, S. (2006). *The child as a thinker: the development and acquisition of cognition in childhood* (2nd edition). London: Routlege.

Michelli, N. & Keiser, D. (Eds.). (2005). *Teacher education for democracy and social justice*. New York and London: Routledge.

Moll, L., Amanti, C., Neff D. & Gonzalez (1992). Funds of knowledge for teaching: Using a qualitative approach to connect homes and classrooms. *Theory Into Practice*, 31 (2), 132–141.

Moll, L. & Gonzalez (2001). Lesson from research with language-minority. *Literacy: A critical sourcebook*. Boston, MA: Bedford/St. Martin's.

Nieto, S. (2003). *What keeps teachers going?* New York, NY: Teachers College Press.

Nieto, S. (2000). *Affirming diversity: The sociopolitical context of multicultural education*. NY: Longman.

Noddings, N. (1992). *The challenge to care in schools*. New York: Teachers College Press, Columbia University

Piaget , J. (1952). *The origins of intelligence in children*. New York: W.W. Norton and Company. Inc.

Piaget, J. (1975). *The development of thought: equilibration of cognitive structures*. New York: The Viking Press.

Rodgers, C.R. (2006). "The turning of one's soul"–learning to teach for social justice:

The Putney Graduate School of Teacher Education. *Teachers College Record*, 108(7), 1266–1295.

Ruddell, R. & Unrau, N. (2004). Reading as a meaning-construction process: The reader, the text, and the teacher. In R. Ruddell & N. Unrau (Eds.), *Theoretical models and processes of reading*. Newark, DE: International Reading Association.

Schon, D.A. (1987). *Educating the reflective practitioner*. San Francisco, CA: Jossey-Bass Publishers.

Siegel, L. and Hodkin, B. (1982). The garden path to the understanding of cognitive development: has Piaget led us into the poison ivy? In S. and C. Modgil, (Eds.) *Jean Piaget: Consensus and Controversy (pp. 57–82)* London: Holt, Rinehart and Winston.

Siegler, R. and Alibali, M.W. (2005). *Children's thinking* (4th edition). New Jersey: Prentice Hall, Inc.

Stanton-Salazar, R. (2001). *Manufacturing hope and despair*. NY: Teachers College, Columbia University.

Tremmel, R. (1993). Zen and the art of reflective practice in teacher education. *Harvard Educational Review*. 63 (4).

Trueba, E. (1999). *Latinos unidos: From cultural diversity to the politics of solidarity*. New York: Rowman & LittleField Publishers.

Valenzuela, A. (1999). Subtractive schooling: U.S.-Mexican youth and the *politics of caring*. Albany, NY: State University of New York Press.

Vygotsky, L. (1978). Thought and language. Cambridge, MA: MIT Press.

Walqui, A. (2010). Interview with Aida Walqui: Scaffolding success. *The Journal of Communication & Education–Language Magazine*, 9 (6), 24–29.

Young, T. & Hadaway, N. (Eds.), 2006). *Supporting the literacy development of English learners: Increasing success in all classrooms*. Newark, DE: International Reading Association.

GLOSSARY OF KEY TERMS

Academic Achievement is a cumulative measurement of academic content that a student has learned in reference to a determined timeframe, learning goals, and instructional standards. Academic achievement is gained dependent on the engagement of students and style of instruction. Commonly, it is reported loosely as student performance in standardized tests.

Achievement Gap refers to the witnessed, continuing disproportion in academic performance or educational attainment between different subgroups of students. These student groups are generally defined by socioeconomic status, race, ethnicity, and gender. Usually, the term has been used to describe the academic discrepancy between Black and Latino(a) students on one side and White and Asian students on the other side based on certain standardized measures of academic achievement.

Capital refers to access to a variety of goods, services, and commodities, both physical and symbolic, that are of value to the upper, middle, and lower classes of society. From Pierre Bourdieu's theory, a capital could be economic, social, or cultural.

Challenges and Coping Strategies pertain to the social element of parental involvement. The challenges connect to a variety of stresses dealing with the economic strain, time, and energy demands, role overload and conflict, and limitation of personal and social choices. In dealing with the challenges, parents continue to utilize *coping strategies* by drawing on previous experiences, skills, and knowledge, as well as informing their children of the disadvantages they would face as part of a minority group.

Class is a way of grouping people who share common political and economic relationships or a way of grouping individuals categorized by socioeconomic indicators, which include concepts of culture, values, politics, and lifestyle. In the United States, there exist lower, lower middle, middle, upper middle, and upper classes.

Class—Behavior Block encompasses both conscious and unconscious actions. This block represents the interaction between the internal factors and external factors, such as school, church, or home, which affect the way in which a person perceives information and makes decisions. As one interacts with teachers, classmates, and administration, his/her way of thinking is affected, and the way he/she sees the world changes.

Class—Identity Block is an internal block that relies on personal networks and relationships. Identity is developed through social connections, political relationships, and learning that occurs through interactions with family, peers, and political associations.

Class—Structural Measures Blocks are external systems of quantifiable measures of economic stability, such as level of educational attainment, occupation, and income.

Critical Race Theory (CRT) is used to describe and define the inequities within the American educational and justice systems as they pertain to race. It was started by legal scholars to bring to consciousness the marginalization of race and racism in the U.S. legal system. It was developed by Derrick Bell and Alan Freeman in response to inequities found in the racial reform and the slow rate at which the law was addressing these race issues during the 1970s. The application of CRT in education is helpful in understanding and addressing the perennial underachievement of African American, Latino, Native American, and some Asian American students in U.S. schools. It is also a methodological and theoretical construct that uses the research tool of counter-storytelling. CRT is used in many fields, including education, in order to more clearly understand, oppose, and expose the systems that subjugate people of color. Some of the central themes of CRT are:

- Interest convergence: The interests of people of color in achieving racial equality will be accommodated only when that converges with the interests of Whites who are in policy-making positions.
- Whiteness as property: Whiteness has a property value in terms of rights and possesses the privilege and benefits to exclude others.
- Voice/Counter-story: Using the personal narratives and stories of the experiences of people of color is a valid form of evidence to document inequity and discrimination.
- Critique of colorblindness: It questions the idea that one is considered fair by treating everybody equally regardless of the students' skin color.
- Social change: Knowledge learned through examination of racial inequity should be used for social justice and to make social change

Cultural Capital refers to the knowledge, skills, education, experiences, and connections one has had through the course of his or her life that promote or hinder success. Cultural capital can exist in three states: embodied, having to do with dispositions or habitus; objectified, having to do with cultural material objects; and institutionalized, having to do with degrees and certificates.

Cultural Deficit Thinking refers to the thought that cultural knowledge, skills, abilities, and networks of students of color have little to no value compared to those of the dominant society's culture.

Cultural Dimension involves the values, norms, knowledge, and beliefs that define what is acceptable to a given society.

Culturally Relevant Pedagogy is a pedagogy grounded in teachers exhibiting cultural competence. Teachers provide opportunity for students to interact with the course content through their cultural context. These teachers are skilled at teaching in a cross-cultural or multicultural setting. It provides an avenue where the cultural understandings of a student can be integrated into the academic practices.

Culturally Relevant and Responsive Instruction. Together, the contributions of Hale, Ladson-Billing, and Gay create a broad understanding of the instructional needs of African American students. In honor of the previous groundwork in culturally relevant and responsive instruction (CRRI) strategies, the two terms "relevant" and "responsive" are used as equal descriptors; however, CRRI adds literacy, multiple literacy, and identities. CRRI also includes writing as a means to preserve, promote, and validate individual student voice and student identity.

Culturally Responsive Teaching, Culturally Responsive Pedagogy, Culturally Relevant Teaching, and Culturally Responsive Instruction are terms that refer to the same theory used to support culture and home language that is infused with core curriculum, instruction, and educational praxis. The intention of using the theory is to include students' backgrounds in the learning process for validation and empowerment. Culturally relevant pedagogy rests on three criteria or propositions: (a) students must experience academic success; (b) students must develop and/or maintain cultural competence; and (c) students must develop a critical consciousness through which they challenge the current status quo of the social order.

Deficit Thinking refers to the practice of having lower expectations for students and parents who do not fit the demographics profile of the traditional context of the school system.

Differentiated Writing is a term used to describe how teachers make writing accessible to all students despite the diversity.

Educational Justice is a term used to convey the understanding that educational opportunities and outcomes should be distributed in a fair and equitable manner. The three principles of justice are: (1) People should be treated fairly, (2) People should be considered according to their need, (3) All people should be given equal opportunity. This term is used to define and describe fairness, access, equity, and care within an educational system. It is also a way of recognizing diversity and fostering respect among teachers, students, administrators, and parents.

Expectations pertain to a cultural element of parental involvement. They connect to a high educational level that the parents hope their child attains. This also connects to the concept of *aspirations*, where parents emphasize the importance of school achievement and moral character to their children.

Field is the space where particular norms or dispositions are more valued than others. There are many different fields; what may be considered valuable in one field might not be considered valuable in another.

Funds of Knowledge are historically accumulated and culturally developed bodies of knowledge and skill essential for household and individual functioning and well-being; skills, experiences, and values students gain from their home experience and family.

Habitus is a system of dispositions, values, expectations, or ways of understanding social or cultural norms that has developed based on one's life experiences.

Holistic Scoring Guide is a type of writing rubric used to assign a numerical value to a writing piece while identifying certain writing qualities.

Latino/Hispanic may be used interchangeably to denote individuals whose ancestry is linked to one of the Spanish- or Portuguese-speaking countries in Mexico, Central, or South America.

Liberatory Pedagogy is a way of teaching, according to Paolo Freire, that places problem posing at the heart of learning, and teachers allow students to become co-investigators of learning in a community of learners.

Literacy is defined as the ability and the willingness to use reading and writing to construct meaning from a printed text in ways that meet the requirements of a particular social context.

Multiple Literacies are the multitude of identities and uses of reading and writing in and outside of the classroom that are socially situated by culture, context, and home language and include cultural literacy, digital literacy, and critical literacies.

NAEP (National Assessment of Educational Progress), otherwise known as the "nation's report card," is a national educational database filled with statistics on the status of American students in the American public school systems.

Parent refers to any familial unit (i.e., guardians, grandparents, parents, aunts and uncles, siblings, etc.).

Parental Involvement refers to any form of support that parents provide their student for education. These supports can be in school or out of school. They can span the range of providing students with the appropriate study space at home, having a supporting attitude about the school their student attends, and actively volunteering at their student's school.

Perceptions are one's understanding or knowledge about an individual, a group, or an idea (example: schooling) based on previous experiences or assumptions.

Practices pertain to how parents engage with their children as a social element of parental involvement. It is connected to the concept of *presence* that describes a parental engagement in the children's schooling, whether in a formal school space or in more personal, informal spaces, including those created by parents themselves.

Resources refer to a social element of parental involvement. This concept is related to *social capital*, which Coleman believes "is a form of capital that exists in the relationship between people." An individual's ties to other people allow him or her to gain access to a broad range of resources.

Social Capital refers to the networks, relationships, and social connections that serve to increase the opportunities or resources available to those who have membership in the group. It is the collective resources associated with a durable network or members of a specific group.

Sociocultural context refers to the cultural and social aspects of a student's background and experience.

Social Dimension pertains to the interactions that exist in the relationships between people.

Student Engagement refers to the learner's commitment to the product and process of learning. It is the visible indicator of motivation. It is a multifaceted construct incorporating various elements of involvement in school or commitment in learning. It consists of the following types of engagement: affective engagement, behavioral engagement, cognitive engagement, and academic engagement.

> *Affective Engagement* refers to how a student feels about learning and school. When students engage affectively, they enjoy going to school and like the learning process.

> *Behavioral Engagement* refers to the efforts that students place on the learning process and their involvement in school activities. When students engage behaviorally, they willingly participate in classroom discussions and activities, as well as participate in other school organizations such as sports, clubs, and events.

> *Cognitive Engagement* refers to the way that students understand the purpose of education or their long-term investment in learning. When engaged cognitively, learning becomes a means for personal development or increasing self-efficacy.

> *Academic Engagement* refers to the student's interest in the subject matter as well as their engagement (relationship) with the teacher.

Transformative Leadership begins with questions of justice and democracy, critiquing inequitable procedures and customs and offering the hope of greater individual achievement as well as a better life lived jointly with others. Transformative leadership consists of the following eight tenets:

- The mandate to affect deep and equitable change
- The need to deconstruct and reconstruct knowledge frameworks that perpetuate inequity and injustice
- A focus on emancipation, democracy, equity, and justice
- The need to address the inequitable distribution of power
- An emphasis on both private and public (individual and collective) good
- An emphasis on interdependence, interconnectedness, and global awareness
- The necessity of balancing critique and promise
- The call to exhibit moral courage

Values and Beliefs refer to a cultural element of parental involvement. They are related to the concept of *social norms*, where parents not only provide rewards for positive behavior, but also exact sanctions for negative behavior.

Voice is a term used to describe an author's tone or personal style used in writing. Voice also refers to an author's ability to maintain and display personal identity in writing. Voice is both a social and cultural experience.

Working Class refers to families that fit one or more of the following criteria: household income level ranges between $15,000 and $45,000 per year, qualification for free or reduced lunch, and households considered by the U.S. census as living in poverty.

Writing As a component of the balanced literacy approach, writing is the ability to effectively communicate thoughts and ideas via paper or electronically using standard English.